DUMBARTON OAKS TEXTS

VIII

THE CORRESPONDENCE OF LEO, METROPOLITAN OF SYNADA AND SYNCELLUS

CORPUS FONTIUM HISTORIAE BYZANTINAE

CONSILIO SOCIETATIS INTERNATIONALIS
STUDIIS BYZANTINIS PROVEHENDIS DESTINATAE

EDITUM

VOLUMEN XXIII

LEONIS SYNADORUM METROPOLITAE ET SYNCELLI EPISTOLAE

RECOGNOVIT, ANGLICE VERTIT,
ET COMMENTARIO INSTRUXIT
MARTHA POLLARD VINSON

SERIES WASHINGTONIENSIS
EDIDIT IHOR ŠEVČENKO

In aedibus Dumbarton Oaks

Washingtoniae, D.C.

MCMLXXXV

THE CORRESPONDENCE OF LEO, METROPOLITAN OF SYNADA AND SYNCELLUS

GREEK TEXT, TRANSLATION, AND COMMENTARY

by

MARTHA POLLARD VINSON

Dumbarton Oaks

Research Library and Collection

Washington, D.C.

1985

Manufactured in the United States of America by
Sheridan Books, Inc., 450 Fame Avenue, Hanover, PA 17331 | (717) 632-3535

LIBRARY OF CONGRESS CATALOGING IN PUBLICATION DATA
Leo, Metropolitan of Synada and Syncellus, 937–ca. 1003.
The correspondence of Leo, Metropolitan of Synada and Syncellus
Greek text, translation, and commentary by Martha Pollard Vinson.
(Dumbarton Oaks texts ; 8) (Corpus Fontium Historiae Byzantinae ; 23)
Includes bibliographical references and indexes.

ISBN 978-0-88402-136-0 (hardcover: alk. paper)
ISBN 978-0-88402-449-1 (paperbound: alk. paper)
LCCN permalink: https://lccn.loc.gov/84004027

1. Leo, Metropolitan of Synada, 937–ca. 1003.
2. Orthodox Eastern Church—Turkey—Bishops—Correspondence.
I. Vinson, Martha Pollard. II. Title.
III. Title: Leonis Synadorum Metropolitae et Syncelli epistolae
IV. Series. V. Series: Corpus fontium historiae Byzantinae; v. 23.
VI. Series: Corpus fontium historiae Byzantinae. Series Washingtoniensis.
BX395.L46 A.4 1985
270.3'092'4 [B] 84-4027

In accordance with the rules adopted by the International Commission for the Edition of Sources of Byzantine History, the text and translation of this volume have been verified by Ihor Ševčenko and L. G. Westerink

EU GPSR Authorised Representative
LOGOS EUROPE, 9 rue Nicolas Poussin, 17000, La Rochelle, France
E-mail: Contact@logoseurope.eu

TABLE OF CONTENTS

ACKNOWLEDGMENTS

The present volume could not have been completed without the kind assistance of many individuals. First and foremost of these is my thesis advisor, L. G. Westerink, who has been an unfailing source of erudition and encouragement from the inception of this project to the final stages of its preparation for publication. The staff at Dumbarton Oaks, particularly Peter Topping, Julia Warner, and the two readers, could not have been more helpful or conscientious and I am most grateful to them. Finally, I should like to thank Phyllis Culham and George Kustas for their moral support and sound advice. It goes without saying that whatever faults remain herein are entirely mine.

INTRODUCTION

Fifty-three letters (one written by Stephen of Nicomedia) and a will form the corpus of Leo of Synada's correspondence. Of these fifty-four documents, only the first thirteen, written during his diplomatic mission to the West (996–98), his will (Ep. 31), and the last two, detailing the political maneuvering prior to the election of the Patriarch Sisinnius II (April 12, 996), can be placed in a historical context and dated with any accuracy or confidence. In between, there are some letters, e.g., Epp. 14–17, for which we can hazard a good guess as to the date of composition and the recipient; others, e.g., Epp. 29, 36, and 43, for which we are, at present, unable to establish the date and in some cases the addressee—regrettably so, since this information would be of interest and help to the historian of the late tenth century; and finally, there are others, "friendly letters," e.g., Ep. 33, about which we know little more, if anything, than what our text tells us, but whose value does not depend upon a precise chronological setting.

The scholarly world has had access to the first nine letters since 1892, when A. Sakkelion published them in Σωτήρ (vol. 15, 117–22). They were taken from a private manuscript, now *Atheniensis B.N. 1896*, and numbered 85–93 according to their order in that manuscript.[1] These letters were known to G. Schlumberger[2] and through him to J. Gay[3] and F. Dölger.[4] Dölger recognized that Schlumberger's chronology of Leo's mission was confused and suggested that a typographical error was responsible.[5] His own account, however, is not much of an improvement: he separates the embassy of which Leo was a member from the one that accompanied Philagathus back to Rome and assigns them to the beginning of 996 and the spring of 997 respectively.[6] P. E. Schramm was the first to make an attempt to reconcile the chronology by a careful analysis of Leo's letters in conjunction with Western sources.[7]

[1] J. Darrouzès, *Epistoliers byzantins du Xe siècle* (Paris, 1960), 39.

[2] G. Schlumberger, *L'épopée byzantine à la fin du Xe siècle*, II (Paris, 1900), 282, note 1.

[3] J. Gay, *L'Italie méridionale et l'empire byzantin* (Paris, 1904; reprint, New York, 1960), 392–93.

[4] F. Dölger, *Regesten de. Kaiserurkunden des oströmischen Reiches*, I (Munich-Berlin, 1924), 101–2.

[5] *Ibid.*, 101.

[6] *Ibid.*, 101–2.

[7] P. E. Schramm, "Neun Briefe des byzantinischen Gesandten Leo von seiner Reise zu Otto III. aus den Jahren 997–98," *BZ*, 25 (1925) 89–105.

Patmensis 706 (=P), from which Sakkelion's manuscript was derived,[8] contains three additional letters which are also concerned with Leo's mission to the West. They provide information on the trip from Constantinople and the situation that greeted Leo in Rome. Together with the other letters, they tend to put Leo's departure from the capital in the fall and his arrival in Rome late in 996, perhaps a month or so earlier than Schramm's January date. Leo remained in the West for two years (Ep. 3.5) and returned to Constantinople in the fall of 998. With the endpoints of Leo's diplomatic tenure more or less firmly fixed, it remained to work out the internal chronology. This has been accomplished, largely due to the efforts of Schramm. However, there are still some points of uncertainty, e.g., the month of the deposition of the anti-pope Philagathus. These will be considered in the notes.

Following the twelve letters in which Leo recounts the events connected with his sojourn in Italy is the one addressed to *ὁ κανικλείου*, which is of crucial importance in establishing the termini of Leo's life since he states in it that he is sixty years old (Ep. 13.5). There are two good reasons, namely, the proximity of this letter to the others and the mention of Italy, France, and Spain (Ep. 13.2–4), for believing that the letter is contemporary with Epp. 1–12. This hypothesis is confirmed by the identification of the addressee of the letter with Nicephorus Uranus who during this period (997) delivered a stunning setback to the Bulgarian Tsar Samuel at the Sperchius River (see *infra*, Ep. 13 and notes). With this knowledge it is possible to establish 937[9] as Leo's date of birth and 1003 as the date of composition for the will, written when Leo was sixty-six and the latest known document from his pen. J. Darrouzès opines that Leo died soon after composing the will, a victim of heart failure or apoplexy,[10] but the actual date and cause of his death remain unknown.

Apparently independently of one another, I. Sycoutres and the team of H. Grégoire and P. Orgels[11] sought to identify the metropolitan of Synada with the historian Leo the Deacon on the basis of the following notice from *Περὶ μεταθέσεων*: *Ἐπὶ τῆς βασιλείας Βασιλείου τοῦ Πορφυρογεννήτου ἐδόθη τῷ μητροπολίτῃ Πατρῶν ἡ ἐπισκοπὴ Κορίνθου, ὡς γράφει ὁ Σεβαστείας Θεόδωρος, καὶ Λέων Συνάδων*.[12] Apart from the problematic nature of this

[8] J. Darrouzès, "Notes d'histoire des textes," *REB*, 15 (1957), 172.

[9] Before the identification of *ὁ κανικλείου* with Nicephorus Uranus permitted a secure date for Ep. 13, Darrouzès posited 937 as Leo's date of birth in "Inventaire des épistoliers byzantins du Xᵉ siècle," *REB*, 18 (1960), 122. This chronology was questioned by N. Panagiotakes in *Λέων ὁ Διάκονος* (Athens, 1965), 40 note 1, on the basis of the uncertainty surrounding the dating of Ep. 13, which Darrouzès elsewhere admitted (*Epistoliers*, 40).

[10] J. Darrouzès, "Un recueil épistolaire byzantin: le manuscrit de Patmos 706," *REB*, 14 (1956), 104.

[11] I. Sycoutres, Letter, EEBS, 9 (1932), 474; but Sycoutres does not mention this identification in his article published the following year, *Λέοντος τοῦ Διακόνου ἀνέκδοτον ἐγκώμιον εἰς Βασίλειον τὸν* B′, EEBS, 10 (1933), 425–34; H. Grégoire and P. Orgels, "La chronologie des patriarches de Constantinople et la 'Question Romaine' à la fin du Xᵉ siècle," *BYZ*, 24 (1954), 177.

[12] G. A. Rhalles and M. Potles, *Σύνταγμα τῶν θείων καὶ ἱερῶν κανόνων*, V (Athens, 1855), 393; PG, 119, col. 905D.

source,[13] the view that Leo of Synada and Leo the Deacon are one and the same person has been successively rejected by Darrouzès, N. Panagiotakes, and M. Sjuzjumov.[14] The arguments against the identification of the two Leos include the disparity between their ages (Leo the Deacon was a *μειράκιον* in 966 when Leo of Synada was thirty-one years old)[15] and that between their treatment of the same individuals (e.g., Stephen of Nicomedia)[16] and events (e.g., Basil II's Bulgarian campaign).[17] The metropolitan of Synada may very well have tried his hand at historiography, but he is not the author of the *Historiae libri decem* ascribed to Leo the Deacon.

Very little is known of Leo's family except that he had a brother (Epp. 46.6 and 47.9) and an uncle who was also a bishop (Epp. 29.16–17 and 42.5–6), but neither their names nor the uncle's see appear in the text. The literary allusions in his letters and Leo's own admission (Ep. 31.19–20) tell us that Leo was an educated man and one devoted to the "classics," but he does not state where this learning was acquired or from whom. Similarly obscure are the dates and circumstances surrounding his appointments to the see of Synada and the office of syncellus.

However short may be the supply of specific names, dates, and places for the events affecting Leo's life, a rich portrait of Leo the individual emerges from his letters. He was a bright and witty man; even better, he had a wonderful sense of humor; better still, he didn't take himself too seriously, despite his confession to the contrary in the will (Ep. 31.22–24). Even if they were not colleagues as syncelli, one would not be surprised to find that the equally witty (and controversial) Stephen of Nicomedia figures in his correspondence. One accepts as routine the elegant (and sympathetic, when the occasion demanded it) letters to his brother bishops and the affectionate personal notes to Byzantium's lesser lights, e.g., the otherwise unknown patrician Methodius. Of more interest are the letters (Epp. 7, 10, 38, 39, 44, and possibly 37) written to four (five?) different officials connected with the fisc, which give the impression that Leo actively cultivated friendships in that branch of the imperial bureaucracy. This would have been a politically wise course of action on Leo's part, even if Synada was not as disadvantaged as he would have us believe in Ep. 43.

But, like everyone else, Leo had his faults, which he enumerates at length in his will. Darrouzès' description of his personality as "apoplectic" does not seem quite fair since the antics of a Philagathus or Arsenius would be enough to try the patience of a saint, which Leo would be the first to admit he was not. Rather, Leo's greatest shortcoming was his judgment, though not of character (e.g., he knew ex-

[13] V. Grumel, "Le Περὶ μεταθέσεων et le patriarche de Constantinople Dosithée," *REB*, 1 (1943), 239.

[14] Darrouzès, "Inventaire," p. 122; Panagiotakes, p. 41; M. Sjuzjumov, *Antichnaia drevnost' i srednie veka*, 7, Seriia istoricheskaia, vyp. 22, Uchenye zapiski, 112 (Sverdlovsk, 1971), 141.

[15] Darrouzès, "Inventaire," 122.

[16] Panagiotakes, 41.

[17] Darrouzès, "Inventaire," 122.

actly what sort of rascal Philagathus was before his appointment to the papal see). His apparent inability to foresee the consequences of a decision involving such doubtful quantities as Philagathus and Arsenius rendered him capable of the kind of gross miscalculation which, barring a minor miracle, could only result in fiasco. Another failure to judge correctly the strength of his own position vis-à-vis the opposition ended in Leo's (temporary?) exclusion from the synod called to elect the Patriarch Sisinnius II. The source of the controversy and the part Leo took in it are still unclear; nor do we know how and when the matter was resolved. Part of the settlement may have included Leo's appointment as head of the legation charged with negotiating the betrothal of Otto III and a porphyrogenita. This ought to have been mutually satisfactory to both Leo and his opponents: Leo's faction would be effectively neutralized by the extended absence of its leading(?) proponent, while at the same time Leo himself could retain a certain amount of dignity by accepting a commission which, to all appearances, was commensurate with his ability and position. However, one should qualify the prestige involved in Leo's new diplomatic status by observing that Basil II's preoccupation with events closer to home had put Italo-Byzantine relations very low on the list of imperial priorities—despite Arab encroachments in southern Italy—and that it was only in the final years of his reign that Basil displayed more than a perfunctory interest in the western territories.[18]

As has been noted above, the first nine letters of the present collection were previously edited by Sakkelion in 1892 and reedited with a historical analysis by Schramm in 1925. A year later there followed K. Dyobuniotes' posthumous publication of Spyridon Lambros' text of the twenty-three letters attributed to Leo which are found in *Vindobonensis phil. gr. 342* (=V) (Epp. 32–54).[19] In 1960 Darrouzès published the thirty letters and the will transmitted under Leo's name in P (Epp. 1–31) and included in his edition Lambros' text of the letters from V.[20] While Darrouzès went far in laying the groundwork for a definitive text of Leo's correspondence, the very nature of his edition, in which Leo's letters appeared as only one of several epistolary collections, meant that there remained much to do. This became apparent during the close scrutiny of the text that is necessary for translation: in other words, what appears to be tolerable Greek often becomes intolerable when one attempts to render it into another language. Further, although Darrouzès did not ignore Leo's rich use of biblical and secular literature, many of these allusions escaped his notice and, one may add, still remain elusive.

While the author acknowledges the contributions of her predecessors to the text of Leo of Synada, this edition is based on a reexamination of the manuscripts, principally P, which contains Epp. 1–31, and V, which contains Epp. 32–54. *Coislinianus 27* (=C) is also valuable for the revised version of Leo's will that it

[18] V. von Falkenhausen, *Untersuchungen über die byzantinische Herrschaft in Süditalien vom 9. bis ins 11. Jahrhundert* (Wiesbaden, 1969), 51–53.

[19] NE, 20 (1926), 324–42.

[20] Darrouzès, *Epistoliers*, 165–210.

contains. Of little importance for this edition are *Atheniensis B.N. 1896*[21] and *Oxoniensis misc. 242* (=O)[22] since they are derivative and the alternative readings they offer are inferior. I have not been able to consult any of these manuscripts directly but have relied on photographs for the three principal ones. This arrangement has proven quite satisfactory except for a very few cases involving P. For example, in the photograph of fol. 207^{v} all that can be read of the word following κορύζῃ in Ep. 13.8 is part of a *chi* because the lower left-hand corner of the page is crumpled. The true readings of P, which are wholly or partially obscure in the photographs for mechanical reasons, have been ferreted out by L. G. Westerink, who was kind enough to examine the folios in question when he was in Greece several summers ago. This represents an unquestionable improvement over the text of Darrouzès who did not have the advantage of inspecting P, either himself or by proxy.

Among the various collections of letters that P contains, there are found in fols. 199^{r}–217^{v} thirty-one letters (including the will) attributed to Leo, metropolitan of Synada and syncellus. P is written on paper and measures 290 × 205 mm. The wire marks average twenty every four centimeters and there are twelve leaves to the quire. It is agreed that P antedates 1201, since it can be identified with a manuscript appearing in the inventory of the library at Patmos which the Higoumenos Arsenius took in this year. The fluid, open style of the script indicates the eleventh century, as has been pointed out by G. Pasquali who used P for his edition of the letters of Gregory of Nyssa. Darrouzès, by supplementing the paleographical evidence with what is known of the library's history and with what can be deduced from the contents of the manuscript, has come to the conclusion that P was written before 1079 in the area around Mt. Latros.[23] In 1079 Christodulus, the library's founder, fled from Mt. Latros to escape the Turks: Christodulus went to Patmos, while his library, of which only a fourth was later recovered, went to Constantinople. Darrouzès notes the presence in P of a collection of letters by John, a monk of Latros, and the lack of any letter or name that is later than the early years of the eleventh century. Darrouzès concludes his argument by observing: "Si l'on ajoute qu'il est témoin unique pour plusieurs correspondances, on comprendra que le recueil n'a pu se former que dans un de ces couvents où se réfugiaient volontiers les plus grands noms

[21] Epp. 1–9 are found in this manuscript which Sakkelion used for his edition (see *supra*). Thereafter it disappeared and was lost until, after a seven-year search, Darrouzès rediscovered it in the National Library at Athens. In his introduction to Leo's letters (*Epistoliers*, 39), Darrouzès says of it: "étant donné que nous avons retrouvé l'original (i.e., *Pat. 706*), cette copie n'a plus aucun intérêt pour l'édition." Cf. also Darrouzès, "Notes," 171–72.

[22] Ep. 4 (to Methodius the Patrician) appears in fol. 213^{r-v} of O, where, however, it is part of a collection of letters written by Nicetas Magistros. The letter was published by S. Lambros in NE, 19 (1925), 187–88, together with other letters attributed to Nicetas which are found in this manuscript and in V. The reference to Leo's diplomatic mission as well as the presence in V of two other letters to the same Methodius (Epp. 40–41), in one of which (Ep. 41) Leo speaks devotedly of Methodius' father, leaves no doubt that Leo is the author of Ep. 4. For the description of O and its contents, see H. O. Coxe, *Catalogi codicum manuscriptorum bibliotheca Bodleianae*, I (Oxford, 1853), 789–800.

[23] Darrouzès, *Epistoliers*, 10–11.

de la magistrature, de l'aristocratie ou des lettres byzantines, parfois avec les souvenirs et les documents de leur vie passée."[24] This is an interesting and plausible theory, but even without it P can be safely assigned to the eleventh or, at the very latest, the twelfth century, which is an acceptable range for P since it is unique.[25]

V, like P, is also composed of a literary collection. Twenty-three letters attributed to the metropolitan of Synada are found in fols. 163^{v}–183^{r}, although one of these letters (Ep. 34, which appears in fols. 164^{v}–165^{v}) was written to Leo by (Stephen) the metropolitan of Nicomedia. V is an eleventh-century parchment manuscript measuring 145/148 × 112/114 mm.[26] There are eight leaves to the quire. Most of the headings and initials are in gold on a red ground. The first and last folios containing Leo's correspondence (163^{v} and 183^{r}) as well as fol. 1^{v} are the only ones to display any additional decoration, which takes the form of a horizontal band of edging, also in gold on red. The border motif of fol. 163^{v} consists of doubled spirals, while that of 183^{r} is an unbroken line of stylized vine tendrils. The letters found in V (Epp. 32–54) have been previously edited by Lambros[27] who also published a complete enumeration of the contents of this manuscript.[28]

C is a parchment manuscript measuring 353 × 258 mm.[29] It is very badly damaged at the beginning and end. C is unusual, in comparison with P and V, in that the bulk of its 251 folios contains a commentary on St. Paul, with catena. Even more unusual is the presence of three folios written by different hands. In one of these, fol. 6^{r}, a revised copy of Leo's will is found. The left-hand side of this folio shows signs of the damage that C has suffered at the beginning: at a few points the writing is so faint as to be almost entirely illegible. The script may best be described as crabbed, and the use of superscription is much heavier than in P and V. One superscript in particular, τ̄(ους), does not appear in either P or V. Since 1003 has been established as the will's date of composition, C (or at least fol. 6^{r}) must be assigned to the very early eleventh century rather than the tenth, as R. Devreesse does. The proximity of the date of the copy to the actual composition raises the possibility that it came from Leo's own papers. Could it be an autograph?

Although the letters in V are attributed simply to the "metropolitan of Synada" (fol. 163^{v}), there is no reason to doubt that he is the same author found in P, "Leo, metropolitan of Synada and syncellus" (fol. 199^{r}). This is confirmed by the presence of the same persons in both collections, e.g., Methodius the Patrician in Epp. 4 (P) and 41–42 (V) and Leo's uncle, the bishop, in Epp. 29.16–17 (P) and 42.5–6 (V);[30] and also by stylistic and chronological considerations: Epp. 53–54 (V) were

[24] *Ibid.*, 11.

[25] Darrouzès, "Recueil," 88–89.

[26] H. Hunger, *Katalog der griechischen Handschriften der österreichischen Nationalbibliotek*, I (Vienna, 1961), 435–37.

[27] *Supra*, note 19.

[28] NE, 19 (1925), 12–27.

[29] R. Devreesse, *Catalogue des manuscrits grecs, II: Le fonds Coislin* (Paris, 1945), 22–23.

[30] The protonotarius to whom Ep. 37 (V) is addressed is probably not the same person mentioned

written only six to eight months before Leo's embassy to the West, the occasion on which the first thirteen letters found in P were written.

There is no overlap between P and V so far as concerns the letters attributed to the metropolitan of Synada. However, P does contain, in fol. 227^{r-v}, under the heading *ἐπιστολαὶ διάφοροι* two letters that appear in V. Both the letters, Epp. 39 and 45, show variations that are the result of editorial revision rather than carelessness on the part of the copyist. While the textual variants in both cases are minor and do not substantially affect the sense, the version of Ep. 45 found in P contains approximately two lines that do not appear in V. This would seem to indicate that, although the letters of P are generally dated later than those of V,[31] the publication of P antedates that of V. This in turn would help explain why the headings in V are, on the whole, less detailed and reliable than those in P.

The critical apparatus has been composed with a view to clarity and succinctness, in that order. Purely orthographical errors do not appear except when they are of interest to the student of linguistics and/or paleography. Corrections and emendations made by previous editors are noted in the apparatus whether they appear in the text or not. One should note that the use of square brackets ([ ]) indicates textual loss due to physical damage, while that of braces ({ }) indicates editorial deletion.[32]

in Ep. 29.18 (P); and the patriarch of Antioch in Ep. 32 (V) may not be the same person as in Epp. 14–16 (P).

[31] Darrouzès, *Epistoliers*, 41.

[32] See M. L. West, *Textual Criticism and Editorial Technique* (Stuttgart, 1973), 80.

BIBLIOGRAPHY

Annales Hildesheimenses, ed. G. H. Pertz, in MGH *SS*, III (Hanover, 1839; reprint, Stuttgart-New York, 1963), 22–116

Annales Quedlinburgenses, ed. G. H. Pertz, in MGH *SS*, III (Hanover, 1839; reprint, Stuttgart-New York, 1963), 22–90

Athenagoras, Metropolitan. Ὁ *θεσμὸς τῶν συγκέλλων ἐν τῷ* Οἰκουμενικῷ Πατριαρ*χείῳ*. EEBS, 4 (1927), 3–38

Bensammar, E., "La titulature de l'impératrice et sa signification," *BYZ*, 46 (1976), 243–91

Bury, J. B., *The Imperial Administrative System in the Ninth Century* (London, 1911; reprint, New York, 1958)

Canard, M., "Deux documents arabes sur Bardas Skléros," *SBN*, 5 (1939), 55–69

Cedrenus, George, and Scylitzes, John, *Opera*, ed. I. Bekker, 2 vols. (Bonn, 1838–39)

Chronicon Venetum, ed. G. H. Pertz, in MGH *SS*, VII (Hanover, 1846; reprint, Stuttgart-New York, 1963), 4–38

Constantine Porphyrogenitus, *De cerimoniis aulae byzantinae*, ed. J. J. Reiske, 2 vols. (Bonn, 1829–30)

Corpus paroemiographorum graecorum, eds. E. L. Leutsche and F. G. Schneidewin, 2 vols. (Göttingen, 1839–51)

Coxe, H. O., *Catalogi codicum manuscriptorum bibliothecae Bodleianae*, I (Oxford, 1853)

Darrouzès, J., *Documents inédits d'ecclésiologie byzantine* (Paris, 1966)

________, *Epistoliers byzantins du Xe siècle* (Paris, 1960)

________, "Inventaire des épistoliers byzantins du Xe siècle," *REB*, 18 (1960), 109–35

________, "Notes d'histoire des textes: 2. Atheniensis 1896, le 'manuscrit de Sakellion,'" *REB*, 15 (1957), 171–72

________, *Recherches sur les* Ὀφφίκια *de l'église byzantine* (Paris, 1970)

________, "Un recueil épistolaire byzantin: le manuscrit de Patmos 706," *REB*, 14 (1956), 87–121

Devreesse, R., *Catalogue des manuscrits grecs. II: Le fonds Coislin* (Paris, 1945)

Diehl, C., "De la signification du titre de 'proèdre' à Byzance," in *Mélanges offerts à M. Gustave Schlumberger à l'occasion du quatre-vingtième anniversaire de sa naissance, 17 Octobre 1924* (Paris, 1924), 105–17

________, "L'étoffe byzantine du reliquaire de Charlemagne," in *Bulićev Zbornik* (Zagreb, 1924), 441–49

Dölger, F., *Beiträge zur Geschichte der byzantinischen Finanzverwaltung besonders des 10. und 11. Jahrhunderts* (Leipzig-Berlin, 1927; reprint, Hildesheim, 1960)

________, *Regesten der Kaiserurkunden des oströmischen Reiches. 1. Regesten von 565–1025* (Munich-Berlin, 1924)

________, and Karayannopulos, J., *Byzantinische Urkundenlehre, 1. Die Kaiserurkunden* (Munich, 1968)

Falkenhausen, V. von, *Untersuchungen über die byzantinische Herrschaft in Süditalien vom 9. bis ins 11. Jahrhundert* (Wiesbaden, 1969)

Gay, J., *L'Italie méridionale et l'empire byzantin* (Paris, 1904; reprint, New York, 1960)

Glykatzi-Ahrweiler, H., *Recherches sur l'administration de l'empire byzantin aux IXe–XIe siècles* (Athens-Paris, 1960)

Grégoire, H., *Recueil des inscriptions grecques chrétiennes d'Asie Mineure* (Paris, 1922; reprint, Amsterdam, 1968)

———, and Orgels, P., "La chronologie des patriarches de Constantinople et la 'Question Romaine' à la fin du Xe siècle," *BYZ*, 24 (1954), 159–78

Grumel, V., "Chronologie patriarcale au Xe siècle," *REB*, 22 (1964), 45–71

———, "Le patriarcat et les patriarches d'Antioche sous la seconde domination byzantine," *EO*, 33 (1934), 129–47

———, "Les patriarches grecs d'Antioche du nom Jean," *EO*, 32 (1933), 279–99

———, "Le Περὶ μεταθέσεων et le patriarche de Constantinople Dosithée," *REB*, 1 (1943), 239–49

———, *Les regestes des actes du patriarcat du Constantinople, I. Les actes des patriarches, fasc. II: 715–1043* (Kadiköy, 1936)

———, "Titulature de métropolites byzantins. I. Les métropolites syncelles," *REB*, 3 (1945), 92–114

Guilland, R., "Etudes sur l'histoire administrative de l'empire byzantin. Le sébastophore: Ὁ σεβαστοφόρος," *REB*, 21 (1963), 199–207

———, "Les logothètes: études d'histoire administrative de l'empire byzantin," *REB*, 29 (1971), 5–115

———, *Recherches sur les institutions byzantines*. 2 vols. (Berlin-Amsterdam, 1967)

Hausherr, I., ed. and Horn, G., trans., *Un grand mystique byzantin: Vie de Syméon le Nouveau Théologien (949–1022) par Nicétas Stéthatos* (Rome, 1928)

Hunger, H., *Katalog der griechischen Handschriften der österreichischen Nationalbibliotek*, I (Vienna, 1961)

Janin, R., *Constantinople byzantine: développement urbain et répertoire topographique*, 2nd ed. (Paris, 1964)

———, "Euchaïtes," *DHGE* (Paris, 1912 ff.)

Jaubert, P. A., *La géographie d'Edrisi*, 2 vols. (Paris, 1836–40; reprint, Amsterdam, 1975)

Krumbacher, K., *Geschichte der byzantinischen Litteratur (527–1453)*, 2nd ed. (Munich, 1897)

Lambros, S., Ἐπιστολαὶ ἐκ τοῦ βιενναίου κώδικος Phil. gr. 342, NE, 19 (1925), 3 ff.; 20 (1926), 324–42

Laurent, V., *Le corpus des sceaux de l'empire byzantin*, V, 1 (Paris, 1963)

Lemerle, P., Guillou, A., Svoronos, N., Papachryssanthou, D., *Actes de Lavra*, I (Paris, 1970)

Leo the Deacon, *Historiae libri decem et liber de velitatione bellica Nicephori Augusti*, ed. C. Hase (Bonn, 1828)

LeQuien, M., *Oriens Christianus*, 3 vols. (Paris, 1740)

Liber Pontificalis, II, ed. L. Duchesne (Paris, 1892)

Lopez, R. S., "Silk Industry in the Byzantine Empire," *Speculum*, 20 (1945), 1–42

Mercati, A., "The New List of Popes," *Mediaeval Studies*, 9 (1947), 71–80

Oikonomides, N., *Les listes de préséance byzantines des IXe et Xe siècles* (Paris, 1972)

Panagiotakes, N., Λέων ὁ Διάκονος (Athens, 1965)
Peter Damian, *Epistulae*, PL, 144 (Paris, 1853)
Poppe, A., "The Political Background to the Baptism of Rus'," *DOP*, 30 (1976), 195–245
Psellus, Michael, *Chronographie*, ed. and trans. E. Renauld, 2 vols. (Paris, 1926–28)
Rhalles, G. A., and Potles, M., Σύνταγμα τῶν θείων καὶ ἱερῶν κανόνων, V (Athens, 1855)
Robert, L., "Les kordakia de Nicée, le combustible de Synnada et les poissons-scies. Sur des lettres d'un métropolite de Phrygie du Xe siècle. Philologie et réalités," *Journal des Savants* (1961), 97–166; (1962), 5–74
Schlumberger, G., *L'épopée byzantine à la fin du Xe siècle*, 3 vols. (Paris, 1896–1905)
Schramm, P. E., "Kaiser, Basileus und Papst in der Zeit der Ottonen," *Historische Zeitschrift*, 129 (1924), 424–75
———, "Neun Briefe des byzantinischen Gesandten Leo von seiner Reise zu Otto III. aus den Jahren 997–998," *BZ*, 25 (1925), 89–105
Scylitzes, John, *Synopsis historiarum*, ed. J. Thurn (Berlin, 1973)
Sjuzjumov, M., *Antichnaia drevnost' i srednie veka*, 7, Seriia istoricheskaia, vyp. 22, Uchenye zapiski, 112 (Sverdlovsk, 1971)
Stoicorum Veterum Fragmenta, III, ed. J. von Arnim (Leipzig-Berlin, 1923)
Sycoutres, I., *Λέοντος τοῦ Διακόνου ἀνέκδοτον ἐγκώμιον εἰς* Βασίλειον *τὸν* Β', EEBS, 10 (1933), 425–34
———, Letter, EEBS, 9 (1932), 473–74
Ex Vita Sancti Nili, ed. G. H. Pertz, MGH *SS*, IV (Hanover, 1841; reprint, Stuttgart-New York, 1963), 616–18
Vryonis, S., Jr., *The Decline of Medieval Hellenism in Asia Minor and the Process of Islamization from the Eleventh through the Fifteenth Century* (Berkeley, 1971)
Wenger, Z., "Ciel ou Paradis," *BZ*, 41 (1951), 560–69
Westerink, L. G., *Nicholas I, Patriarch of Constantinople: Miscellaneous Writings*, Dumbarton Oaks Texts, VI (Washington, D.C., 1981)
Yahya-Ibn-Sa'id, *Histoire de Yahya-Ibn-Sa'id d'Antioche*, ed. and trans. I. Kratchkovsky and A. Vasiliev, Patrologia Orientalis, 23 (1932), 371–520
Zepos, J. and P., *Ius graecoromanum*, I (Athens, 1931)
Zonaras, John, *Annales*, ed. Pinder, 3 vols. (Bonn, 1841–97)

ABBREVIATIONS

BYZ:	*Byzantion*
BZ:	*Byzantinische Zeitschrift*
CPG:	*Corpus paroemiographorum graecorum*, ed. Leutsch and Schneidewin
DHGE:	*Dictionnaire d'histoire et de géographie ecclésiastique*
DOP:	*Dumbarton Oaks Papers*
EEBS:	Ἐπετηρὶς Ἑταιρείας Βυζαντινῶν Σπουδῶν
EO:	*Echos d'Orient*
MGH *SS*:	Monumenta Germaniae Historica, *Scriptores*
PG:	Patrologiae cursus completus. Series graeco-latina, ed. Migne
PL:	Patrologiae cursus completus. Series latina, ed. Migne
NE:	Νέος Ἑλληνομνήμων
REB:	*Revue des études byzantines*
SBN:	*Studi bizantini e neoellenici*
SVF:	*Stoicorum veterum fragmenta*, ed. von Arnim

SIGLA

TEXT

⟨ ⟩	addenda
{ }	delenda
[ ]	supplenda in lacuna codicis
...	lacuna statuenda
α̣	puncto notantur litterae incertae

APPARATUS

C:	*Coislinianus 27*, s. XI
P:	*Patmensis 706*, s. XI–XII
O:	*Oxoniensis misc. 242*, s. XVI
V:	*Vindobonensis phil. gr. 342*, s. XI

TEXT and TRANSLATION

ΛΕΟΝΤΟΣ ΜΗΤΡΟΠΟΛΙΤΟΥ ΣΥΝΑΔΩΝ
ΚΑΙ ΣΥΓΚΕΛΛΟΥ ΕΠΙΣΤΟΛΑΙ

1. Ἰωάννῃ ὀστιαρίῳ τῷ τοῦ πρωτοβεστιαρίου Λέοντος

Γελᾷς ἄρτι τὸν πλατὺν γέλωτα, ὦ καλὴ κεφαλή, ὦ καλὴ ψυχή, ὁ μηδενὶ πώποτε κακοῦ γεγονὼς αἴτιος, πολλοῖς δὲ μᾶλλον πολλὰ ἀγαθὰ προξενήσας καὶ εἰς τοῦτο, ὡς εἰπεῖν, τὸ εὖ ποιεῖν, πᾶσι προκείμενος. Ὁ Φιλάγαθος ἐκεῖνος ὅς, ἵνα συνέλω, οὐδένα εἶχε τὸν ἰσοστάσιον, "οὗ ἀρᾶς τὸ στόμα καὶ πικρίας ἔγεμε" καὶ βλασφημίας καὶ πονηρίας καὶ λοιδορίας, ᾧ παρόμοιος οὐδείς, ὃν τίνι ἀντιτάξομεν οὐ γινώσκομεν, οὗτος ἐκεῖνος ὁ παλαμναῖος πάπας, ὁ σοβαρὸς καὶ ὑπέροφρυς, ὦ θεὲ καὶ δίκη καὶ ἥλιε, συμποδισθεὶς ἔπεσε. Καὶ τί μὴ τῷ ἀδελφῷ λέγω καὶ τὸ τοῦ πτώματος εἶδος; Πρὸ παντὸς ἀνάθεμα γέγονε τῆς δυτικῆς Ἐκκλησίας, εἶτα τοὺς ὀφθαλμοὺς ἐξωρύχθη, τὴν ῥῖνα τρίτον ἐξετμήθη καὶ τὸ χεῖλος τέταρτον, πέμπτον τὴν γλῶτταν τὴν πολλὰ καὶ ἄρρητα λαλοῦσαν καὶ ἄμαχον· ἐπόμπευσεν ἐπὶ τούτοις ἕκτον ὀνίσκῳ πτωχῷ σεμνυνόμενος οὐροκρατῶν καὶ τοῦτον, τὴν δὲ κεφαλὴν ἔσκεπε ἀσκοῦ παλαιοῦ τεμάχιον τὰς προτομὰς ἔχον ὀρθίους· τὸ δ' ἕβδομον εἰς κρίσιν ἦλθε, κατεψηφίσθη, τὴν ἱερατικὴν ἐνεδύθη καὶ ἐξεδύθη στολήν, ὀπισθοφανῶς ἐσύρη ⟨κατὰ⟩ τὸν ναὸν αὐτόν, τὸν πρόναον, τὴν φιάλης αὐλὴν καὶ ὡς εἰς ἀναψυχὴν εἰς τὸν κάρκαρον ἐνεβλήθη.

Εἶπόν σοι, ἀδελφὲ ἰσόψυχε, τὰ συμβάντα τῷ ταπεινῷ Φιλαγάθῳ μηδὲν ἢ προσθεὶς ἢ ἀποκρυψάμενος, ἀλλὰ καὶ πᾶσι λέγω μὴ τολμᾶν οἷα ἐκεῖνος· ἡ δίκη γὰρ οὐ καθεύδει. Σὺ δέ μοι χαῖρε καὶ εὖ πρᾶττε καὶ διηνεκῶς ὑπερεύχου καὶ μέμνησο· ἴδοιμί σε τάχιστα χαίροντα καὶ εὐοδούμενον.

1: 6 cf. Rom. 3.14

1: P 199r.

6 *πικρίας* Schramm: *πονηρίας* P || 17 add. Schramm || 19 *κάρκαρον* Sakkelion: *βάρκαρον* P

THE CORRESPONDENCE OF LEO, METROPOLITAN OF SYNADA AND SYNCELLUS

1. To John the Ostiarius, (Nephew) of the Protovestiarius Leo

Just now you're enjoying a good laugh, you lovely fellow, you lovely soul, you who have never caused anyone trouble; on the contrary, you have effected many good things for many people, and for this purpose, I mean your good works, you are available to all. That Philagathus who, to be brief, had no equivalent, "whose mouth was full of cursing and bitterness," blasphemy, wickedness, and abuse, who was unique and, as far as we know, without parallel, that murderous pope, that pompous and haughty creature—O God and Justice and Light of the Sun—has fallen, bound hand and foot. Why don't I tell my brother what his fall was like? First of all, he was pronounced anathema to the Western Church; second, his eyes were put out; third, his nose and fourth, his lips were cut off; fifth, his overpowering tongue which constantly babbled unmentionable things. Sixth after this, he led a procession solemnly riding a shabby little donkey which he held by the tail, too. A shred of an ancient goatskin with its head upright covered his own. Seventh, he went to trial, was condemned, was dressed in and stripped of his ecclesiastical garb, was dragged out backwards through the very nave, the narthex, the courtyard with the fountain, and was thrown in the dungeon as a respite.

I've told you, my brother and soul mate, what happened to unfortunate Philagathus, neither adding nor omitting anything, and furthermore I advise everyone against that fellow's brand of audacity. Justice does not sleep. Farewell, goodbye, pray for us constantly and remember us. I hope to see you well and happy very soon.

2. Μιχαὴλ μαγίστρῳ

Ὄντως "σοφὸν ἓν βούλευμα τὰς πολλὰς χεῖρας νικᾷ," ἐγὼ δὲ καὶ "γνώμας," ὦ Εὐριπίδη, λέγω καὶ "ὁρμὰς" καὶ "πράξεις" αὐτὰς καὶ οὐ μεταμέλομαι τοῦτο λέγων. Σοῦ ἕνεκεν, ὦ θαυμάσιε καὶ καλὲ μάγιστρε, πρὸς ἐκεῖνον τὸν σοφὸν ἀπετείναμεν· σὺ γὰρ καλὸς εἶ, καὶ προβουλευόμενος καὶ τοῖς κακῶς βουλευθεῖσι καλῶς ἐπιβουλευόμενος· οὐκ ἂν ἁμάρτοι τις καὶ "Γερήνιον καὶ πατέρα λαοῦ" σε καλέσας καὶ πᾶσαν ἀγαθὴν κλῆσιν ἐπιφημίσας σοι. Ἐγὼ γοῦν τοῦτο μόνον οἶδα σοφὸν βουλευσάμενος, τὸ σὲ προστάτην τοῦ ἐμοῦ οἴκου ποιήσασθαι καὶ αὐτὰς τὰς ψυχικὰς κινήσεις μου. Εἴ τις οὖν ἔλεος, εἴ τις φιλανθρωπία, εἴ τις χρηστότης, εἴ τις ἀγάπη, "εἴ τις παράκλησις ἐν Χριστῷ" σπεῦσον μὴ "κενωθῆναι τὸ καύχημά μου," ἀλλὰ τοῦ σοῦ Λέοντος ἐπ' ἀγαθοῖς μνημόνευε καὶ πιστεύω τῷ θεῷ ὡς οὐδὲν δυσχερὲς ἀπαντήσει μοι.

Ἵνα δὲ τὰ ἡμέτερα γνῷς πῶς ὁ Θεὸς ᾠκονόμησεν, ἰδοὺ κἀκεῖνα γράφω σοι. Ἤλθομεν ἐν Φραγγίᾳ δι' ὅλου τοῦ αὐγούστου καὶ τοῦ σεπτεμβρίου καὶ τοῦ ὀκτωβρίου· ἐξήλθομεν διὰ τῶν ἑτέρων τριῶν τοῦ νοεμβρίου καὶ τοῦ δεκεμβρίου καὶ τοῦ ἰαννουαρίου καὶ ἐποιήσαμεν ἐν τῇ Ῥώμῃ μῆνας τέσσαρας καὶ εἴδομεν, ἃ εἴδομεν· ἀλλ' ὁ Θεὸς περιεφύλαξεν ἡμᾶς ἀβλαβεῖς καὶ ἀνυπονοήτους, ἐφ' οἷς πρότερον καὶ ἐβουλευσάμεθα καὶ ἐγράψαμεν· καὶ ἐξήλθομεν ἀποκρισιάριον λαβόντες, ἐλάττονα μὲν πρὸς τὸ παρόν, μείζονα δὲ ἕτερον ἐκδεχόμενοι εἰς Ἱδροῦντα, δι' ὅλου τοῦ σεπτεμβρίου. Ὅμως πάντα οἶδας ὅσα περιεῖχε τὸ σύμφωνον· ἐρώτησον τὸν τὰ γράμματα ἐπιδιδόντα ἄνθρωπον ἡμῶν καὶ παρ' ἐκείνου μαθήσῃ πάντα· εἴ τι δύνασαι, βοήθησον ἡμῖν ὑπὸ τοῦ Θεοῦ βοηθούμενός τε καὶ συνεργούμενος.

2: 2 Trag. Gr. Frag. no. 200 ex Euripidis *Antiope* ‖ 7 Hom., *Il.*, 2.336 ‖ 11–12 Phil. 2.1 ‖ 12 I Cor. 9.15

2: P 199^{v}.

2. To Michael the Magister

The saying is true that "one wise plan conquers many enemies." But I, Euripides, add as well "ideas," "initiatives," and even "actions," nor do I regret this addition. For your sake, wonderful and good Magister, I refer to that wise poet; for you are good, have foresight, and plot successfully against evil conspirators. One would not be far wrong if he called you "Nestor and the father of his people" and bestowed upon you every good name. I know that I have formed this single wise resolve: to make you guardian of my household and (to confide to you) even the inclinations of my heart. If, then, there is any pity, any human kindness, any goodness, any affection, "if there is any comfort in Christ," take care lest "my glorifying become void"; but remember your Leo to his advantage, and I trust in God that nothing unpleasant will happen to me.

That you may know how God has managed our affairs, here I am writing to you about them. We traveled to Frangia during all of August, September, and October. We returned during the next three months (November, December, and January) and stayed in Rome for four months and saw what we saw. But God preserved us unharmed and unsuspected of what we planned and wrote previously. We left, taking a legate with us, a less important one for the present, and waited for one of greater stature at Hidrous all of September. At any rate, you know everything the agreement included. Ask our agent who gives you our letter and you will learn everything from him. If you can, help us with God's help and with him as your coworker.

3. Τῷ Ἁγιοζαχαρίτῃ

Ἡ γραφή σου, ὑπέρλαμπρε καὶ θαυμάσιε ἄνθρωπε, "ὑετὸς ἐπὶ γῆν διψῶσαν" ἐγένετο ἐν τῇ καρδίᾳ μου καὶ ἐκόρεσε καὶ ἐγλύκανε καὶ εὔφρανε καὶ ἐπιλαθέσθαι πεποίηκε τῶν λυπηρῶν καὶ ἀηδῶν ἐκείνων, ὧν εἰς διετῆ χρόνον μετέσχομεν. Τὴν γὰρ πρώτην γεῦσιν, ἣν ἐν τῇ Πόλει ἐπέμψαμεν (οἶδας ὃ λέγω ὁ νοῦς ὁ ὀξύτατος) γνόντες ὡς ἀηδὴς ὑμῖν φανεῖται, ἑτέραν μετήλθομεν τὴν τῆς συμπενθερίας καὶ ἐν Φραγγίᾳ διὰ τριῶν μηνῶν ἀπὸ Ῥώμης εἰσήλθομεν καὶ τὰ τῆς συμπενθερίας ἐλαλήσαμεν καί, εἰ μὴ ἡμεῖς ἐκωλύσαμεν, οὐδὲν ἂν ἐκώλυε τοῦ μὴ τὴν συμπενθερίαν διὰ μιᾶς εὐκόλως προβῆναι.

Τοῦ Θεοῦ οὖν καλῶς καὶ φιλανθρώπως τὰ ἡμέτερα οἰκονομήσαντος, ἐξήλθομεν εἰς Λογγιβαρδίαν καὶ ἀποκρισιάριον ἕνα μὲν καὶ τὸν ἐλάττονα ἀπεστείλαμεν πρὸς τὸν βασιλέα ἡμῶν τὸν ἅγιον· ἕτερον δὲ ἐκδεχόμεθα δι' ὅλου τοῦ σεπτεμβρίου τὸν ἄρχοντα καὶ ἐπίσκοπον Μεδιολάνου, εἴτε μεθ' ἑαυτῶν τοῦτον εἰσάξοντες, εἴτε καὶ μόνον ἀποστελοῦντες, ὡς ὁ διακριτικώτατος νοῦς τοῦ ὑψηλοῦ καὶ ἁγίου ἡμῶν βασιλέως τυπώσειέ τε καὶ προστάξει. Σὺ οὖν, συνετώτατε καὶ καλὲ φίλε καὶ προστάτα, μέμνησο τοῦ σοῦ Λέοντος τοῦ δυστυχ[οῦς] μέν, ὀρθοῦ δὲ φίλου καὶ ἀνυποκρίτου καὶ πλέον σοι προσκειμένου ἢ ἐμοὶ αὐτῷ. Ἀξιωθείην καὶ ἰδεῖν σε καὶ προσκυνῆσαι καὶ περιπλακῆναι καὶ συγχαρῆναί σοι καὶ οὕτως τὸν παρόντα βίον ὑπεξελθεῖν.

4. Μεθοδίῳ πατρικίῳ

Μὴ νομίσῃς, ἔνδοξε κύριε καὶ πνευματικὲ ἀδελφέ, ἧττόν σου λυπηθῆναί με ἐπὶ τῇ τοῦ κοινοῦ πατρὸς στερήσει, ἀλλ' εἰ μὴ πλέον, τέως ἴσον πληροφορήθητι. Διδάσκειν οὖν σε ἢ παραμυθεῖσθαι οὐχ οἷός εἰμι καὶ ὀλιγόνους καὶ ἀπόδημος καὶ τοσοῦτον διεστηκώς, Θεὸς δὲ ὁ μέγας καὶ σκεπαστὴς καὶ βοηθὸς γένοιτό σοι παραμυθία καὶ

3: 2–3 cf. Job 29.23

3: P 201ᵛ.
17 *τυπώσει* Schramm || 19 supplevi: *δυστυχ* [ˆ] P

4: P 202ʳ. O 213ʳ.
2 *ἐνδοξότατε κύριέ μου* O || 3 *κοινοῦ λαοῦ πατρὸς* O || 5 *οἷος τ'* O *ὀλίγος ὢν* O || 6 *βοηθὸς καὶ σκεπαστὴς* O

3. To Hagiozacharites

Your letter, illustrious and marvelous man, was "rain upon the thirsty earth" to my heart and satisfied, sweetened, and cheered me. It made me forget those lamentable and unpleasant things that have been my lot for two years. Since we realized how unpleasant the first taste, which we sent to the City, would appear to you—you know what I mean, my sharp-witted friend—we went after a second and spent three months away from Rome in Frangia and discussed the marriage agreement; and, unless we had prevented it, there would be no reason for the marriage not being brought to an easy and successful conclusion in a day.

With God beneficently managing our affairs, we set out for Longobardia and sent the less important legate to our saintly emperor. We waited for the other, the prince-bishop of Milan, during the whole month of September, either to bring him with us or to dispatch him alone, as the most discerning mind of our exalted and saintly emperor should ordain and decree. But you, my most wise and dear friend and guardian, remember your Leo who, while unfortunate, is a loyal and sincere friend and one who is more devoted to you than to himself. May I be judged worthy to see you, pay my respects to you, embrace you, and rejoice in your company and so leave this present life.

4. To the Patrician Methodius

Don't imagine, my esteemed lord and spiritual brother, that the loss of our common father caused me less sorrow than you; believe me when I say my grief is equal to yours if not greater. I am unable to offer you guidance or comfort since my intelligence is limited and I am so far away from home and from you. But I pray that God, the great protector and helper, will be for you a source of comfort and aid and

ἀντίληψις καὶ πατὴρ ἀθάνατος ἀντὶ πατρὸς ἐκείνου τοῦ μακαρίου μέν, θνητοῦ δέ.

Τὰ ἡμέτερα οὐχ ὡς οἱ ἡμέτεροι ἤλπιζον προέβη, ἀλλ' ὡς ὁ Θεὸς ὁ καλὸς καὶ πάνσοφος καὶ ἰσχυρὸς ᾠκονόμησε καὶ οὕτως ἐγὼ λέγω ὡς οὐκ ἐγὼ προσεδόκησα ἢ ἄλλος τις· καὶ γὰρ πρῶτον μὲν ἐκεῖνα ἃ ἤκουσας ἐμελετήθησαν καὶ ἐσκευάσθησαν, ἔπειτα ἐν Φραγγίᾳ συνελθόντες τὰ τῆς συμπενθερίας ἐνηργήσαμεν.

5. Τῷ [*κῦρ*] *Μύρωνι*

Οὐκ ἐμὸν ἐγένετο, πνευματικὲ ἀδελφέ, τὸ τούτῳ ἢ ἐκείνῳ προσρυῆναι ἀλλ' οὕτω συμβάντι ἐγὼ ἠκολούθησα· τὸ δ' οὖν ἐμὸν πρόθυμον εἶχε καὶ σὲ καὶ ἤθελέ σε προΐστασθαί μου καὶ προέστης καὶ ἐβοήθησας· ὁμολογῶ τοῦτο καὶ ἀπ' αὐτῆς τῆς Ῥώμης. Σὺ οὖν μὴ ὅτι ἐγὼ κακός, ἀλλ' ὅτι σὺ ἀγαθὸς σκοπῶν, ὑπερμάχου μοι καὶ ἐξομάλιζε τὰ τραχέα καὶ βοήθει μοι καὶ Θεὸν εὑρήσεις βοηθὸν καὶ συναγωνιστὴν καὶ συλλήπτορα.

6. *Ἰωάννῃ ὀστιαρίῳ τῷ τοῦ πρωτοβεστιαρίου*

Γελᾶν μὲν οἶδά σε, καταγελᾶν δὲ νῦν ὑπονοῶ σε ἀκούσαντα ὅτι πάπαν τὸν Φιλάγαθον προεχειρισάμην, ὃν ἔδει με καὶ ἀποπνῖξαι καὶ προσεπειπεῖν τὸ ἄξιος, τὸν μυρίων σκηπτῶν ἄξιον. Ὁρῶ σε τούτοις ἐπιγελῶντα καὶ χαίρω καὶ εὔχομαι ἀεὶ γελᾶν σε. Πάντως ἢ

---

7 *μακαρίτου* O || 9 *οἱ ἡμέτεροι* om. O || 10 *καλὸς ὁ πάνσοφος ᾠκονόμησε* O || 11 *οὐδ'* O *πρῶτα* O || 12 *ἤλπισας ἐμελετήθη καὶ ἐσκευάσθη* O || 13 *Φραγγείᾳ εἰσελθόντες* O post *ἐνηργήσαμεν* lac. indicavit Schramm

---

5: P 202^{r}.
1 supplevi || 7 *τραχέα* Sakkelion: *βραχέα* P

6: P 202^{v}.

an immortal father in place of your father who, while saintly, was nevertheless mortal.

Our affairs have turned out not as our friends had hoped but as God the good, the omniscient, and the mighty beneficently ordained—I mean in a way that neither I nor anyone else expected. First those things of which you've heard were taken care of and arranged, then we had a meeting in Frangia and negotiated the marriage contract.

5. To [Lord] Myron

I did not intend (on this occasion), spiritual brother, to take refuge with this or that one, but I bent with the wind. Yet at least I was eager and willing for you to become my guardian and you did guard and help me; I assert this even from Rome herself. You, then, considering not the fact that I am bad but that you are good, be my ally, make the rough smooth, and help me, and you will find that God is your supporter, fellow combatant, and helper.

6. To John the Ostiarius, (Nephew) of the Protovestiarius (Leo)

I know that you're laughing at me but I suspect that you'll roar when you hear that I appointed Philagathus pope—when I ought to have strangled him and said "serve him right!" He ought to be struck by lightning a thousand times! I can see you laughing and I'm glad and I hope you'll always laugh. This much is certain:

οὐδὲν σεαυτῷ σύνοιδας ἢ πολλὰ σύνοιδας καὶ δι᾽ ὑπερβολὴν θἀτέρου γελᾷς· μόνον εἰ τοῦτο καὶ μόνον, λέγω δὴ τὸ γελᾶν, ἁμαρτάνεις, οὐδ᾽ οὕτω μακάριος—"οἱ γὰρ πενθοῦντες, τοῦτο"—πλὴν συγγνωστός, εἴ γε ἐπὶ τῷ γελᾶν ποτε καὶ κλαύσειας ἑκὼν εἴτε καὶ ἄκων· τὸ δ᾽ οὖν παρὸν καὶ χαῖρε καὶ γέλα καὶ εὖ πρᾶττε καὶ ἔρρωσο καὶ μέμνησο ἡμῶν. Ἡ Ῥώμη ῥώμης δεῖται καὶ ῥωμαλέου καὶ στιβαροῦ ἀνδρὸς καὶ ἐμβριθοῦς φρονήματος, ἅπερ, οἶδα, ὁ ἡμέτερος μέγας καὶ ὑψηλὸς βασιλεὺς κέκτηται τῶν προλαβόντων πλέον, ὡς καὶ αὐτὸς πλέον τῶν ἄλλων οἶδας, πλέον καὶ συνομιλῶν καὶ τῶν ἀπορρήτων κοινωνῶν τοῖς βασιλεῦσι. Σὺ δὲ μὴ δόξῃς παίζειν, ἀλλ᾽ ἀληθεύειν ταῦτά με γράφοντα.

7. Τῷ γενικῷ

Εἰ παράδοξον εἴπω τι, μηδαμῶς ἀπιστήσῃς· κἀμοὶ γάρ, ὅπερ εἴπω, παράδοξον φαίνεται. Εἰμὶ μὲν ἐν Ῥώμῃ, πλὴν καὶ σοὶ σύνειμι καὶ μᾶλλον σοὶ σύνειμι ἤπερ εἰμὶ ἐν Ῥώμῃ, τὸ μὲν γὰρ ἑκὼν καὶ φιλῶν, τὸ δ᾽ ἄκων καὶ ἀποστρεφόμενος. Εἰ οὖν μάθω καὶ καλὰ εἶναι τὰ κατὰ σὲ καὶ ὡς ἐγὼ θέλω, τότε μοι καὶ ἡ ἀποδημία ὡς ἐπιδημία λογισθήσεται καὶ κοῦφα τὰ δυσχερῆ καὶ ὁμαλὰ τὰ ἀνώμαλα καὶ οὐδέν, εἰ καὶ θάνοιμι, σκυθρωπόν μοι ὑπολειφθήσεται.

Δήλου ταῦτα καὶ εὖ πρᾶττε καὶ ἔρρωσο, τῶν συνετῶν συνετώτερε. Τὰ καθ᾽ ἡμᾶς ἀπὸ τοῦ κυροῦ Καλοκυροῦ γνώσῃ σαφέστερον καὶ ἐν οἷς ἐσμεν καὶ οἷα ἐπράξαμεν καὶ οἷα ἐγράψαμεν. Ὁ γραφεὺς καὶ εἰς τὰ τοιαῦτα ὑπηρετῶν ἡμῖν τέλει τοῦ βίου ἐχρήσατο καὶ ἀναγκάζομαι καὶ τοῖς φίλοις προσκρούων καὶ τοῖς κυρίοις μου. Ἴδοιμί σε ὡς ἐγὼ θέλω καὶ βούλομαι· θέλω δὲ ἄλυπον, ἄνοσον, ὑγιῆ, εὐημεροῦντα καὶ εὐπραγοῦντα.

8. Τῷ κῦρ Στεφάνῳ τῷ ἐν μοναχοῖς ἀσυγκρίτῳ

Ἰδού σοι καὶ πάπαν, ἵνα μὴ πάνυ χαίρῃς ἢ σφόδρα χαίρῃς, εὐαγγελίζομαι τὸν Φιλάγαθον· σκόπησον καὶ αὐτὸς τίνι δώσεις τὴν τῶν τοιούτων φοράν, Θεῷ ἢ καιρῷ; Καὶ τίς ἐκέρασεν, εἰπέ, ἀντιστρό-

---

6: 8 cf. Matt. 5.4. **7:** P 203^{r}. **8:** P 203^{r}.

either you are completely in the dark or else you are pretty well informed and are laughing only because of the excess of one or the other. So long as this is your only sin—I mean the laughter—even then you aren't blessed (that is reserved for those who mourn); but you can be forgiven because after laughing you may at some time shed tears whether you want to or not. For the time being, at any rate, be glad, laugh, good luck, farewell, and remember me. Rome stands in need of power, a powerful and mighty man, one with an authoritative spirit, which, I realize, our great and exalted emperor has acquired in greater measure than his predecessors, as you yourself know better than anyone else, being on more intimate terms with the emperors and privy to confidential affairs. Don't think that I'm joking; I'm being quite serious.

7. To the Genicus

If what I say is incredible, don't be sceptical, for it seems incredible even to me. I am in Rome but I am also with you; I am with you even more than I am in Rome: the former, because I want to and am willing; the latter, despite the fact that I am unwilling and detest it. If I hear that you are well and as I hope you are, then I will reckon even this absence as a presence, the difficult will seem easy, the rough smooth, and even if I die I shall have no regrets.

Report these things, and to you, who are wiser than the wise, success and good health. You will get a more exact report of my doings from the Lord Calocyrus —what sort of situation I'm in, what I've done and written. The secretary who worked for us in this capacity passed on and I'm in a bind—and offensive to both my friends and my superiors. May I see you as I hope and wish, without pain and sickness and enjoying prosperity and good luck.

8. To the Lord Stephanus, Incomparable among Monks

I report to you the joyful news, so that you don't rejoice too much or excessively, that Philagathus is our new pope. Who do you think should get credit for such a thing—God or circumstance? Who has brought two opposites together and

φως τὰ πράγματα καὶ τίς τὰ ἄμικτα ἔμιξεν, ἵν' ἡ μὲν Πρεσβυτέρα καὶ ὑπὲρ λῆξιν νέον λάβῃ σφριγῶντα καὶ ὀργῶντα καὶ πηδῶντα τὰ νέα—δεῖ γάρ με συννεωτερίσαι τῷ πάπᾳ ὅσον περὶ τὰς λέξεις—ἡ Νέα δὲ σχῇ, ἵνα τι καὶ ψυχρολογήσω, τὸν ἀποσφριγάσαντα καὶ ἐξαυδήσαντα; Εἰ μὲν οὖν κατὰ λόγον ταῦτα, ἀθύμει· εὐθυμεῖν γάρ ἐστι τὸ ἀθυμεῖν οὕτως· εἰ δ' οὐ κατὰ λόγον, γέλασον, ἴσον γάρ ἐστι τῷ θρηνῆσαι· εἰ δ' ὑπὲρ λόγον, θαύμασον καὶ τὸ θαῦμα στέναξον καὶ τῷ στεναγμῷ δάκρυσον, ἵνα εἰδῇς ἄνθρωπος ὢν καὶ μηδ' αὐτὰ εἰδῇς τὰ ἀνθρώπινα.

Ταῦτά σε πειθέτω τῆς ἀρετῆς ἔχεσθαι, ᾗ συνετράφης, ᾗ συνηυξήθης, ᾗ καὶ ἐποιώθης, ᾗ καὶ συναπέλθοις· θρόνον δέ, εἰ σὺν Θεῷ, λάβε καὶ κόσμησον· εἰ δ' οὐ σὺν Θεῷ, φύγε καὶ μάκρυνον, ἵν' ἀμφοτέρωθεν θρόνος σοι δοθῇ ὁ οὐράνιος. Ἀπὸ τοῦ κυροῦ Καλοκυροῦ γνώσῃ τὰ ἡμέτερα καὶ οἷα ἐπράξαμεν καὶ οἷα ἐγράψαμεν. Τοὺς χειροτονηθέντας οὔπω καὶ νῦν οἵτινές εἰσιν ἔγνων· εἰ μὲν οὖν ἴσοι τοῖς προαπελθοῦσιν, ὃ οὐκ ἄν ποτε εἴποις, δήλωσον, εἰ δ' οὐκ ἴσοι, σίγησον, εἰ δὲ κρείττους, κήρυξον, εἰ δ' ἀσυγκέραστοι κἀκεῖνοι καὶ ταῖς χηρευούσαις ἀνάρμοστοι, σκυθρωπάζων μέν, πλὴν οὕτως ἔξειπε, εἰδὼς ὡς ἡμῖν ὀλιγοδρανέουσιν ἀντίδοτος τὸ γράμμα γενήσεται ἀναψύχουσα. Ἐρρωμένον, ἀπαθῆ, διηνεκῶς εὔχεσθαί σε εὔχομαι.

9. 〈 〉

Εἰ καὶ ἔδοξα ἀργῆσαι, θεοφιλέστατε πάτερ καὶ δέσποτα, ἀλλ' οὐκ ἤργησα· τὴν γὰρ Ῥώμην εἶδον, πρᾶγμα μέγα, σοφὸν καὶ ὑπέρογκον καὶ ἄνδρα μὴ ἔχουσαν· ἄνδρα αὐτῇ δέδωκα τὸν ἀρχιεπίσκοπον Φραγγίας τὸν τῷ ἰουλίῳ τὴν εὐχήν σου λαβόντα. Τοῦτο μὴ θαυμάσῃς· ἔδει γὰρ οὕτω προβῆναι, ἄλλως δ' ἀποβῆναι· τὰ γὰρ ἐξ ἀρχῆς ἀνυπόστατα ῥᾴδια πάντως καὶ εὐχερῆ πρὸς καθαίρεσιν. Ἡ οὖν Ῥώμη τὸν ἴδιον ἔχει πάπαν, πρὸς καιρὸν μὲν ἐκδιωχθέντα βίᾳ καὶ ἀνάγκῃ πλὴν καὶ τὸν μοιχὸν εὑρήσοντα καὶ μετὰ ζήλου τιμωρήσοντα. Τὰ οὖν καθ' ἕκαστον ὡς ἐπράχθη ταῦτα καὶ τὰ μείζονα παρὰ τοῦ κυροῦ Καλοκυροῦ μαθήσῃ. Εἰ οὖν καλῶς ὑποδέξεται τὴν δουλείαν ἡμῶν ὁ βασιλεύς, εὖ ἂν ἔχοι· εἰ δ' οὐκ ἀποδέξεται καὶ τῶν ἀνθρώπων ὅσοι τὸ διακριτικὸν ἀκέραιον ἔχουσιν —αὐτὸς δὲ σκόπησον—τί ἂν ἐγὼ εἴποιμι αὐτὸν μὴ ἀποδεχόμενον εὑρίσκων; Ὑγιαίνων, εὐθυμῶν, τῆς ἡμῶν ὑπερεύχου ταπεινώσεως.

9: P 204r.

5 ἰουλίῳ coni. Dölger in ed. Schramm: τυλίῳ P ‖ 14 αὐτὸν scripsi: τὸν P

reconciled the irreconcilable in order that: 1) the Old Rome take, in excess of what is due to her, a young pope, full of vigor, lusty, and jumping from one novelty to another (for I must follow the pope's revolutionary style); and 2) the New Rome have (if I may make a feeble joke) one who has lost his vigor and his voice? If these events seem reasonable, despair, for such despair is the same as cheer; and if they seem unreasonable, laugh, since it's the same as mourning; and, if they seem beyond reason, be astonished and express your amazement in moans and weep with moaning, so that you may know that you are a man and that you don't even know the ways of mankind.

Let these things persuade you to hold on to the virtue with which you were brought up, grew up, and developed your character and with which I hope you will die. As regards a see, take one and be an honor to it, if God be willing. If he is not, flee far away so that in both cases the heavenly throne may be granted to you. You will learn about us, both what we have done and what we have written, from the Lord Calocyrus. Even now I do not know who have been elected. If they are equal to their predecessors, which you could never say, report it; if not, keep it quiet. If they are better, proclaim it. If they too are those unsocial men, unfit for widowed churches, though you are upset, nevertheless, speak out, in the knowledge that your letter will be a refreshing remedy for us who are half-dead. I hope that you are in good health and free from troubles; I beg you to pray for me constantly.

9. ⟨ ⟩

Even if I seem to have been idle, most pious father and lord, still I have not been idle: I saw Rome, a great power, wise and enormous and in need of a man. I gave her one, in the person of the archbishop of Frangia, who was the recipient of your prayer in July. Don't be surprised at this; it had to happen like this but end up otherwise. For that which from the beginning had no substance is necessarily easy and ready to be destroyed. Rome has her own pope who, for the time being, is expelled by violence and necessity, but he will find and punish the adulterer with a vengeance. You will learn the details of what was done and more important things from the Lord Calocyrus. If the emperor accepts my services with good grace, it would be well. But if he and all those who have faultless judgment reject them, you yourself look into the matter. What objection could I make if he refuses to accept them? Be healthy and happy and pray for our humility.

10. Τῷ μαγίστρῳ καὶ σακελλαρίῳ

Τὰ κρίσιμα μὴ αὐτόθεν ἐπιφαίνεσθαι παλαιόν ἐστι παράγγελμα, ᾧ καὶ σὺ πείθου, ὁ συνετὸς ἐν συνετοῖς καὶ διαφέρων ἐν φρονίμοις. Καὶ ἄλλοι σοῦ λέγοντος ἐπείθοντο ὡς ἔμαθον. Τὰ γοῦν ἐμὰ ὡς εἰπεῖν ἀφ' ἑστίας καὶ ἀπὸ βαλβῖδος καὶ ἀπὸ τῆς ἀφετηρίας αὐτῆς κέκριται· ἅμα γὰρ ἐλύσαμεν ἐκ τοῦ Σοφίας λιμένος καὶ ἡ ναῦς περιερράγη καὶ μικροῦ περιετράπη. Ἔδοξεν οὖν κακὸς οἰωνὸς τὸ γενόμενον, ἀλλ' οὐκ ἦν ἐμὸν ἀποβῆναι, μόνον δὲ μεταβῆναι τὴν ναῦν καὶ τὴν ἐκείνης, ὅ φασι, τύχην ἤπερ ἐκείνης ἀλλάξασθαι. Τὰ δ' οὖν ὅσα ἐναυαγήσαμεν καὶ ἐκινδυνεύσαμεν καὶ ἐταλαιπωρήσαμεν καὶ ἐνοσήσαμεν καὶ διεμερίσθημεν, οἱ μὲν τῷ βίῳ καταλειφθέντες, οἱ δὲ τῷ Ἅιδῃ παραπεμφθέντες, οἱ δ' εἰς Ῥώμην διασωθέντες, ἐάσθω. Τὰ δ' ἐπ' ἐκείνοις, ὅσα ἐχειμάσθημεν πηλῷ καὶ τέλμασι καὶ ποταμοῖς κάτωθεν καὶ τῷ ἄνωθεν ὑετῷ καὶ χιόνι καὶ ὄμβροις ῥαγδαίοις διηνεκέσι βαλλόμενοι, σιγῇ κεκρύφθω πρὸς τὸ παρόν, ἵνα μὴ δόξω σωθεὶς ἀχαριστεῖν καὶ τὴν πρόνοιαν ἐρεθίζειν ἢ διυπνίζειν ἥμερον ὕστερον βλέψασαν. Τὰ δ' εὐφημότερα λεγέσθω καὶ ἀπαγγελλέσθω τῷ κυρίῳ μου.

11. Τῷ πατριάρχῃ

Εἰ καὶ ἑτέρῳ τοῦτο συνέβη τὸ καὶ ἰδεῖν ἐν ταὐτῷ καὶ λιπεῖν καλὸν τοιοῦτον, τὴν θεσπεσίαν σού φημι κεφαλήν, καὶ γεύσασθαι μέν, μὴ ἐμπλησθῆναι δέ, ἀλλ' ὅσον προγεύσασθαι καὶ ἀποσχέσθαι, θεομακάριστε δέσποτα, ἀγνοῶ· πλὴν οὐκ οἶμαι οὕτω τινὰ ὡς ἐμὲ δυστυχῆσαι, διὰ τοῦτο "ἐξέλιπον οἱ ὀφθαλμοί μου," "ἐξέλιπε δὲ ἡ ζωή μου ἐν ὀδύνῃ" θρηνοῦντος καὶ στένοντος καὶ διανοουμένου "πότε ἥξω καὶ ὀφθήσομαι τῷ προσώπῳ σου;" Εἰ μὲν οὖν μὴ καὶ εἶδόν σε,

---

10: 5 *ἀπὸ βαλβῖδος CPG*, I, 33

10: P 204ᵛ.
1 *τῶ μαγίστρω* in textu, *τῶ μαγίστρω καὶ σακελλαρίω* mg. P || 14 *τῶν* P, corr. Darrouzès || 17 *βλέψασαν* scripsi: *βλάψασαν* P

11: 6 Ps. 68.3 || 6–7 Ps. 30.10 || 7–8 Ps. 41.2

10. To the Magister and Sacellarius

That the signs of a crisis are not immediately visible is an old rule upon which even you should act, you who are considered wise among the wise and preeminent among men of good sense. And others have followed your advice, as I've heard. In my case the crisis has taken place from the beginning, as it were, from the gate, from the very start. For at the same time as we cast off from the Port of Sophia, the ship cracked and nearly capsized. This seemed to be an evil omen, but it was not my fate to disembark, only to change ships and the luck of that one, as they say, for another. To what extent we were shipwrecked, how great were the dangers we faced and the hardships we endured, how sick we were and how we were divided—some surviving, others escorted to Hades, others coming safe to port at Rome—I let all this go unsaid. What came next—how we passed the winter, inundated by mud and slime, by rivers from below and rain from above, by snow and continuous violent rainstorms—I leave cloaked in silence for the present lest I seem ungrateful for having arrived safely and lest I provoke or rouse Providence which looked upon me kindly later on. I prefer to give my lord a more auspicious report than this.

11. To the Patriarch

Whether it has befallen anyone else to see and at the same time leave such a fine man, I mean your divine self, and to taste yet not be sated, but only to get a foretaste and be separated, I don't know, most blessed lord. But I don't think anyone is as unfortunate as I, hence "mine eyes fail and my life is spent with grief," lamenting, groaning, and thinking: "When shall I come and appear before you?" If I

μὴ καὶ ἀνεμιμνησκόμην σου, μὴ καὶ ἐν τῇ καρδίᾳ μού σε περιέφερον πλήρη καὶ ἔνσωμον, τάχα ἂν κάλλιόν μοι καὶ ἀπονώτερον. Ἐπεὶ δὲ ἐγένετο, τί μὴ ἐπέσχες τὴν μακρὰν ταύτην καὶ δολιχὴν πορείαν; Τί μὴ ἐξωμάλισας τὴν ὁδόν; Τί μὴ ταχεῖαν τὴν ἐπάνοδόν μοι ἐπηύξω; Τί μὴ ἔγνως; Τί μὴ προεῖπας; Ἢ πάντως προέγνως μέν, ἀφῆκας δὲ παιδευθῆναι; Ἀλλὰ νῦν γοῦν μεταμελόμενος, αἴτησαι ταῦτα καὶ ὑπὲρ τοῦ σοῦ πρόσευξαι Λέοντος, ἵν' ἴδῃ καὶ προσκυνήσῃ σε καὶ ὑπακούσῃ εὐχομένῳ σοι καὶ τῆς δεξιᾶς ἀντιλάβηται, καὶ τὸ γῆρας ὑπέρεισον.

Τὴν Ῥώμην ὑπὸ χεῖρας ⟨καὶ⟩ πόδας τοῦ μεγάλου καὶ ὑψηλοῦ ἡμῶν βασιλέως τοῦ Θεοῦ θέλοντος καὶ ἀγαγόντος καὶ ἐγὼ διάκονος ἐγενόμην, τὴν καρδίαν τοῦ κρατοῦντος Κρισκένζου ἐκείνου μὲν εὐθύναντος, δι' ἐμοῦ ⟨δὲ⟩ τοῦτο ποιῆσαι θελήσαντος. Τὰ οὖν καθ' ἕκαστον καὶ τὰ ἐπὶ λεπτῷ διὰ τοῦ ἀποκομιστοῦ μαθήσῃ σαφέστερον· ὑπογραφέως δὲ μὴ εὐπορῶν κινδυνεύω καὶ φίλοις καὶ δεσπόταις προσκρούων, γέρων αὐτὸς ὢν καὶ ὄκνῳ εἴκων καὶ ῥαθυμίᾳ. Τὴν ἱερὰν ἐκείνην καὶ θαυμασίαν γραφήν, ὡς εἰπεῖν στήλην ὀρθοδοξίας, οὐδεὶς εὑρέθη πάπας ἄξιος ἀξίως ὑποδέξασθαι καὶ τιμῆσαι, ἀλλ' ὁ πρὸς ὃν ἡ ἐπιστολὴ Ἰωάννης μετῆλθεν· ὁ δὲ μετ' ἐκεῖνον Γρηγόριος οὐδ' ὅσον συγχωρηθεὶς εὔξασθαι ἀπῆλθε, τῇ τοῦ προέχοντος ἐν Ῥώμῃ Κρισκένζου δυνάμει τοῦ τε θρόνου καὶ τῆς ἀξίας ἀπελαθείς· ὁ δ' ὑπεισῆλθεν ὁ μηδὲ ζῆν ἄξιος, ὁ ἐμὸς φόρτος, ὁ θρασὺς Φιλάγαθος, ὁ πάντολμος, ἡ ̣γηδύς, ὁ ῥύπος, ἡ κηλίς, ὃν ὡς εἶδον ἐπιβαίνοντα—καὶ σὺ [ἐ]μακροθύμεις—ἴδοιμι, Χριστέ, καὶ ἀποβαίνοντα.

Τ[ούτῳ] τοῦ τοιούτου τὴν ἀρετήν, τοῦ τοσούτου τὴν δόξαν, τοῦ ἀνυπερβλήτου, τοῦ ἀσυγκρίτου, σοῦ, τοῦ θεοειδοῦς, τοῦ ἐνθέου, γραφὴν ἐπιδοῦναι, ἴσον ἐνόμισα "χοίρῳ καὶ κυνὶ μαργαρίτας καὶ ἅγια" προσρῖψαι. Προσῆξα τοίνυν τὸ σεβάσμιον ἐκεῖνο γράμμα καὶ προσεπαττάλωσα τῷ τάφῳ τοῦ Κορυφαίου καὶ οἰκείᾳ χειρὶ τὸ τίμιόν σου ὄνομα προσέγραψα, ἀνάξιον κρίνας μνημονεύεσθαί σε καὶ ἀναφέρεσθαι παρ' ἐκείνου τοῦ μοιχοῦ, τοῦ βδελυροῦ, τοῦ μισητοῦ, τοῦ θεοστυγοῦς. Τὸ οὖν ἐκείνου παραινῶ ἀποτρόπαιον ὄνομα μηδὲ ἐν τῷ προνάῳ, μηδὲ ἐν τοῖς προθύροις, μηδὲ ἐν τοῖς προαυλείοις, μηδὲ ἔσω τειχῶν, ἀλλ' ἔξω καὶ εἰς αὐτὸ τὸ ἐξώτερον ἀπογραφῆναι σκότος· πλὴν οἰκονομίας ἕνεκεν, ὧν ἐγράψαμεν,

---

35–36 Matt. 7.6

11: P 205^{r}.

9 *ἀνεμνησκόμην* P, corr. Darrouzès ‖ 18 add. Darrouzès ‖ 21 add. Westerink ‖ 30 *φόρτος* lectio dubia: *φίλτατος* Darrouzès ‖ 31 *̣γηδύς* P: *μιαρία* Darrouzès ‖ 32 supplevi ‖ 33 suppl. Westerink ‖ 34 *θεειδοῦς* P, corr. Darrouzès ‖ 38 *προέγραψα* P, a. corr. ‖ 39 *ἀναφαίρεσθαι* P, corr. Darrouzès

had not even seen you, nor remembered you, nor carried you in my heart, as large as you are, it would perhaps be better for me and less painful. But since it has happened, why didn't you prevent this long and distant journey? Why didn't you smooth the way? Why didn't you pray for my speedy return? Why didn't you know (that it would be so long)? Why didn't you tell me beforehand? Or did you know all along but abandoned me to learn my lesson? Now, at least, change your mind, ask for these things and pray for your Leo, that he may see you and fall at your feet and listen to you as you pray and take your hand; and be a support for his old age.

Rome is under the hands and feet of our great and exalted emperor, with God willing and directing it—I myself was the instrument while he guided the heart of her ruler Crescentius—and wishing to do this through me. You will learn the particulars and fine details more exactly from the messenger. Since I don't have a secretary, I run the risk of offending my friends and lords—I am old and prone to procrastination and sloth. That holy and marvelous letter, a veritable pillar of orthodoxy, no pope has been found worthy to accept and honor now that John, the person to whom it was sent, has passed away. Gregory, his successor, left without being allowed so much as a prayer, driven from his see and office by the might of Crescentius, the most powerful man in Rome. The one who crept in, who is not even worthy to live, my personal burden, bold Philagathus, the rogue, the paunch, the filth, the blight whom just as I saw him ascend—while you, Christ, were bearing this patiently—so may I also see him step down.

I considered handing over (to him) the letter of so virtuous and illustrious a person, the letter of an incomparable man, you, godlike and divine, to be like "casting pearls and holy things before swine and dogs." I brought that venerable letter and nailed it to the tomb of St. Peter and with my own hand I added your honored name, thinking you unworthy to be commemorated (in liturgical prayer) and entered (in the diptychs) by the adulterer, the abomination, the man who hates and is hated by God. I do not advise that man's abominable name to be listed even in the narthex, even in the doorway, even in the courtyard, nor inside the walls, but outside, that is, in the outer darkness. But for diplomatic reasons, I recommend that the

σβεσθῆναι καὶ κατασιγασθῆναι πρὸς τὸ παρὸν ἐγὼ συμβουλεύω, τὴν τοῦ καλοῦ καὶ μεγάλου ἡμῶν βασιλέως εὐδοξίαν πραγματευόμενος, ᾗ καὶ συνεργεῖν δοκεῖ καὶ κατατίθεσθαι ὁ ἀλιτήριος, οὔτι "ἑκών, ἀλλ' ἄκοντί γε θυμῷ," γεωμετρικαῖς, ὅ φασιν, ἀνάγκαις, ἢ μᾶλλον Κρισκενζικῷ κατεχόμενος φόβῳ, Ἑρμοῦ ἕνεκεν ζῶν.

Προστεθείη σοι ἵν' ἴδω σε καὶ τὰ τῆς ἀποδημίας ἐξείπω σοι καὶ τὰ τῆς μεγαλοδόξου Ῥώμης ἀναγγείλω σοι, ὡς καὶ αὐτὸς ὑπὲρ ἐμοῦ εὔξῃ.

12. Τῷ Σάρδεων

Τὰ μὲν ἄλλα μοι κοῦφα καὶ ὡς εἰπεῖν εὔφορα, τό τε τῆς ὁδοῦ μῆκος καὶ τὰ ἐνθαλάσσια ναυάγια καὶ τὰ ἐν τῇ χέρσῳ κλώσματα· τὸ δ' αὐτῆς τοσοῦτον διαστῆναι τῆς καλῆς σου ὄψεως καὶ θέας καὶ ὁμιλίας, τίς ἐνέγκοι ψυχή; Τίνι φορητὸν τὸ ἀφόρητον; Οὐκ οἶμαι παρηγορίαν εἶναί τινα τοῦ τοσούτου κακοῦ, οὐδ' ἂν αὐτὴν εἴποι τις τὴν ἄκραν εὐδαιμονίαν· εὐχῶν οὖν χρεία, εὐχῶν "εἰς αὐτὰ τὰ ὦτα Κυρίου Σαβαὼθ εἰσερχομένων," οἷαι πάντως αἱ σαὶ τοῦ θεοτιμήτου δεσπότου μου. Εἰ οὖν ὑγιαίν[εις] ḳạị εὐεκτεῖς, ὡς αὐτὸς εὔχομαι, εὔχου καὶ αὐτὸς ἡμῖν καὶ αἰτοῦ τὴν ἐπάνοδον· εἰ δέ τι λυπεῖ σε τῶν ἀπὸ ἐγκρατείας γινομένων σοι, ἀμφότεροι σοῦ ἕνεκεν προσευχώμεθα· προτιμητέοι γὰρ σοὶ κατὰ πάντα καὶ διὰ πάντα.

Τὴν Ῥώμην εἶδον καὶ εἷλον καὶ τὸ ἐμὸν ἔδειξα πρόθυμον, τοσοῦτον τολμήσων ἢ τολμήσας, ὅσον οὐδ' εἰς νοῦν ἂν ἐβάλετο ἕτερος. Εἰ μὲν οὖν καὶ βασιλεὺς ὁ μέγας χωρήσοι τοῦτο, καλὰ καὶ ἐπὶ καλοῖς ἐμοχθήσαμεν· εἰ δ' ἀνάξιον κρίνῃ τοῦτο τῆς αὐτοῦ βασιλείας, σοὶ καταλιμπάνω σκοπεῖν. Τί ἂν ἐγὼ εἴποιμι; Τὸν κακῶς γνωρισθέντα καὶ κολληθέντα μοι ἐπὶ κακῷ τῆς ἑαυτοῦ κεφαλῆς πάπαν πεποίηκα, τὸν ἐκ Καλαβρίας ἢ Σικελίας ἢ καὶ αὐτῆς τῆς Αἴτνης, τὸν ἐξ ἧς ἐκριφῆναι ἢ ἐνριφῆναι ἄξιον, τὸν ἀβέβαιον, τὸν ἄφιλον, τὸν τοῦ ψεύδους ἀρχηγὸν καὶ πατέρα καὶ θύλακον, τὸν πάν-

---

46–47 Hom. *Il.*, 4.43 || 47 cf. *γραμμικὴ ἀνάγκη* Olympiodorus in Grg. 102.12 ed. Westerink et *Διομηδεία ἀνάγκη* Plato, *Rep.*, 493D

12: 7–8 cf. Ps. 17.6; Is. 5.9; Jac. 5.4

12: P 206r.

3 *κλώσματα* P: *κωλύματα* coni. Darrouzès || 9 supplevi || 10 *αἰτοῦ* Westerink: *αὐτοῦ* P *δέ τι* scripsi: *δ' ἔτι* P || 11–12 *προσευχόμεθα* P, corr. Darrouzès || 12 fort. *προτιμητέος γὰρ σὺ*

contents of my correspondence be suppressed and hushed up for the time being, out of concern for the good reputation of our noble and great emperor with whom the sinner seems to be cooperating and assenting, but by no means willingly, and with geometrical necessity, as they say, or, rather, dominated by fear of Crescentius and living for the sake of gain.

May (your life) be increased so that I may see you and tell you about my trip and report on the status of celebrated Rome. You, too, pray for me.

12. To the Metropolitan of Sardes

The rest—the length of the journey, the shipwrecks at sea, the entanglements on land—is light and almost easy for me to bear. But what soul could endure so long a separation from your noble face, presence, and company? Who can bear the unbearable? I don't think there is any alleviation for such misery, not even if someone should mention complete happiness itself. We need prayers, prayers that will reach the very ears of the Lord of Hosts, prayers exactly like yours, my lord honored by God. If you are enjoying vigorous and robust health, as I hope, pray for us too and ask for our return. If you are bothered by any aftereffects from your fasting, let's both pray for you. For you ought to prefer us in every way and for every reason.

I saw Rome and took it and showed that I would eagerly venture more (or, rather, have ventured more) than would even occur to someone else. If, then, the great emperor should approve of this, our efforts have been good and to the good; but if he should consider it unworthy of his imperial majesty, I leave it to you to consider (what will happen). Why should I tell you myself? I have made my bad friend and associate pope, to his misfortune. He's from Calabria, or Sicily, or even Mt. Aetna itself, from which he ought to be thrown out or in, the unreliable, the unfriendly, the author, father, and pack of lies, the unscrupulous, blasphemous,

τολμον, τὸν λοίδορον, τὸν βλάσφημον, τὸν κύνα, τὸν δεινόν, τὸν θρασύν, τὸν περιπετῆ, τὸν τὸν Θεὸν ἀπειπάμενον, τὸν τὸ λαϊκὸν τοῦ μοναχικοῦ ἀντικαταλλαξάμενον, τὸν τὸ μέγα καὶ σχῆμα καὶ ὄνομα ὡς βαρὺ ἀποσεισάμενον, τὸν αἰσχροπαθῆ, τὸν αἰσχρολόγον, τὸν ῥυπαρόν, τὸν ὅλον φθόνον, τὸν ὅλον δόλον, τὸν ξυρόν, τὴν μάχαιραν, τὸν ἔμμυσον, τὸν βέβηλον, τὸν αὐτοκακίαν, τὸν αὐτορυπαρίαν, τὸν ὄφιν, τὴν δολίαν γλῶτταν, τὸν τρόπον ἀνώμαλον, τὸν λαιμόν, τὴν κοιλίαν, τὸν αὐτόχρημα κοπρίαν, τὸν γαστέρα, τὸν τὰ ὑπὸ γαστέρα Θεὸν ἡγησάμενον, τὸν πάσης ἄξιον βλασφημίας, τὸν πάσης κολάσεως, τὸν πάσης τιμωρίας, τὸν βόρβορον, τὸν εὐτράπελον, τὸν φλύαρον, τὸν υἱὸν τῆς ἀπωλείας, τὸν μιαιφόνον, τὸν χαιρέκακον, τὸν αἱρετικόν, τὸν ἀβάπτιστον, τοῦ ἐναντίου πνεύματος ἔμπλεων, τὴν ἀπάτην, τὴν χλεύην, τὴν γλωσσαλγίαν, τὸν τοῦ Θεοῦ καὶ ἁγίων ἐχθρόν, τὸν τὴν ἄρρητον φθορὰν καὶ μίξιν ὑπὸ δώδεκα παθεῖν καυχησάμενον, τὸν τρισκαιδεκάτην προσθέντα τὴν ὑπὸ διδασκάλου, τὸν διδάξαντα ἅπερ ἔμαθε, τὸν ἄθλιον—ἄθλιος γὰρ ὃς καὶ ποιήσει ταῦτα καὶ διδάξει—τὸν ἔτι καὶ νῦν τοῖς αὐτοῖς τούτοις ἐπιμένοντα, (τοιοῦ⟨τον⟩ γὰρ ἡ ἐξ ἁπαλῶν ὀνύχων τῶν τοιούτων παί[δευ]σις), τὸν νομοθέτην τῶν ἄλλων, ἃ φυσικὰ καλεῖν οὐκ αἰσχύνεται, τὸν ἔτι καὶ νῦν ἐπὶ παλαιῶν γεγονότα [κα]κόν, τὸν οὐδὲν ἢ φαγεῖν καὶ πιεῖν καὶ ὅσα ἐκεῖνος οἶδε καλὸν καὶ ἡδὺ τιθέμενον, τόν, ἵνα συνέλω, υἱὸν διαβόλου.

Ἐγὼ δὲ τὸν ἐκ τῶν κατ' αὐτὸν καὶ περὶ αὐτὸν τοιοῦτον εἶναι καταμαθών, τῷ μεγάλῳ καὶ ἀποστολικῷ ἐνιδρῦσαι θρόνῳ ὅλος καὶ πᾶς ἐγενόμην, οὐ χηρεύοντι—ἢ γὰρ ἂν πρὸς καλοῦ τῷ ἀσεβεῖ τούτῳ ἐγένετο—ἀλλὰ ζῶντος τοῦ ἀνδρός, μοιχὸν καταστῆσαι τοῦτον διανοησάμενος. Οὐκ οἶμαι γὰρ κάλλιον ἐκεῖνον περὶ τῶν ἑαυτῷ λυσιτελούντων σκέψασθαι, ἢ ἐμὲ περὶ τοῦ πῶς ἐκεῖνον ὑποσχεῖν τῶν πολλῶν ἀσεβημάτων δίκας· καὶ νῦν οἰμώζει καὶ τὴν ἐκ Θεοῦ καὶ τὴν ἐξ ἀνθρώπων καὶ τὴν ἐκ τοῦ Ὤτου καὶ τὴν ἐκ τοῦ πάπα ἐλπίζων ὑφέξειν τιμωρίαν. Ὁ γὰρ πάπας ἐκεῖνος ὁπλίζεται "μεστὸν ζήλου θυμὸν" ἔχων, οἶμαι δὲ ὡς οὐ φείσεται, οὐδὲ ἀλλάξεται, οὐδὲ μὴ διαλυθῇ πολλῶν δώρων· ὁ δ' ὑποπτήσσει καὶ δέδιε καὶ τρομαλέος ἐστὶ καὶ μερμερίζων ἀνήνυτα. Τὸ γὰρ ψεῦδος ἐπέλιπεν αὐτῷ, αἱ δὲ εἰς Θεὸν ἐλπίδες οὐδ' εἰς νοῦν αὐτῷ ποτε ἐπεισῆλθον· "εἶπε γὰρ ὁ ἄφρων ὡς οὐκ ἔστι Θεός," τῇ μοιχείᾳ δὲ ἐπιμένων, τί καὶ προσεύ-

52–53 cf. Prov. 6.34 ‖ 56–57 cf. Ps. 13.1; 52.1

23 τὸν λαϊκὸν P, corr. Darrouzès ‖ 28 τρόπῳ Darrouzès ‖ 39 add. Westerink suppl. Westerink ‖ 41 παλαιῶν P: πλέον coni. Westerink: παλαιὸν Darrouzès [κα]κόν suppl. Darrouzès ‖ 44 δὲ τὸν P: fort. δ' αὐτὸν

abusive dog, the sly, audacious, fickle, a man who has renounced God, who has traded the status of a monk for that of a layman, as though the glorious habit and calling of the former were oppressive, a man who lets himself be used for foul ends, foul-mouthed, (the) sordid, thoroughly jealous and treacherous, the cutthroat, the hatchet, defiled, profane, all wickedness, the utter sordidness, the snake, the smooth talker, unstable, the greed, the gluttony, the excrement itself, the paunch, the man whose god is what's below his paunch, a man worthy of every curse, punishment, and retribution, the slime, the trickster, the babbler, the son of perdition, the murderer, a man who rejoices at another's misfortune, the heretic, the unbaptized, a man possessed by the evil spirit, the fraud, the joke, the chatterbox, the enemy of God and the saints, a man who boasts that he has been monstrously raped and seduced by twelve, whose experience with his schoolmaster brings the number to thirteen, the man who teaches exactly what he's learned, the wretched, for a man who not only does but also teaches these things is wretched, a man who even now continues these same practices (for this is what it means to be brought up in such things from childhood), the man who laid down the law on other practices, which he does not hesitate to call natural, a man who has become a sinner of long standing, (a man) who considers nothing good and pleasant except eating and drinking and (all the) other things he is expert in, and, in a word, the son of the devil.

Even though I learned that such is his character from his affairs and associates, I committed myself completely to installing him in the great and apostolic see, although she was not widowed (otherwise it would have been to the good for this impious man), but I planned to make an adulterer of him while her husband was still alive. I don't think he could deliberate about his own advantages better than I could about the punishment for his many impieties. Even now he laments, anticipating punishment from God, man, Otto, and the pope. For that pope, "with his heart full of jealousy," has armed himself. I don't think he will give any quarter, or change his mind, nor will he ever come to terms even at the price of many gifts. But the other is cowering and afraid, he trembles, and is considering all kinds of impossible plans. His lying has been to no purpose, but hope in God has never even occurred to him. "The fool says that there is no God," and what kind of prayer will he pray who

ξεται; Μετάνοιαν ποίαν ἐπιδείξεται τῆς ἀσελγείας, οἵας ἂν εἴποις, μὴ ἀφιστάμενος;

Εὔχου μοι, θαυμάσιε δέσποτα, καὶ σὲ ἰδεῖν τάχιον καὶ σοῦ πρῶτον ἰδεῖν τὸν ὄλεθρον αὐτοῦ· ἐγὼ γὰρ σπεύδω τοῦτο καὶ εὔχομαι καὶ οὐδ' αὐτῶν τῶν σαρκῶν μου φείσομαι, ἕως ἂ̣ν̣ καθαιρήσω καλῶς ὃν κακῶς ᾠκοδόμησα.

13. Τῷ κανικλείου

Ἤχησε τὰ ἔργα σου, θαυμάσιε στρατηγέ, κατὰ τὴν Ἰταλίαν πᾶσαν—πολλὴ δέ ἐστιν, ὡς οἶδας, καὶ καλὴ καὶ μεγάλη—καὶ ἀκουστά, ἃ ἐγένετο, κατ' αὐτὰς τὰς Γαλλίας, Ἱσπανίας. Τί τούτου μεῖζον ἑξηκοντούτης ἐγὼ τυγχάνων ἢ εἶδον ἢ ἤκουσα; Ἀλλ' οἱ πρὸ ἐμοῦ φήσουσιν ὡς εἶδον, οἱ δὲ πρὸ ἐκείνων αὐχήσουσιν ὡς ἤκουσαν—αὐτοὶ δ' οἱ γέροντες, οἱ ψυχρολόγοι, οἱ μυθολόγοι οἰήσονται σὺν τῇ κορύζῃ χάναι καὶ φάναι· μὴ ἐμβλέψαι εὔχομαί τ[ι] τούτων ἢ αὐτὸ τὸ μηδὲ ὂν γενέσθαι. Σὺ δὲ φανερὸν καὶ ἔνδηλον ἅπασι ποιήσας, ὡς ὁ ποιήσας, ὡς ὁ σοφὸς καὶ στρατηγός ἐστι καὶ πᾶν ἐστιν ὅπερ ἐστὶ καλόν, φύγοις τὰς τοῦ φθόνου βολὰς καὶ μὴ ἐπεγχάνοι μῶμος στρογγύλως οὕτως βιοῦντί σοι καὶ ἀλήπτως. Ἀλλ' ἐπείπερ καὶ τὸν ἀκμαιότατον χρόνον ἐγκρατῶς ἐδαπάνησας, οὐδ' ὅσον οὐδ' εὐλαβῶς ἡδονῇ πλησιάσας, καὶ τὴν φρονοῦσαν ἡλικίαν καλῶς διέρχῃ καὶ ἀμέμπτως, φθάσαις καὶ γῆρας τῷ νεωτέρῳ βίῳ συνόμοιον, λιπαρόν, ἄνοσον, εὐαίσθητον, τέλειον· τοιαῦτα γὰρ ὡρίσαντο οἱ πάλαι δεινοὶ σωφροσύνης εἶναι καὶ βίου ἀρίστου γνωρίσματα.

13: 10 ff. cf. *SVF*, III, 164.23–26

13: P 207ᵛ.

7 *οἰήσονται* scripsi: *ἴσον τι* P ‖ 8 *τι τούτων* Darrouzès: *τ[]τοῦτον* P ‖ 9 *μηδὲ ὂν* scripsi: *μὴ δέôν* et ·/· mg. P ‖ 10 *ποιήσας* P: fort. *ποιητής* Westerink ‖ 14 *ἡλιακήν* P, correxi ‖ 15 *φθάσαις* scripsi: *φθάσαι* P ‖ 17 *γνωρίσματα* scripsi: *γνώρισμα* P

persists in adultery? What sort of repentance will he show for his debauchery, whatever kind you mean, so long as he doesn't break with it?

Pray, admirable lord, that I may see you soon and, before I see you, that I may see his destruction first. I am bent on this and pray for this, nor shall I spare my very flesh until I (shall) tear down the man whom I have very badly built up.

13. To the Keeper of the Imperial Inkstand

Your deeds, marvelous general, have resounded throughout all of Italy—it is, as you know, a big place, lovely and impressive, too—even France and Spain have heard about what you've done. I've never seen or heard anything to top this, and I'm sixty years old. My elders, however, will claim that they saw and their elders will boast that they heard—but these old men, babblers and storytellers that they are, will suspect that they gape and prate like dotards: please don't give a thought to any of these things or to the very one that cannot be. But since you have made it clear and manifest to all, as the man of action does, that the wise man is also a general and everything that is desirable, I hope that you may avoid the shafts of envy and that no disapproving stare may reproach you who live so simple and blameless a life. But, since you have temperately spent even the best years of your life without so much as coming near pleasure, not even in the most cautious way, and since you are now passing through the age of reason honorably and irreproachably, I pray that you attain an old age similar to your youth, hale, healthy, sharp, and perfect. For the clever men of old defined such things as the marks of temperance and an excellent life.

14. Τῷ πατριάρχῃ Ἀντιοχείας

Ἦν ὡς ἀληθῶς ὡς ταύρου μυκηθμὸς γεγωνότερος, ἔτρεψε τὸν Ἀντίταυρον, καὶ λέοντος βρυχηθμὸς τῇ ἀλκαίᾳ ὑποθυμούμενος ὑπότρομα τὰ ἄτρομα κατεστήσατο· καὶ στρατηγοῦ ἢ στρατοῦ ἢ ναυάρχου ὁρμῶντος ἢ καὶ ὀργῶντος εἰς μάχην οἶδα τὸ θαρραλεώτερον προφώνημά τε καὶ ἐμβόημα τοὺς ἐναντίους τρέπειν. Ταῦτα, ἃ ἔδρασας ἐπ' ἐμοί, πατριαρχῶν γενναιότατε—οὐ γάρ σε τοῖς νερτερόχρωσιν ἢ πυξοπροσώποις εἴσκω, ζώσιμον ὄντα καὶ βιώσιμον, ἢ ἔμβιον, ἐμπρόσωπόν τε καὶ ἅγι[ον]. Τί οὖν ἔδρασας, ἐγὼ δὲ ἔδεισα; Μυκησάμενος, βρυχησάμενος, ἐκκραγὼν καὶ πνεύσας, πολὺς πλησίστιος ἐλθών, ἐμβολὴν δούς, ἔτρεψας, ἐξέπληξας, εἶδες τὰ νῶτα, εἰς βυθὸν ὦσας, εἴπω τι καὶ γήϊνον, ἐξεπρέμνισας. Τοιοῦτος εἰ καὶ στιβαρῷ τινι ἐπῆλθες, μή τί γε τῷ δειλῷ ἐμοί, τίς ἂν ὑπέστη σου τὴν ὁρμὴν καὶ οὐχὶ ἐκσεισθεὶς ἐπατήθη καὶ κατηλοήθη; Ἐγὼ δ' ὁ μέλεος καὶ κατ' ἐμοῦ πάντως γενναῖος καὶ τῆς φωνῆς τὸ τραχὺ καὶ δύσηχον ἀπεμιμούμην καὶ τὸ "ὑπόδρα ἰδὼν" καί, ἵν' ἐξάρω σέ, δέσποτα κράτιστε, φοβερός τις ἤμην καὶ ἀκαλλής σε ποσῶς ἐκμιμούμενος.

Ταῦτ' εἴθ' ὡς παίζοντος, εἴθ' ὡς θαυμάζοντος ἐκδέξῃ ὁ δεσπότης μου, σὺ μὲν οὐχ ἁμαρτήσεις, ἐμοὶ δὲ πάντως συγγνωμονήσεις, φιλάνθρωπος ὤν, καὶ ἡ φαινομένη μέν, μὴ οὖσα δὲ νομιζομένη δεινότης. Πλὴν εἰ καὶ τὸ ἀποστολικὸν εἰπὼν αὐτὸς τὰ ἐμαυτοῦ σαφηνίζω, τὸ "οὐ γὰρ ἄλλα γράφομεν ὑμῖν ἢ ἃ ἀναγινώσκεται καὶ ἐπιγινώσκεται" στήσω τὴν ἄλην τοῦ μὴ κενεμβατεῖν ἕνεκα. Τί οὖν ἀντιστήσω σοι τῷ θαυμαστῷ Θεουπολίτῃ; Τίν' εὑρήσω φερέγγυον σοί γε τῷ λόγοις σοφῷ, τῷ τρόποις χρηστῷ, "τῷ δώροις ἁπλῷ," "οὗ μὴ ἄξιος ὁ κόσμος," οὗ ἀρετὴ τοῖς ἀνθρώποις ἐκάλυψεν, ὃν ὑπερκόσμιον τὸ κόσμιον ἀποδείκνυσιν, ὃς ἀμίμητος, ὃς ἀπαράβλητος, ὃς ἀπαράμιλλος; Ἐάσθω μόνος ἀσύγκριτος, ἰσόθεός τις ὢν καὶ ὑπερνέφελος ἄνθρωπος· τούτου εἰ ἅψαιτο βάσανος, τούτῳ εἴ τι τῶν ἀβουλήτων προσπέσῃ, τολμήσας εἴπω, ἄδικος σύ, Δίκη, ἢ ἄχολος, ἢ καθεύδεις καὶ ῥέγχεις.

Ἡμεῖς μὲν οὖν, εἰ καὶ ἀφρόνως ἐπαίξαμεν, ἀλλὰ σωφρόνως ἐσπουδάσαμεν. Σὺ δ' ὦ θεσπέσιε δέσποτα, καὶ ῥάβδον ἔχεις καὶ μάστιγας ἔχεις, τοὺς ἱερούς σου λόγους καὶ παιδευτὰς τῶν ἀφρόνων·

14: 16 cf. Hom., *Od.*, 8.165 || 22–23 cf. II Cor. 1.13 || 25 cf. Jac. 1.5 || 26 cf. Heb. 11.38

14: P 208r.

2 ἀληθῶς Darrouzès: ἀληθὲς P || 9 supplevi || 16 ἰδὼν scripsi: ἐδίδων P || 21 εἰπὼν scripsi: εἴπω P || 25 ἁπλῷ scripsi: ἁπαλῶ P || 30 σύ scripsi: σὺν P || 32 ἐπάξαμεν P, corr. Darrouzès

14. To the Patriarch of Antioch

It was truly like the deafening bellows of a bull, putting Antitaurus to flight, or when the roaring of a lion, angrily switching its tail, makes the fearless quiver. When a general, an army, or an admiral is eager or even wild for the fray, I know that their confident yells and cries rout the enemy. These are the things, most noble of patriarchs, that you have done to me: I don't mistake you for the cadaverous or pasty-faced (corpses of your predecessors?) since your chances for survival look good, or, rather, you are very much alive, in the flesh, and holy. What then did you do to terrify me? Bellowing, roaring, shouting, snorting, attacking under full sail and ramming, you put to flight and thoroughly shook me up; you saw my tail and pushed me into the deep; and, if I may change the metaphor to the land, you rooted me out. If you had attacked even a strong man in such a way, much less craven me, who would have sustained your onslaught and not been shaken up, trampled, and crushed to a pulp? Yet I, the hapless and ever brave at my own expense, tried to imitate the harsh discord of your voice and the Homeric "angry look," and, to enhance your greatness, most powerful lord, I pretended to be ugly and awful, imitating you to a certain extent.

Whether you take this as a joke or as a sign of my admiration, my lord, you will not misunderstand and you will surely pardon me since you are kindhearted and your supposed brusqueness is only apparent, not actual. Yet if I explain myself by adding the Apostle's words, "for we write none other things unto you than what is read or acknowledged," I shall put an end to your error so that there will be no (further) false steps. What object of comparison shall I find for you, the admirable citizen of God's own city? Whom shall I find equal in worth to you who are eloquent in speech, excellent in character, "liberal in giving," "of whom the world is not worthy," whose virtue overshadows mere mortals, who by his decency is raised above the world, inimitable, incomparable, unrivaled? Let us say that he alone is peerless, a godlike and celestial man, and leave it at that. If any torment were to afflict this man, if something undesirable should befall him, putting it boldly, you, Justice, are unjust or a milksop or noisily asleep on the job.

τούτοις νύξον, τῦψον, πλῆξον τὸν ἀμούσως καὶ παρατέ[χν]ως ᾄδοντα, μόνον ἐλθὲ καὶ ἐπίφανον ἡμῖν τοῖς μὴ ἐνιαύσιον χρόνον ἀλλ' αἰώνιον ἡγησαμένοις τὴν ἀπουσίαν σου.

15. Τῷ *αὐτῷ*

[Τ]*ί δ' ἐγώ—ἐγὼ δὲ εἰπών, εὐτελὲς τὸ ἐγώ, ὡς ὁ* Χριστὸς *καὶ σύ, ἔδοξα—ἆρ' ἐπιστελῶ καὶ τοῦτο τολμήσω καὶ πρῶτος τοῦτο, καὶ οὐχ ὕβριν ἡγήσῃ καὶ δυσπετήσεις, μακάριε, ὡς πολὺ παρὰ σοὶ τὸ μακάριος, εἰ καὶ μέχρις ἐμοῦ καταβήσῃ;* Ἀλλ' *ἤδη σοι καὶ τοῦτο εἴργασται καὶ σφόδρα ὑπερυψώθης καὶ προσγειότερος ἐμοὶ γεγονὼς καὶ μνησθείς μου διὰ μετεξετέρου γραφῆς σ*[*ου*], *τῆς πρὸς τὸν θαυμαστὸν* Δημήτριον, Δημήτριον *τὸ καλὸν χρῆμα, τὸ τῆς σοφίας τέμενος, τὸ τῆς ἀρετῆς ἄγαλμα, ὃν εὐχῆς ἐκτενεστέρας ποιοῦ, θεῖος ὢν καὶ ταῦτα θεῖος, ζῆν τε καὶ ἐρρῶσθαι καὶ κόσμον εἶναι τοῦ κόσμου.* Τῆς *οὖν ὅτι ἐμνήσθης μου παρὰ τοῦ* Θεοῦ *μνήμης τυγχάνων, πανάγιε καὶ θεσπέσιε δέσποτα, καὶ νῦν ἔρρωσο καὶ μεταστὰς ἐκείνην λάχε λῆξιν τὴν τοῦ* Θεοῦ *ἐγγύς.* Τὸ *δ' οὖν νῦν σῴζοιο, οὐ σοῦ τοσοῦτον, ἡμῶν δὲ χάριν ὡς σοῦ ἕνεκεν· καὶ πάντας δίκαιον, ἀλλὰ καὶ σὲ ὑπερεύχεσθαι ὥσθ' ἡμᾶς μὲν διὰ σοῦ, σὲ δὲ δι' ἡμᾶς τῷ σεμνῷ βίῳ ἐμπολιτεύεσθαι.* Στήριζε *οὖν ταῖς εὐχαῖς, τῷ λόγῳ δίδασκε, τῇ βακτηρίᾳ ποίμαινε, τῇ ῥάβδῳ παίδευε καὶ τὴν κατ' ὄψιν ἐντυχίαν διὰ τῆς θερμῆς πρὸς* Θεὸν *ἐντυχίας διάπραττε καὶ δὸς ἐν καιρῷ τὴν ἐνδημίαν σου πρὸ τῆς πρὸς τὸν* Κύριον *ἐκδημίας σου· ὄφελος γὰρ οὐ μικρὸν τοῦτο τοῖς ἀπὸ τῶν σῶν μικρῶν ὠφελουμένοις τὰ μέγιστα.*

---

35 suppl. Darrouzès

15: 10–11 cf. Const., *App.*, 7.34.6

15: P 209r.

2 [Τ]*ί* suppl. Darrouzès || 3 *ἄρ'* P, correxi || 7 supplevi || 10 *κόσμον* corr. Darrouzès: *κόσμος* P || 11 *τῆς* Westerink: *τίς* P *ὅτι* P: ὅς Darrouzès || 17–18 *κατόψιν* P, corr. Darrouzès || 18 *εὐτυχίαν* P, corr. Westerink

We, then, even if we are silly in our jokes, still are sensible in matters of gravity. You, reverend lord, hold the rod and the scourge which are your pious words, the chastisers of fools. Use them to prod, poke, and jab me for croaking off-key; just come and present yourself to us who think you've been gone not for a year but an eternity.

15. To the Same (the Patriarch of Antioch)

Who am I to be so bold as to write this "I" and put it first as well? For I, just as Christ and yourself, considered "I-ness" a trifling matter. Won't you be insulted and get out of temper, saintly man? For there must be a good deal of the saintly about you, if you stoop even to my level. Yet you have already done this and have been mightily exalted both because you have come down to earth on my account and because you mentioned me in a certain letter to the wonderful Demetrius, Demetrius the good, the temple of wisdom, the image of virtue. Make him the subject of even more fervent prayer, as you are his uncle (and a holy one, too), to live, to be well, and to be "an adornment of the world." Thus, being remembered by God because you remembered me, all-holy and divine lord, farewell for the present, and when you pass on, take your place near God. For the present, however, may you be kept safe, not so much for your sake as for ours. Furthermore, everyone, and you in particular, ought to pray that we, by your help, and you, for our sake, devote ourselves to the sacred life. Bolster us with your prayers, teach us with your words, watch over us with your staff and chastise us with your rod. By your ardent prayers to God, obtain that we may meet you face to face, and while there is still time, let us enjoy your presence here, before you exchange your sojourn here for your return to God. For this is no small help to those who benefit to the greatest extent from your small kindnesses.

16. Τῷ αὐτῷ

Ἀτυχῆ μέ τις οἶδ' ὅτι ἐρεῖ, ἐγὼ δὲ εὐτυχῆ. Τίς γὰρ ἐγὼ πρὸς τὸν Θεουπόλεως, ὅτι καὶ γράψαι αὐτῷ ἐτόλμησα; Ἀλλὰ σοί γε χάρις πολλὴ τῷ διακομίζοντι, μὴ ἐπιδόντι τὴν γραφήν· μηδέ γε ἐπιδοίης, ὦ βέλτιστε, ἀλλ' ἐμβραδύναις πλαζόμενος, καὶ πανηγυρίσω πᾶσαν πανήγυριν, ἢ καὶ αὐτὸς ἐξ ἀνθρώπων γένοιο καὶ ἄνοστος. Ἐγὼ δ' ὁ γράφων ἀλλ' ἀπολογούμενος, θαυμάζεις ἴσως, θεοτίμητε δέσποτα, τίς ὢν τίνι γέγραφα· ἀλλ' ἴσθι ὡς ἐμὲ θαῦμα ἔχει καὶ πρὸς ἐμαυτὸν ἐγὼ λέγω ὅτι "οὐκ ἔμεινας εἴσω τῶν ὅρων. Τί προέδραμες; Τί πρῶτος ὥρμησας, προπετέστατε; Λαβεῖν γὰρ ἔδει σε μίαν ἢ καὶ δευτέραν καὶ τότε γράψαι· ἐπεὶ δ' ἀντέστρεψας τὴν τάξιν, γράψον πολλὰ συγγνώμην αἰτῶν. Τίς [ἄφη]σεν ἢ ἀφήσοι τὸ πάσης συγγνώμης ἁμάρτημα μεῖζον; Θεουπολίτης ἐκεῖνος ἀνήρ." Εἰ μὲν οὖν ἀφῇς, ἀφήσω κἀγὼ σιγήν· εἰ δέ σοι "χόλος ἐν στήθεσι μετόπισθε" λέλειπται μένειν, [ἀ]λ̣λ' ἐγώ σε βιάσομαι γράφων γράψαι τότε μοι, ὅτι "κακῶς, ὦ Λέον, γέγραφας." Εἴτε οὖν γράψεις, εἴτε καὶ μὴ γράψεις, ἐπεύχου μοι σῶος, ἔντιμος, ὑγιής· τρία γάρ σοι ταῦτα ἐπεύχομαι.

17. Ἀρσενίῳ Ἡρακλείας

Τί φῄς, Ἀρσένιε μικρόφρον ἢ ἔκφρον ἢ παντελῶς ἄφρον; ⟨Σὺ⟩ τὸν σύγκελλον εἰς ἀγῶνας, σὺ τὸν ἵππον, ὅ φασιν, εἰς πεδίον, σὺ τὸν λέοντα νύσσεις καθεύδοντα, δεῖλος καὶ ἄκικυς καὶ παιδίον μᾶλλον ἢ ἀνὴρ ὤν; Οὐ σὺ μὲν Ἀρσένιος, Λέων δ' ἐγώ; Οὐ σὺ τοῦ σκότου καὶ τῆς γωνίας, τοῦ φωτὸς δ' ἐγὼ καὶ τῆς Ἐκκλησίας; Οὐκ ἀδάμας ἐγώ, σὺ δ' Ἡρακλεία λίθος; "Οὐ μακρόθυμος ἐγώ, σὺ δ' ἰσχυρὸς ἄφρων;" Οὐ "Βαρὺ λίθος καὶ δυσβάστακτον ἄμμος"; Τὸ γὰρ "ὀργὴ δὲ ἄφρονος βαρυτέρα ἀμφοτέρων," σοὶ δίδωμι νοεῖν, εἴ γε ὅλως νοεῖς. Οὐ Θεοῦ

16: 14 cf. Hom., *Il.*, 1.82–83

16: P 209ᵛ.
11 *γράψαι* Westerink: *λαβεῖν* P ‖ 12 suppl. Darrouzès ‖ 15 supplevi

---

17: 3–4 cf. *CPG*, I, 191, n. 65; II, 483, n. 99 ‖ 7 cf. Prov. 14.29 ‖ 8–9 Prov. 27.3

17: P 210ʳ.
2 addidi ‖ 8 *ὀργὴ* Darrouzès: *ὁρμὴ* P

16. To the Same (the Patriarch of Antioch)

I fully realize that someone will say that I am unlucky, but I say that I am lucky. For what is my connection with the patriarch of the city of God that I have dared even to write him? A thousand thanks to you, postman, for not delivering the letter; I hope, my good man, that you will not do so either, but lose your way and take forever—I'll jump for joy—or I hope even that you leave this world and do not return to it. As for me, the writer of the letter or rather the apology, perhaps you wonder, reverend lord, who I think I am, and to whom I have written. Rest assured that I am amazed at myself and wonder out loud: "You've overstepped the bounds. Why were you the first to rush forward, impetuous man? You should have received a letter or two and then written back. But since you've gone out of turn, write and beg his pardon fervently. Who has forgiven or could forgive an unpardonable sin? That man, the citizen of Theopolis, that's who!" If, then, you should forgive me, I will break my silence; but if "any rancor is left behind to dwell in your heart," by writing I will compel you to write me, if only to say "you did a bad thing in writing, Leo." Whether you write or not, pray for me, in safety, in honor, and in health, for these are the three things I pray for you.

17. To Arsenius, (the Metropolitan) of Heraclea

What do you mean, Arsenius, you nitwit—are you only out of your wits or are you completely witless? Are you trying to provoke the syncellus? You're inviting the cavalry onto the plain, as the saying goes; you're goading a sleeping lion, you, the cowardly weakling—you're a child, not a man. Are you not merely Arsenius (the boy), while I am (the great) Leo? Are you not a man of the shadows and crannies, while I am of the light and the Church? Am I not a diamond and you a rock from Heraclea? Am I not a man of patience and you a brawny fool? Is it not true that "a stone is heavy and sand cumbersome"? I leave it to you to think of the rest—"a fool's wrath is heavier than both"—if you can think at all. Am I not a

μὲν ἐγώ, σὺ δ' ἐμὸν δημιούργημα; Οὐ τοσοῦτον ἀπέχεις τῶν λοιπῶν ἀνθρώπων, ὅσον ἐγὼ τοῦ Θεοῦ; Τίς ὀνάριον τὰ ὑπὲρ σὲ ἔπεισε φαντάζεσθαι; Καλά σοι τὰ τῆς Ἡρακλείας ἐπιβατήρια καὶ σοβαρὰ αὐχήματα καὶ κόμπος καὶ γένειον καὶ ἀκροχειρισμὸς καὶ χάσμα καὶ ἄνοια, παλμοὶ μελῶν καὶ ἄστατος ποὺς καὶ φρενῶν ἔκστασις. Εἰ δέ μου τὴν ὑπὲρ σοῦ σπουδήν τις ὀνειδίσει, ἀλλ' ἐγὼ τὸν τοῦ ζωγράφου πίνακα σὲ ἀναστρέψας, τὸν πρότερον θέοντα νῦν ἀλινδούμενον ἐπιδείξω ἡμίονον καὶ ἐπιγελῶν ἐπιφθέγξομαι τὸ "Τοιοῦτος ἡμῖν ἔπρεπεν ὁ τῆς Ἡρακλείας ἀρχιερεύς," κωφός, βωβός, ἄναυδος, ἔμπνοος στήλη, λαλῶν οὐ λαλῶν—τί γὰρ ἰχθὺς λαλήσει;—φρονῶν οὐ φρονῶν—τί γὰρ λίθος φρονήσει; νοῶν οὐ νοῶν—πῶς γὰρ ἄνους νοήσει; Οὐκ εἰς ἀναβολὰς τοίνυν φανεὶς τοιοῦτος, μένε τοιοῦτος· ἀλλοῖος γάρ, οὐδ' εἰ πάνυ σπουδάσειας, γενήσῃ.

18. Τῷ αὐτῷ

Ὅτι μὲν οὖν κοῦφος ἦς καὶ εὐρίπιστος, πάτερ Ἀρσένιε, ᾔδειμεν —οὐκ ἦν γὰρ βαθὺ τὸ γνῶναι τοῦτο οὐδὲ Πυθίου δεόμενον—ὅτι δὲ καὶ ἀχάριστος καὶ ἀγνώμων καὶ ἀσυνείδητος, εἰ καὶ ἐλάνθανες, ἀλλ' οὖν περιφανῶς καὶ ταχέως ἐξ ἀφροσύνης πάντως ἑαυτὸν ἐφανέρωσας καὶ ὅπερ οὐκ ἂν σοί πολλοί τινες ἐχθρῶς διακείμενοι εἰργάσαντο, τοῦτο σὺ κατὰ τῆς ἑαυτοῦ κεφαλῆς καὶ ψυχῆς ἔπραξας καὶ οἱονεὶ τίτλον τῇ κορυφῇ σου ἐπέθηκας, ἁδρῶς ἐγχαράξας τὸ "Ἀρσένιος, ὁ κολοφὼν τῶν ἀχαρίστων." Ἐγὼ μὲν οὖν ὑπ' αἰσχύνης ἐγκαλυπτόμενος καὶ αὐτήν μοι διαστῆναι τὴν γῆν εὔχομαι τὸ "σὺ τοῦτον" ἀκούων καὶ "ὅλως ἐκεῖνος πρὸς σέ." Καὶ "πῶς ὁ μεγαλόνους τὸν μικρόνουν οὐκ ἐφώρασας ἐκ τῶν ἐπιτηδευμάτων; Οὐκ ἐγνώρισας τοὺς ζωγραφοῦντας, οὐκ ᾔδεις τοῦ Ἀρσενίου δούλους—τοὺς τέκτονας, τοὺς μαγείρους, τοὺς ἀπεμπολουμένους εἰς τὸν πρόεδρον, εἰς τὸν σεβαστοφόρον, εἰς τὴν δέσποιναν, τοὺς καλοὺς ἀγρούς, τὸ οἰνοφόρον προάστειον;" Ταῦτα ἰδεῖν τότε καὶ νῦν ἀκούω καὶ διὰ σοῦ λανθάνω καὶ τοῖς καλοῖς ἀπιστεῖν· σὺ δὲ ἐγενεαλόγησας οὕτως ἐκ-

---

16 cf. Plut., *De Pythiae oraculis*, 396E || 17–18 cf. Heb. 7.26

18: P 210ᵛ, 236ʳ⁻ᵛ.
6 *διακειμένου* P, corr. Darrouzès || 17 *ἐγενεαλόγησεν* P, corr. Darrouzès

creature of God, while you are a creature of mine? Aren't you as distant from the rest of mankind as I am from God? Who persuaded you, little jackass that you are, to dream of things beyond you? Well suited to you are the welcoming ceremonies of Heraclea, the pompous pretense, the empty rhetoric, the flowing beard, the arm wrestling, the yawning, the idiotic behavior, the trembling of limbs, the faltering steps, and the signs of mental derangement. If anyone criticizes my support of you, I will turn upside down the portrait that you are and point out that the mule which was previously running is now an ass rolling in the dust, and I will remark with a chuckle, "That's the sort of high priest for Heraclea that suits us"—deaf, dumb, speechless, a living slab of stone, talking—no, not talking—what does a fish have to say? Thinking without thinking—for what can a stone think? Intellectual—no, not intellectual—what intellect does a moron have? Since you have wasted no time in proving yourself to be such a man, remain so; you will not change no matter how hard you try.

18. To the Same (Arsenius of Heraclea)

That you were fickle and easily swayed, Father Arsenius, we have known—this knowledge isn't hard to come by nor does it require an oracle—but that you are ungrateful, inconsiderate, and unscrupulous (even if you used to get away with it), still by your thoughtlessness you have really shown your true colors conspicuously and without delay. This, which not even a host of enemies would do to you, you yourself have done against your own life and soul. It's as though you'd put on your head a big sign in bold relief: "Arsenius, King of the Ingrates." I am embarrassed to death and wish the very earth would swallow me up when I hear: "You had him appointed." "That creature is entirely dependent on you." "How is it that you, mental giant that you are, did not see through that mental midget from his doings? Didn't you hear about the artists? Didn't you know about Arsenius's personal servants, the carpenters and the cooks, the sale of the good farmland to the proedrus, the sebastophorus, and her ladyship, the wine-producing estate?" Even now I hear it said about me that I must have seen these things then and because of you I've slipped into the habit of distrusting even good men without realizing it. You are at

δραμὼν ἀπ' αὐτῆς τῆς βαλβῖδος καὶ τῆς ἀφετηρίας φθάσας εὐτυχῶς καὶ τὴν νύσσαν αὐτὴν καὶ τὴν εὔριπον καὶ τὸν τοῖς ἀχαρίστοις διδόμενον κομίσοιο στέφανον καὶ μὴ ἄλλο τι κατὰ σοῦ εὔξασθαι τοὺς νοῦν ἔχοντας ἢ τοιαύταις φήμαις ἐγκαλινδεῖσθαί σου τὴν σεμνότητα καὶ τοῖς ὁμοίοις ἔργοις ἐνρυπαίνεσθαι.

19. Τῷ *αὐτῷ*

Εἰ καὶ πολλοὶ πολλὰ καταλέγουσι καὶ ἀξιοῦσι πιστεύεσθαι, Θεὸν προβαλλόμενοι μάρτυρα, ἀλλ' οὖν βούλομαι καὶ σέ, 'Αρσένιε, *ἐρέσθαι τε καὶ συγκάταινον λαβεῖν καὶ τοῖς ἄλλοις ἐκείνοις καὶ πίστεως ἀξίοις ὅτι ἀληθεύουσι συνθέσθαι.* Καὶ *φασί σε κατὰ τὰς ἐπισκοπάς σου διερχόμενον τυραννικήν τε καὶ σοβαρὰν ἐξαπαιτεῖν τὴν δεξίωσιν, οἶνον εὐώδη καὶ παλαιὸν καὶ κηρὸν καὶ ἄρτον εἰλικρινῆ καὶ κροκίζοντα καὶ ἕνα σεμνὸν καὶ τοῦτον ἐκ τοῦ ὅλου μοδίου γινόμενον, ὄρνιν κατὰ κεφαλήν, γαλαθηνὰ χοιρίδια καὶ χῆνας, σύνδυο μὲν τοῖς πρώτοις, σύντρεις δὲ τοῖς μέσοις, χοίρους καὶ πρόβατα ἐκλεκτὰ καὶ πιότατα· ἰχθύας ἀποβάλλεσθαί σέ φασι τοὺς μικροὺς καὶ τοὺς μέσους, ἀπαιτεῖν καὶ τοὺς ὑπερλιπεῖς καὶ μεγάλους· καὶ τούτου τεκμήριον τὸν τοῦ* 'Ραιδεστοῦ *προάγουσιν ἐπίσκοπον, ὃς ἐν τῇ θαυμαστῇ σου πρεσβείᾳ τοῖς εὑρεθεῖσι δεξιωσάμενος τὴν ὑπέρφυτον ἀρετήν σου, αὐτὰ ἐκεῖνα κατὰ κόρρης ἐδέξατο τὰ ἰχθύδια προσριφέντα.* Τούτοις *σιωπῶν δοκεῖς μὴ ἀντιλέγειν· ἐλεῶ σε τοίνυν τοῖς ἀνοήτοις ἴσα καὶ ὡς ἀνοίᾳ καὶ ἀπονοίᾳ, κακοῖν δυοῖν, ἐνισχόμενον οἰμώζειν ἐγὼ συμβουλεύω.* 'Αλλά *μοι ἔρρωσο καὶ εὐθύμει· εὐθυμοῦσι γὰρ οἱ οὕτω φρονοῦντες.*

---

21 *ἐνκαλινδεῖσθαι* P, correxi

19: P 211r, 236v.

4 *συγκάταινον*: *σύμβουλον* mg. P || 12 *καί*¹: fort. δὲ || 13 *τὸν τῆς* P, corr. Darrouzès || 14–15 *ὑπέρφυτον* P: fort. *ὑπερφυῆ*

the bottom of it: since you did so well right from the starting post, I hope that you will also successfully make the turning point and the second half of the race and get the crown for ingratitude. Sensible men pray nothing else against you than that your eminence may wallow in such reports and be sullied by similar deeds.

19. To the Same (Arsenius of Heraclea)

Even if many men make numerous reports and, thinking them worthy of credence, call upon God as their witness, still, Arsenius, I want to ask you yourself and I want you to agree that those other trustworthy men are telling the truth. They say that you've been going around to your bishoprics and demanding hospitality like a haughty tyrant: wine, aged and with a good bouquet, candle wax, pure, golden bread (a single grand loaf, and this made from a whole bushel of flour), a chicken apiece, suckling pigs and geese (those of the first rank share two-ways, while those of the intermediate rank share three-ways), pigs and mutton, choice and plump. As regards fish, they say that you reject the little and medium-sized fish and demand really big and fat ones. They produce the bishop of Rhaedestus as proof of this; this man who, on the occasion of that glorious mission of yours, honored your admirable excellence with the fish he happened to have, got those selfsame fish back—thrown at his head. By your silence you seem not to disprove these charges. I pity you like I pity fools and I advise you to howl because you are caught in the net of two evils, lack of common sense as well as lack of moral sense. Good-bye and be cheerful, since people who think like you do are cheerful.

20. Τῷ αὐτῷ

Τοιαῦτα, πάτερ ὅσιε, τὰ ἀνθρώπινα, τοιαῦτα, τίμιε δέσποτα, τὰ μὴ κατὰ Θεὸν αὐτέγκλητα καὶ αὐθύβριστα καὶ ἀφ᾽ ἑαυτῶν αἰσχυνόμενα· τοιοῦτοι καὶ οἱ τῶν νῦν ἐπιλήσμονες, τῶν δὲ ἐπὶ τῶν ἄνω χρόνων μνήμονες. Σὲ οὖν, ὦ θαυμάσιε, ἐκ ψυχῆς πάσης ἀφίημι μέμψεως ἅπαξ ἀγνωμονήσαντα (δεῖ γάρ με, εἰ σωφρονῶ γε καὶ φρονῶ, καὶ πλείονα ἐλπίσαι καὶ μείζονα) ἐμὲ δὲ αἰτιῶμαι καὶ πάντες καὶ τότε ὑπερλαλήσαντα καὶ ἄρτι καταλαλήσαντα. Εἰ οὖν οἱ ἔπαινοι ἡμῶν ὡς ἀραὶ ἐλογίσθησαν, δεχθήτωσαν αἱ ὕβρεις ὡς ἔπαινοι· οὕτω γὰρ ἄνω καὶ κάτω στρεφόμενος ὁ πίναξ ὀρθώσῃ τὰ γεγράμμενα. Τὸν οὖν λαμπρόν, ὡς ἔφης, εἴπερ αὐτὸς ἔφης, ἔα Φωκίωνα τῆς αὐλῆς ἔξω, τοῖς δὲ ἔσω μᾶλλον πείθου πολλὰ περὶ ἀγάπης εἰποῦσί τε καὶ διδάξασι· τούτοις ἐντρέφου, τούτοις ἐντρύφα, τούτοις πείθου καὶ χριστομαθῶς ἢ καὶ χριστοθελῶς ἄγε τὸ ποίμνιον, ἵνα μὴ ὁ τῆς ἀγάπης Θεὸς βλασφημούμενος κἀγὼ τοῖς ὀνείδεσι βάλλωμαι καὶ οὐκ ἐπὶ τοῖς σοῖς κατακρίνωμαι· εἰ δὲ τοῖς αὐτοῖς ἐπιμείνοις, σὺν τῷ λαμπρῷ σου κατακριθήσῃ Φωκίωνι.

21. Τῷ αὐτῷ

Εἰ μὲν ᾔδειμεν, Ἀρσένιε, εἰδότα σε ὅτι οὐδὲν οἶδας ⟨...⟩ ἀνίατα νοσεῖν σε καὶ ἀθεράπευτα κρίνομεν καὶ ἀπολεγόμεθα αὐτόν σε σεσυλημένον τὸν νοῦν καὶ τὸ φρονεῖν ἀφῃρημένον καὶ ταῦτα τῶν κρισίμων ἔσωθεν. Καὶ ἰατροὶ γάρ φασι τοῦτο καὶ Πλάτων πρὸς τὸν Ἀλκιβιάδην, οἱ μὲν χειρίστην νόσον λέγοντες τὴν ὅτι οὐκ οἶδεν ὅτι νοσεῖ ὁ κάμνων (οἶσθα δὲ πάντως ὁποίᾳ, ἱκανῶς ταύτῃ ἐνισχημένος), ὁ δ᾽ ἐν ἐρωτήσει διδάσκων καὶ πείθων.

20: P 211r.
7 *πάντως* Darrouzès ‖ 9 *ἀραῖς* P, corr. Darrouzès ‖ 10 fort. *ὀρθώσει* ‖ 15 *βλασφημῆται* Darrouzès

---

21: 3–5 cf. Galen, *In Aph.*, I.12 (XVII B, 396.5–397.6, ed. Kühn)

21: P 211v.
2 lac. statui post *οἶδας* ‖ 5 *φησὶ* P, correxi

20. To the Same (Arsenius of Heraclea)

Such, holy father, are the ways of man; such, honorable lord, are the ways contrary to God—they indict, accuse, and disgrace themselves; such, also, are men who are forgetful of the present but mindful of the remote past. With all heartfelt sincerity, I relieve you, excellent sir, of all blame for being inconsiderate on one occasion (for I must, if I have any common sense, expect more and greater offenses), and I blame myself, as all the others do, for speaking on your behalf then and for maligning you more recently. If, then, our praises are reckoned as curses, let the insults be taken as praises. For if the picture is thus turned upside down, it will show correctly what has been painted. Leave the "illustrious Phocion," as you said, if those were your own words, outside the fold and listen instead to those inside when they speak and teach at length about charity. Nourish yourself with them, take delight in them, obey them, and lead the flock as befits a disciple of Christ or, rather, according to Christ's will; otherwise the God of charity is blasphemed against and I too will be the target of reproaches, and it won't be for your activities that I am condemned. But if you should persist in these same things, you will be condemned along with your "illustrious Phocion."

21. To the Same (Arsenius of Heraclea)

If we knew, Arsenius, that you know you know nothing, ⟨you would not be a hopeless case; as matters stand⟩, we consider you to be incurably, terminally ill and we write you off as delirious and out of your senses, and this within the critical period. The doctors say this, and Plato says it as well to Alcibiades: the former call the worst illness that which the diseased man doesn't know he has (you know quite well what sort of ailment they are talking about since you've got a severe case of it yourself); the latter teaches and persuades in the form of questions. "Are you un-

Πότερον σαυτὸν λέληθας ὅτι οὐκ ἐπίστασαι τοῦτο, ἢ ἐμὲ ἔλαθες μανθάνων καὶ φοιτῶν εἰς διδασκάλου, ὅς σε ἐδίδασκε διαγινώσκειν τὸ δικαιότερόν τε καὶ ἀδικώτερον;

Τί δ' εἰ μὴ ἔχω; οὐκ ἂν οἴει με ἄλλως εἰδέναι περὶ τῶν δικαίων ⟨καὶ⟩ ἀδίκων;

Ναί, εἴ γε εὕροις.

'Αλλ' οὐκ ἂν εὑρεῖν με ἡγῇ;

Καὶ μάλιστα, εἴ γε ζητήσειας.

Εἶτα ζητῆσαι οὐκ ἂν οἴει με;

Ἔγωγε, εἰ οἰηθείης μὴ εἰδέναι.

Τὰ δ' ἄλλα, ἵνα μὴ μακρηγορῶ, οἶσθα, σοφώτατε· εἰ μὲν οὖν προσδοκᾷς τὴν καθέδραν διδάξαι σε ἃ ἀγνοεῖς—πολλὰ δέ εἰσιν ἢ μᾶλλον πάντα—τοῦ παντὸς ἁμαρτάνεις καὶ "διώκεις ἀκίχητα"· εἰ δὲ οὐκ ἀρνούμενος τὴν νῦν καθέδραν καὶ ὧν ἀξίως προκάθῃ (πολλοὶ δέ εἰσιν, ὡς ὁρᾷς, ἀναίσθητε, καὶ σοφοὶ καὶ τίμιοι καὶ εὐλαβεῖς καὶ σεβάσμιοι καὶ οἷοι μηδὲ ἐκδουλεύεσθαι παρὰ σοῦ ἀνεχόμενοι) ὑπεραναβῆναι σπεύδεις καὶ τῶν συγκέλλων, κἂν ὑπόσχου τοῦτο πρῶτον, μαθεῖν ὅτι οὐδὲν οἶδας, οὐδεὶς ὢν καὶ οὐδέσι συναριθμούμενος· καὶ ἀναπλασθῆναι ζήτησον καὶ ἀναχωνευθῆναι ὡς ἀνδριάς τις παλαιὸς καὶ κατιωμένος καὶ πυρωθῆναι καὶ σφυρηλατηθῆναι καὶ τῷ ἄκμονι συνδαρῆναι. Εἰκὸς γάρ σε καὶ νέον πάλιν ἀνδριάντα γενέσθαι τῷ προτέρῳ ὅμοιον· οὕτω σὺ καὶ διὰ παντὸς {τὸ} παλαιὸς καὶ νέος, οἰόμενος μέν, μὴ εἰδὼς δὲ μηδέν, ἀλλὰ μηδ' ὤν τις πλὴν οὐδείς.

22. Νικολάῳ μητροπολίτῃ Νεοκαισαρείας

Τῶν ὁμολογουμένων καὶ βεβαίως συγκειμένων ἕν τι, δέσποτα, καὶ τὴν ἡμῶν ⟨ἡγοῦ⟩ φιλανθρωπίαν καὶ ἴσθι ὡς καὶ συναπήραμέν

9–11 Plato, *Alc. I*, 109D ‖ 12–18 *Alc. I*, 109E ‖ 21 Hom., *Il.*, 17.75 et *CPG*, I, 345

---

12 ἄλλως Pl.: ἄλλο P ‖ 13 addidi ‖ 14 ναὶ Pl.: καὶ P ‖ 16 καὶ μάλα γε, εἰ ζητήσειας Pl. ‖ 18 γε post οἰηθείης Pl. ‖ 19 οἶσθα Darrouzès: ἦσθα P ‖ 22 δὲ scripsi: ὡς P ‖ 30 delevi ‖ 31 μηδέν Westerink: μὴ δὲ P

22: P 212r.

3 add. Westerink: ⟨εἶναι νόμιζε⟩ post φιλανθρωπίαν add. Darrouzès ‖ 7 σου P, corr. Darrouzès

aware that you don't know this or did you learn it without my knowledge by going to a master who taught you to distinguish between the more just and the more unjust?" "What if I don't have one? Don't you think I could acquire knowledge of the just and unjust some other way?" "Yes, if you should find it." "Don't you think I could find it?" "Certainly you could, if you made it a subject of investigation." "Don't you think I would do that?" "I do, indeed, if you thought you didn't know."

In short, you know the rest, O Brilliant One. If you suppose that your see has taught you what you don't know—that's a lot, everything, in fact—you are absolutely mistaken and "you're on a wild goose chase"; but if, while being truthful about the kind of see you hold and those over whom you worthily preside (they are numerous, as you see, you numbskull, intelligent, honorable, pious, venerable men, the kind who wouldn't put up with being made your slaves), if, I say, you are still in a hurry to surpass the syncelli, at least promise to learn this first of all, that you know nothing because you are a nobody and you belong in the ranks of nobodies. Ask to be reformed and smelted over again like some rusty old statue, melted down, hammered, and beaten out on an anvil. For even as a refurbished statue, you will probably look the same as before: you will be like that forever, old or new, thinking that you know but not knowing anything, not even being a somebody but a nobody.

22. To Nicholas, the Metropolitan of Neocaesarea

Consider our (sincere feelings of) sympathy, my lord, to be one thing agreed upon and firmly resolved: to be sure, we set sail with you, suffered with you, and

σοι καὶ συνηλγήσαμεν καὶ τῶν τῆς λαχούσης σε ἀνιαρῶν καὶ συμμετέσχομεν καὶ εἴ τις καὶ νόσος τοῦ ἱεροῦ σώματος ἥψατο, κἀκείνης καὶ ἡμεῖς ἐκοινωνήσαμεν· καὶ νῦν πρὸς τὴν βασιλεύουσαν τὴν ὁρμήν σοι λαβόντι καὶ προσυπαντήσομεν καὶ "καλῶς ὁ ἐμὸς δεσπότης ἦλθες" προσείπωμεν καὶ τὰ φιλικά σε καὶ ἐνδιάθετά σε κατασπασόμεθα. Μόνον ἔλθοι συντόμως τὸ ἐλθεῖν σε καὶ συντμηθείησαν ἢ καὶ "κολοβωθείησαν αἱ μεταξὺ ἡμέραι," ἵνα τι κατ' αὐτῶν εὐξώμεθα σοῦ ἕνεκεν καὶ τῆς ἀσπαστῆς ἡμέρας ἐκείνης, ἐν ᾗ σε ἴδωμεν.

Ἤδη γάρ μου καὶ τὰς αἰσθήσεις πάσας ἡ γραφή σου κεκίνηκεν, ὀρθὰ τὰ ὦτα πρὸς τὴν ἀγγελίαν τῆς παρουσίας σου στήσασα, τοὺς ὀφθαλμοὺς πρὸς ἀνατολὰς ἀτενῶς ὁρᾶν πείσασα, ἀλλὰ καὶ χρωτὸς ἐκείνου τοῦ συνήθους καὶ εὐώδους ῥινηλατεῖν παρεσκευάσασας. Ἡ δὲ ψυχὴ πῶς δοκεῖς διάκειται "ὀσσομένη φίλον ἐσθλόν, εἴ ποθεν ἐλθὼν" ὅλους ἡμᾶς τῆς θυμηδίας ἐμπλήσαιεν; Εἰ οὖν ἡ ἐλπὶς οὕτως, ἣν χαρὰν πρὸ χαρᾶς οἱ περισσῶς ἐξωνόμασαν σοφοί, σκόπησον αὐτὸς τίς ἐπὶ τῇ παρουσίᾳ σου γένωμαι. Ἐγὼ δοκῶ τι καὶ τῶν ἀπευκτῶν ὑφ' ἡδονῆς παθεῖν, ἐκεῖνος ὥσπερ ὁ τοῦ Ὀδυσσέως· ἀλλ' "αὐτίκα τεθναίην" ὑγιῆ σε ἰδὼν καὶ ἀγρυπνίας ἀπηλλαγμένον, κακῆς νόσου κακοῖς μᾶλλον πρεπούσης· τὴν γὰρ σὴν ὁποιανδήποτε διάθεσιν ἐγὼ ἐμὴν κρίνω κατ' ἐκείνην τὴν ἀπόφασιν τὴν "κοινὰ τὰ τῶν φίλων" γνωρίζουσαν.

23. Μαλακεινῷ πρωτοσπαθαρίῳ

Πέμπτος ἤδη χρόνος οὗτος ἀφ' οὗ συνωψίσθημεν τῇ ἀγάπῃ σου—εἰ βραχὺς ἢ πολύς, αὐτὸς κρίνῃς, ὁ κριτὴς ἡμῶν. Τοίνυν ἐπεὶ ἐξήλθομεν καὶ ἐπεὶ ἀνήλθομεν, ἐπεὶ ἰδεῖν σε προσδοκῶμεν, ὀλίγον τὸν πολὺν λογιζόμεθα καὶ τῶν κακῶν ἐν λήθῃ γινόμεθα· μὴ πεῖραν λάβῃς τοιούτων σύ, μηδ' ἄλλος ὁ καλός γε καὶ ἀγαθός, οἷος σύ, ἀλλ' ὅστις οἷος ἐγὼ τετύχηκα, οἵων ἐγώ.

10–11 *τί . . . εὐξόμεθα* P, corr. Darrouzès || 14 *στήσαντα* P, corr. Darrouzès || 18 *τῆς θῦ μηδίας* P, corr. Darrouzès || 19 *ἡ χαρὰ* P, corr. Westerink *ἐξωνόμησαν σοφόν* P, corr. Darrouzès

22: 10 cf. Matt. 24.22 || 17–18 cf. Hom., *Od.*, 1.115 || 20–21 alludit ad Hom., *Od.*, 24.345? || 22 Hom., *Il.*, 18.98 || 24–25 Plato, *Lysis*, 207 C; Suda, K 2500 (ed. Adler, 3,200); *CPG*, I, 196; II, 76; et alibi

23: P 212v.
6–7 *ἄλλος τίς* P, corr. Westerink || 7 fort. *τετυχήκοι* Westerink

continue to share the troubles of the church which has received you as her lot. And whatever illness has afflicted your holy body, we shared that burden as well. Even now, since you are on your way to the capital, we shall come to meet you, we shall say in greeting, "Welcome, my lord," and we shall give you a hearty and affectionate embrace. I only hope that your arrival will be soon and that "the intervening days will be shortened and diminished," if we may put some kind of curse upon them for your sake and for that welcome day on which we shall see you.

Already your letter has stirred all my senses: it made my ears prick up at news of your arrival, it persuaded my eyes to look steadily toward the East, and further, you caused my nose to sniff out a trace of that familiar and fragrant skin. As for the soul, how do you think it reacts as "it looks for a noble friend to see if he will come from somewhere" and completely fill us with joy? If such is my hope, which the exceeding wise call "joy before joy," imagine how I will act upon your arrival. I think something terrible might happen to me from sheer delight, just like Odysseus' father. "But I would be willing to die on the spot" if I saw you healthy and free from insomnia, a bad malady more suited to bad men. In accord with the old saw, "Friends share and share alike," I consider your condition, whatever it may be, mine.

23. To Malacinus the Protospatharius

It has now been four years since we saw (you), your charity—you yourself, our judge, judge whether the time has been long or short. Ever since we left (the capital) and returned (to it), those years seem short and we are oblivious to our misfortunes because we may expect to see you there. I hope that you (or anyone else as fine and good as you) don't meet with the sort of things I've been through; let them happen to a man like myself.

24. Τῷ αὐτῷ

Πρότεροι ἐγράψαμεν καὶ πρότεροί σε ἠσπασάμεθα· ἅμα γὰρ ἤλθομεν, ἅμα σοὶ καὶ ἐπεστείλαμεν καὶ τὰ ἡμέτερα ἐκδιδάσκοντες καὶ τὰ σὰ ἐκδιδαχθῆναι ζητοῦντες, πρὸς τούτοις καὶ τὰ συμβάντα τῷ εὐλαβεστάτῳ Γερασίμῳ ἀναγνωρίζοντές σοι. Ἐπεὶ ⟨δ'⟩ οὐχ ὁμοίων διακομιστῶν ἐτύχομέν σοι, ὁ μὲν ἐμὸς εἴσω τοῦ Ἀνατολικοῦ ἔμεινε μηδὲν πλέον ἐλπίσας, ὁ δὲ σὸς ὑπερεθεμάτισε· ἀνάγκη γὰρ αὐτὸν ἤπειγεν ἄλλη, δι' ἣν οἶμαι σὲ πρὸς τὴν γραφὴν κατεπεῖξαι, ἐπεὶ πολλὰ ἀνεκράξαμέν τε καὶ ἐγράψαμεν, ὥστε σὲ πρὸς τοῦτο ἐκκαλέσασθαι.

25. Τῷ κριτῇ τῷ Μιτιληναίῳ

Ἐγὼ καὶ σιγῶν φιλῶ καὶ λαλῶν ἀγαπῶ· σὺ δὲ μικρὰ λαλῶν, βοᾷς ὅτι λαλεῖς, καὶ μίαν φιλικὴν γράψας, ἔκραξας ὅτι ἔγραψας πάμπολλα, ἡμεῖς δὲ οὐδ' ὅτι ἐγράψαμεν οὐδ' ὅτι ἐπράξαμεν ἐγρύξαμεν. Ταῖς οὖν προτάσεσι ταύταις σὺ ἐπάγαγε τὸ συμπέρασμα, ὁ σοφὸς τὰ τοιαῦτα καὶ εὔστροφος· εἰ οὖν ὀρθῶς συλλογίσῃ, ἔχω τὴν νικῶσαν ἐγώ, εἰ δ' ἄλλως ἐπάξεις τὸ συμπέρασμα, ἄλλος τὴν ἐσφαλμένην ἀποίσεται νίκην. Τί οὖν; Εἰ καὶ πολλὰ γράφεις καὶ σιγᾷς ὅτι γράφεις, ἀλλ' ὀλίγα γράφων πλείονα λέγεις γράφειν· ἡ δευτέρα εἶχε τὴν περὶ τοῦ προαστείου ὑπόθεσιν· ἡ τρίτη σιωπὴν εἶχεν καὶ σιγήν, ἀλλ' ἐλέγξω κἀκείνην ὅτι ψευδής σοι, μετὰ τὴν ὑπόσχεσιν πλείονα λαλήσαντι τῶν πρώην. Μὴ οὖν ὅτι ἐπαίξαμεν σὺ λυπηθῇς, ἀλλ' ὅτι ἠληθεύσαμεν αἰσχύνθητι καὶ πολλὰ γράψον ἀπολογούμενος, μὴ εὑρεσιλογῶν καὶ πλαστολογῶν, ἀλλ' ὅλος τῆς ἀληθείας γινόμενος.

24: P 213^{r}.
5 addidi || 10 *ἐκαλέσασθαι* P, corr. Darrouzès

25: P 213^{r}.
2 *σιγῶν* scripsi: *σιγῶ καὶ* P || 8–9 fort. *Τί οὖν οὐ καὶ πολλὰ . . . γράφειν*; Westerink || 9 fort. lac. post *γράφειν* || 11 *σου* P, corr. Darrouzès

24. To the Same (Malacinus)

We were the first to write and the first to send you our greetings: as soon as we arrived, we sent you a letter informing you of our doings and asking to be informed about yours in return. In addition, we reported the news about that most pious Gerasimus. Since our couriers were affected by different circumstances, mine remained in the Anatolikon theme without expecting anything further, while yours crossed the theme limits. He apparently had other urgent business and it was because of this, I think, that he made you write hurriedly—after all, we did a lot of shouting and writing to provoke you to reply.

25. To the Judge Mitylenaeus

Whether I write you or not, I like you and am your friend. When you've hardly made a peep you claim that you're a real chatterbox, and when you've written a single friendly note you shout that you've been writing all the time; we, on the other hand, don't breathe even a word about what we've written and done (on your behalf). Draw your conclusion, then, from these premises, since you're (so) clever and well-versed at that sort of thing. If, then, your logic is sound, the prize is mine; but if you come to a different conclusion, someone else will carry off the trophy undeservedly. How can that be? Even granted that you write a lot, still you fail to write because you do write, but only a few words stating that you write a great deal more. Your second letter had as its subject the affair of the manor; the third concerned itself with "silence," but I will prove that letter was false since after this promise you actually said more than in the preceding ones. Don't be offended because of my little joke; be embarrassed because it's true and write us a long letter of apology. And don't make up a lot of excuses and skirt the issue; be completely truthful.

26. Μιχαὴλ *μητροπολίτῃ* Εὐχαΐτων

"Εὐχαριστῶ τῷ Θεῷ ὅτι" *πάντα κατὰ νοῦν σοί γε ἀπήντηκε καὶ ἐμοὶ ἀπηγγέλη διὰ γραφῆς σου, σεβάσμιε καὶ ἅγιε δέσποτα· ἀλλὰ καὶ ὅσα δυσχερῆ καὶ ὅ[σα] ἀνώμαλα περὶ τὴν λαχοῦσάν σοι εὗρες ἐκκλησίαν, κἀκεῖνα σὺ* "*διὰ τῆς πρὸς* Θεὸν *εὐχαριστίας*" *ἐξομάλισον, οὕτως γὰρ ἐκελεύσθημεν* "*διὰ τῶν δεξιῶν,*" *φημί,* "*καὶ τῶν ἀριστερῶν*" *εὐχαριστεῖν αὐτῷ. Ὅτι δὲ μνήμης ἠξίωσας ἡμᾶς, ὅτι γραφῆς, τοῦτο ὑπὲρ πᾶσαν ἀγάπησιν, ὑπὲρ πᾶσαν φιλαδελφίαν ἐλογισάμεθα καὶ ἡγησάμεθα· καὶ σὲ εὐχόμεθα μένειν οὕτω καλόν, οὕτως ἀγαθόν, οὕτως ἥμερον καὶ τίμιον καὶ κόσμιον,* "*φωστῆρα,*" *ὡς εἰπεῖν,* "*ἐν κόσμῳ, λόγον ζωῆς ἐπέχοντα.*" Πιστεύω *γὰρ τῷ* "*μακάριοι* [*οἱ*] *πρᾳεῖς ὅτι αὐτοὶ κληρονομήσουσι τὴν γῆν,*" *ἥντινα δὴ* "*γῆν*" *ταύτην ὑποληπτέον.* Νῦν *μὲν οὖν δῴη ὁ* Θεὸς *γράφειν σε καλὰ καὶ ὡς ἐπὶ τὸ βέλτιον μετεβλήθη σοι τὰ πράγματα, ἔπειτα δὲ ἔλθοις καὶ αὐτὸς τὸν πόθον ἡμῶν ἀποπληρώσων διὰ τῆς χαριεστάτης σου ὁμιλίας καὶ ὄψεως.*

27. Γρηγορίῳ *μητροπολίτῃ* Νικαίας

Ἔοικε καὶ τοῦτο εὔλογον, ὦ θαυμάσιε Νικαίας, *τοῦ δυσπεπτῆσαι τὴν ἐπιστολήν σου καταφαγόντα· ἁπαλῷ γὰρ ὄντι μοι καὶ νηπίῳ καὶ* "*δεομένῳ γάλακτος ὅσον εἰς γνῶσιν, στερεὰν δοὺς αὐτὸς τροφὴν*" *καὶ οἷον εἰπεῖν βόειον, ἐξώγκωσάς με καὶ κατέβλαψας, ὀδύνας τε καὶ στρόφους ἐπινοησάμενος καὶ ἐνσκευασάμενος.* Τί *τοῦτο πεποίηκας, ἀπειρόκακε, γέροντα* Ἀβραάμ; Τὸ *γὰρ σοφῶς ἐμπεσεῖν τισιν ἴσον ἐστὶ τῷ σφοδρῶς, τὸ δὲ σφοδρῶς ταὐτὸν τῷ καταβαλεῖν·*

26: 2 cf. I. Cor. 1.14; II Thess. 2.13; Apoc. 11.17 ‖ 5 cf. II Cor. 9.12 ‖ 6–7 cf. II Cor. 6.7 ‖ 10–11 cf. Phil. 2.15–16 ‖ 12 cf. Matt. 5.5

26: P 213ᵛ.
4 supplevi ‖ 12 supplevi

27: 2–3 cf. Apoc. 10.9–10 et Ezech. 2.9–3.3 ‖ 4–5 cf. Heb. 5.12

27: P 214ʳ.
2 *εὔλογον* Westerink: *τὸ λογίον* P ‖ 7 fort. *ἀπειρόκαλε* Westerink *γέροντος* P, correxi ‖ 8 *καταβαλεῖν* scripsi: *καταλαβεῖν* P ‖

26. To Michael, the Metropolitan of Euchaïta

I thank God that everything has gone according to your wishes and that it was your letter, reverend and pious lord, which informed me. As for all the difficulties and rough spots that you have found in your assigned church, smooth them out by thanking God, for thus we have been directed to offer thanks to him "in prosperity and adversity." That you took the time to remember us, that you wrote, is something which, in our estimation, surpasses all affection and brotherly love. It is our prayer that you remain so noble, so good, so gentle, honorable, and decent, "a light," one may say, "in the world, holding forth the word of life." I believe in that beatitude, "Blessed are the meek, for they shall inherit the earth," whatever is meant by this "earth." For the present, I hope that God will allow you to report the good news that your situation has changed for the better; next, I hope that you will come in person to fulfill our wishes with your charming conversation and presence.

27. To Gregory, the Metropolitan of Nicaea

It was natural for me to get indigestion after gulping down your letter, marvelous Metropolitan of Nicaea. Since I am a tender babe, and "have need of milk" as far as knowledge is concerned, you, by giving me solid food (you might say a big steak), have made me bloated and done a good deal of harm by thinking up and preparing recipes for pangs and colic. Why have you, an innocent, done this to old man Abraham? A sally of wit against some people is equivalent to a violent assault, and a violent assault is as good as a downfall: you knocked me off my feet with your

σὺ οὖν καὶ σφοδρῶς καὶ σοφῶς γράφων ἐξέσεισάς με τῆς ἕδρας μου καὶ μηδ' ὅποι μηδ' ὅπως στῆναι κατέλιπες. Ἕρπων οὖν καὶ ἀσκωλιάζων μέμνημαί σου καὶ ἐρῶ σου κατὰ πνεῦμα μᾶλλον ἢ σάρκα· (ἔοικας γὰρ ἄλλῳ)· καὶ ὁρῶ σε κατὰ συνέχειαν καὶ φιλῶ σε κατὰ ἀνάπνευσιν. Καὶ τί ἐπῳκοδόμησα τῇ νεοπαγεῖ, ὡς ἔφης, φιλίᾳ, οὐκ οἶδα, οὐκ ἔχω, οὐ μὰ τὰ πολλὰ καὶ λεπτὰ τῆς Ἀσκανίας λίμνης κακέμφατα κορδάκια. Τῷ μεγίστῳ καὶ δεσπότῃ βασιλεῖ ὡς πολλά σου εὐχαριστοῦντος εὐχαρίστησα πλείονα, πρὸς δὲ καὶ ὅσα ἥρμοζε ὑπὲρ φίλου φίλον εἰπεῖν, κἀκεῖνο τὸ "καλός ἐστι, σοφός ἐστι, συμπεφυκὼς ἔχει τοῖς χείλεσιν οἶμαι καὶ τῇ καρδίᾳ"· σὺ δ' ὄντως ἁρμοσθεὶς ἢ μᾶλλον σαυτὸν ἁρμόσας ὥστ' ἀκούειν τοιαῦτα, καὶ χαῖρε καὶ γράφε καὶ ἔρρωσο.

28. Τῷ πατριάρχῃ

Ψιλὸν καὶ ξηρόν, ὡς εἰπεῖν, κόμμα ἢ τεμάχιον γραφῆς ἐδεξάμην, μήτ' ἐπτυγμένον, μήτ' ἐμφαῖνον τίνος ἢ πρὸς τίνα, τοῦτο μόνον αὐταῖς λέξεσι περιέχον· "Εἰσήλθομεν ἡμεῖς"—τὸ δ' ἦν κούλουρον, πλὴν παρ' ἡμῶν ἀνεμετρήθη—"εἰσελθέτω καὶ ὁ σύγκελλος εἰ μέλει αὐτῷ τῶν ψήφων· εἰ δὲ μέλλει καὶ ἀναβάλλεται, μηνυσάτω τὴν αἰτίαν τῆς μελλήσεως." Ἐγὼ δ' ἐκείνῳ τάδ' ἀντιλέγω· τίς ὤν, σοφώτατε, τίνι ταῦτα ἀπεσχεδίασας καὶ περὶ ποίου ᾐνίξω συγκέλλου καὶ τίς τὸ "εἰσελθέτω" προστακτικῆς ὂν ἐγκλίσεως τολμηρῶς εἴποι τῷ συγκέλλῳ; Οὐδείς, ὡς οἶμαι, τοιαῦτα τολμᾷ πρὸς σύγκελλον φθέγξασθαι, πλὴν εἰ μὴ μανείη καὶ ἔξω φρενῶν. Τὸ δ' "εἰ μέλει αὐτῷ τῶν ψήφων" μικροῦ καὶ ἐξεγέλασα καὶ ἐξεκάγχασα, εἰς δέ γε τὸ "εἰπεῖν τὴν τῆς μελλήσεως καὶ τῆς ἀναβολῆς αἰτίαν" ἐλθὼν κάτθανον ὑπὸ γέλωτος.

Οὗτος ἐκεῖνος ὁ γράψας, γελαστὸς ἦν μᾶλλον ἢ γελαστής· ἐγὼ δ' αἰτίαν ἔχων εἰπεῖν, διὰ τὴν ἀγάπην οὔτε μέλλων ἢ ἀναβαλλόμενος ἑτέρως ἰσοστάθμου ἢ καὶ πληρεστάτου ἀντέγραψα· "Ἐξήλθετε ὑμεῖς πρώην, ἐξήλθομεν ἡμεῖς ἀρτίως· εἰ μέλει ὑμῖν τῶν ψήφων,

---

12 ἄλλῳ scripsi: ἄλλως P || 15–16 *σοι εὐχαριστοῦντες* P, corr. Westerink

---

28: P 214^{v}.

6–7 *μέλει . . . ἀναβάλεται . . . μελήσεως* P, corr. Darrouzès || 9 *ἐγκλίσεως* scripsi: *ἐγκλήσεως* P || 13 *μελήσεως* P, corr. Darrouzès || 15 *γελαστὸς* corr. Darrouzès: *γελαστῆς* P || 16 *ἀναβαλόμενος* P, corr. Darrouzès || 17 fort. *πληρέστατον*

violently witty letter and didn't even leave me a place or the wherewithal to stand. Crawling and hopping, I think of you, and my passion for you is of a spiritual rather than a physical nature; for you seem transformed (into a spirit) and I see you constantly and love you with every gasp. What I built on the newly laid foundations (as you put it) of our friendship, I don't know, I swear I don't understand, by the many tiny "kordakia," with their scabrous name, of the Ascanian swamp. Thanking his majesty the lord emperor in your name, I added my own thanks more profusely. Above and beyond all the things it befitted a friend to say on a friend's behalf, I mentioned that famous saying "He is good, he is learned, and, in my opinion, his words and thoughts are one." You are truly fit, I mean you have made yourself fit, to hear such things said of you. Good-bye, and write.

28. To the Patriarch

I have received a bare and lean scrap of a letter (it was more like a sliver), not folded, no indication of sender or addressee, and this is all it contained, verbatim: "We have come in." It was truncated, but we completed it: "The syncellus must come in too if he is interested in voting. If he delays and procrastinates, let him give the reason for the delay." I have this to say to him: Who do you think you are, my learned friend, and to whom did you jot off that note? To what kind of syncellus were you alluding? Who would have the nerve to say to the syncellus "come"—and in the imperative mood? In my opinion, nobody but a raving madman would dare to say such a thing to a syncellus. The part that goes "if he is interested in voting" almost made me roar with laughter; and, when I got to that business about "the reason for the delay and procrastination," I nearly died laughing.

The fellow who wrote that note is a joke, not a jokester. I, on the other hand, since I am able to give a reason, have answered out of (brotherly) love, without procrastination or delay, in slightly longer or even quite expansive terms: "You left some time ago, we left just now. If you are interested in voting, vote; I am the first

ψηφίσασθε· πρῶτος γὰρ ἐγώ, καὶ παρὼν καὶ ἀπὼν συμψηφίζομαι· εἰ δέ γε μελλήσετε καὶ ἀναβαλεῖσθε, δίκην δώσετε τὴν ἐσχάτην, ἐφ' ὅσας ἡμέρας καὶ μέχρι τοῦ νῦν καὶ ἀπὸ τοῦ νῦν ἀργήσετε, ὡς ἔξω τῆς ἐκκλησίας καὶ τῆς πόλεως χρονοτριβοῦντες." Ἀλλ' εἰ πρὸ τῆς ψήφου τοιαῦτα ἐξυβρίσθημεν, τίς ἂν ἐνέγκοι τὰ μετὰ τὴν ψῆφον ἐμπτύσματα; Ταῦτ' ἔκφορα μήτε πρὸς τὸν μειζότερον ποιήσῃς. Ἀλλ' εἰ τὰ μετ' ἐπιτιμίου ἐξέφρασας, θαυμάζω εἰ μὴ ἐκφράσῃς τὰ χωρὶς ἐπιτιμίου· ἔρρωσο, ὅστις ἂν ᾖς.

29. Ἑτέρα

Εὐχαριστῆσαι τῷ κυρῷ μου προθέμενος, ἐπεὶ μὴ ἀξίως τοῦτο ποιῆσαι ἴσχυσα, συγγνώμην αἰτῶ δηλῶν ὡς ἐβουλήθην μὲν καὶ προεθυμήθην καὶ ὥρμησα, ἐπεσχέθην δὲ τῇ ἀδυναμίᾳ καὶ τῷ μεγέθει τῆς εὐεργεσίας σου. Σὺ γὰρ ταχύτερον ἢ ἐκλήθης καὶ ὀξέως ἐβοήθησας καὶ οὔτε ἡ ἀνωμαλία σε τῶν πραγμάτων οὔθ' ὁ καιρὸς εἰς στενὸν κομιδῇ συνηγμένος οὔτε ἄλλο προέστη σοι τῶν ἐμποδίων. "Τομωτέρα" σοῦ γὰρ ἡ πρὸς τὸ εὐεργετεῖν ἐστι σπουδὴ "πάσης διστόμου μαχαίρας" καὶ ξίφους ἠκονημένου. Ταῦτα καὶ ἐννοοῦντι καὶ ἀναλογιζομένῳ μοι πρόθεσις μὲν ἦν πολλοὺς συμπαραλαβεῖν ὥστε πλέξαι σοι τὸν εὐχαριστήριον· μόνῳ γάρ μοι ἀτόλμητον κατεφαίνετο. Ἀλλ' ἐπεὶ οὐ πρὸς τὸ εὐχαριστεῖν ἀπεῖδες, ἀλλ' εἰς Θεὸν ἔσ[χες] τὰς ἐλπίδας σου, δίκαιον ἔκρινας ὁλόκληρον ἐκεῖθεν τὴν ἀντιμισθίαν ἀπολαβεῖν καὶ μὴ περικόψαι ταύτην διὰ τῆς μικρᾶς ἡμῶν εὐλογίας τε καὶ εὐφημίας, μᾶλλον καὶ πολυπλασιάσαι διὰ προσθήκης ἑτέρας χρυσοβουλλίου τοῦ ἁγιωτάτου ἐπισκόπου καὶ θείου ἡμῶν, ἀνδρὸς οἵου εὔχεσθαι καὶ εὐχομένου ἀκούεσθαι. Οὗτος τὸ χρυσοβούλλιον καὶ τὰ πρὸς τὸν πρωτονοτάριον γράμματά σου καὶ ὅσα ὁ πρωτονοτάριος ἱερὰ ἀφείλετο ἀπολαβών, σὺν ἐμοὶ στήσεται καὶ ὑπερευξόμεθά σου καὶ τὰ ἀγαθά σοι αἰτησόμεθα τῆς ἄνω Ἱερουσαλήμ· καὶ ὁ Θεὸς οἴδαμεν ὅτι ἐπινεύσει, οὐχ ἡμῖν τοσοῦτον, ὅσον σοῦ ἕνεκεν καὶ τοῦ ἀνεπιλήπτου σου βίου καὶ καθαροῦ. Φυλαχθείης ὑπὸ Θεοῦ καὶ στηριχθείης, σωτηρία τῷ κόσμῳ καὶ μέγα τυγχάνων παραμύθιον.

---

20 μελήσετε P, corr. Darrouzès   ἀναβάλεσθε P, correxi

29: 8–9 cf. Heb. 4.12

29: P 215[r].
10 συμπαραλαβεῖν Westerink: συμπεριλαβεῖν P ‖ 13 ἔσ[χες] suppl. Darrouzès

and my vote counts whether I'm there or not. If you dawdle and delay, you will pay the harshest possible penalty for every day, up to the present and afterwards, that you spend doing nothing, because you are wasting your time outside your church and city." However, if we were handled so rudely before the vote, who could endure the abuse after it? Don't let even your superior in on this. But since you have reported (secrets) when a penalty was attached, I'll be surprised if you don't report them now that there is none. Good-bye, whoever you are.

29. Another (Letter)

Since I was unable to thank you properly, my lord, as I had planned, I ask your pardon. I had every wish and intention of doing it, I even started to but was thwarted by my own ineptitude and the generosity of your benefaction. You rushed to my aid faster than you were called and you let neither the precariousness of the situation, the short notice, nor anything else stand in your way. Your zeal for good works is "sharper than any two-edged sword" or finely honed blade. It occurred to me as I was reflecting upon these things to call a great number of others to my aid to plait for you a garland of gratitude: this was too great a venture for me by myself. However, since you did not act with the expectation of receiving thanks but instead had all your hopes in God, you deemed it right to receive your entire reward from him. (You decided) not to diminish this reward by our insignificant blessings and praise but rather even to increase it by the further addition of the golden bull of our most holy bishop and uncle, a prayerful man, and one whose prayers are heard. After this man has received the golden bull and the (copy of) your letter to the protonotarius and has recovered all the sacred objects that the protonotarius took away, he will stand by my side and together we shall pray for you and ask for you the blessings of the heavenly Jerusalem. We know too that God will grant them, not so much because of our efforts as because of yourself and your blameless and pure life. May God protect and strengthen you who are a saving grace for the world and a great source of comfort.

30. Τοῖς νοταρίοις

Οἱ λόγοι τὴν φύσιν ὑπόπτερον ἔχουσιν, διὰ τοῦτο σημείων χρῄζουσιν ἵνα ἱπταμένων αὐτῶν λάβῃ τὸ τάχος ὁ γράφων. Σὺ οὖν, ὦ παῖ, τὰ χαράγματα τέλεια ποίει καὶ τοὺς τόπους ἀκολούθως κατάστιζε· ἐν γὰρ μικρᾷ πλάνῃ πολὺς ἡμάρτηται λόγος, τῇ δὲ ἐπιμελείᾳ τοῦ γράφοντος κατορθοῦται τὸ λεγόμενον.

31. Ἡ διαθήκη τοῦ Συνάδων

Ζωὴ καὶ θάνατος ὡς ἡμέρα καὶ νύξ, φαιδρὰ τὰ πρῶτα, σκυθρωπὰ τὰ δεύτερα, ἀλλὰ ταῦτα καὶ Θεοῦ ἐστι πρόσταγμα καὶ οὐ παρελεύσεται γινόμενα καὶ ἀπογινόμενα· τὸ δὲ τίς ὁ λόγος οἴδαμεν μὲν καὶ ἡμεῖς εὑρεσιλογήσαντες, τὸν δ' ἀληθῆ μόνος οἶδεν ἐκεῖνος. Ἐγὼ γοῦν ζήσας ἤλπισα καὶ θανεῖν—ὡς μὴ ὤφελον ἑκάτερον, ἐπείπερ οὐκ ἦν ὑπαλλάξαι τὸ ἕτερον. Ἓξ καὶ ἑξήκοντα βιώσας ἐνιαυτούς, ἡμέρας εἶδον καὶ "ἡλίους μοι ἐπιφαύσαντας" ἐνενήκοντα πρὸς τοῖς τετρακισχιλίοις καὶ δισμυρίοις, οὓς αἱ νύκτες ἐδιπλασίασαν, ὡς εἶναι καὶ τὴν ὅλην ἀναμετρουμένην χάρυβδιν, ἡμέρας φημὶ καὶ νύκτας, ὀγδοήκοντα καὶ ἑκατὸν πρὸς ταῖς ὀκτακισχιλίαις καὶ τετρακισμυρίαις, ὧν ἀναμάρτητον οὐδεμίαν διῆλθον—εἴθε καὶ μονοαμάρτητον, ἀλλὰ μὴ πολυαμάρτητον. Ἢ γὰρ εἶδον κακῶς, ἤ τι καὶ ἄσεμνον ἤκουσα, ἢ περισσῶς ἔφαγον, ἢ καὶ ὁμοίως ἔπιον, ἢ καὶ ἀμφότερα, ἤ τι καὶ ἐνενόησα πονηρόν, ἢ καὶ ἔδρασα, ἢ καὶ ἑκάτερα, ἢ ὄσφρησις ἐθήλυνέ με, ἢ ἁφὴ κατεμαλάκισεν, ἢ ἔλεξα ἀργῶς, ἢ

30: P 215v.

1 Haec epistula eadem est atque Basili Caesariensis, *Ep. 333* (PG, 32, col. 1076C–D; vol. III, p. 201, ed. Courtonne [Paris, 1966]), ubi titulus habet *νοταρίῳ*

31: 8 cf. Job 31.26

31: P 215v–217v. C 6r.

1 *Λέοντος μητροπολίτου Συνάδων ἐπὶ τῇ ἰδίᾳ ἐπιτάφιος τελεύτῃ* inscripsit C ‖ 4 *τὲ* post *γινόμενα* add. C ‖ 5 *μὲν* om. C ‖ 6 *ὤφελεν ἑκάτερα* C ‖ 7 *ὑπαλλάξαι* P: *καταλύξαι* C: *ὑπαλύξαι* Darrouzès *δὲ* post *ἓξ* add. C ‖ 10 *καὶ*[1] om. C ‖ 10–11 *χάρυβδιν . . . νύκτας* P: *ὡς εἰπεῖν χάρυβδιν* C ‖ 11 *τοῖς ὀκτακισχιλίοις* C ‖ 11–12 *τετρακισμυρίους* C ‖ 12–13 *μονοαμάρτητον* C: *μόνον ἀναμάρτητον* P ‖ 13–14 *ἤ . . . ἤκουσα* P: *ἢ καὶ ἀσέμνως* C ‖ 14 *καὶ* ante *περισσῶς* add. C ‖ 15 *καὶ*[3] om. C ‖ 16 *ἐθήλυνέ με* C: *ἐθήλυνεν* P *κατεμαλάκι(σεν)* C: *κατεμαλάκησεν* P

30. To the Notarii

Words have a flighty nature; they need symbols so that the writer can catch them as they whiz by. You, then, my boy, form your letters perfectly and put your punctuation marks in the correct places. For many a word loses its meaning completely when a small mistake is made; but, if the writer is careful, what he says will be what is meant.

31. The Will of the Metropolitan of Synada

Life and death are as day and night: the former are bright, the latter, dark. Yet these things, too, are God's commandment and will not cease coming into being and passing away. And though we, too, have employed ingenious arguments to answer the question of (this) natural law, he alone possesses the true knowledge. Speaking for myself, even as I have had life, I also expected death; I wish I'd had neither since it is impossible to change the latter. In my sixty-six years, I have seen 24,090 sunlit days shining on me, which, doubled by the nights, gives a grand total of 48,180 for the Charybdis I have crossed, I mean the days and nights. Of these, I did not get through a single one without sin—if only there had been just one transgression a day instead of many! I either viewed (something) maliciously or I heard something base; I either ate or drank too much, or both; I either thought or did something wicked, or both; I succumbed to the sense of smell or touch; or I spoke

ἔπραξα ὃ μὴ ὤφειλε, ἢ λοιδοροῦντος ἤκουον, ἢ καὶ αὐτὸς ἐλοιδόρησα, ἢ ἀμελῶς ἔψαλλον, ἢ οὐδ' ὅλως ηὐξάμην, ἀλλὰ πανημέριος ἐματαιοπόνουν, ἢ λόγοις οὐκ ἐσχόλασα θείοις, ἢ τοῖς ἔξω πλέον ἐν[ε]διέτριψα καὶ τοῦ μέτρου, ἢ προσπαθῶς ὑπέρ τινος εἶπον, ἢ ἐμπαθῶς ἠμυνάμην, ἢ ὠργίσθην, ἢ ἔτυψα, ἢ καὶ ἀμφότερα, ἢ ἐμετεωρίσθην, ἢ ἐπήρθην καὶ ἐφυσήθην καὶ διὰ μέσης ἐπόμπευσα τῆς ἀγορᾶς, συγγαυριῶν τῷ ἵππῳ καὶ σεμνυνόμενος καὶ οἷον εἰπεῖν ὡραϊζόμενος· ἢ οὐδ' ὅλως ἠλέησα, ἢ γλίσχρως ἠλέησα καὶ ἀναξίως, πάντως εἰς ἁμαρτίαν καὶ τοῦτο.

Πόσους παρεῖδον ἕλκεσι βρύοντας; Πόσους τὸν Θεὸν ἐπιβοωμένους παρῆλθον; Πόσους τὸ τῆς Θεοτόκου ὄνομα καὶ εἰς δέησιν προτεινομένους καὶ κάμψαι δι' αὐτῶν τὴν ἀμείλικτον καὶ ἀσυμπαθῆ καὶ σκληρὰν καὶ λιθώδη καὶ αὐτόχρημα πῶρον καρδίαν μου, οὐδ' ἐπεστράφην ἀλλ' ὀξυποδήσας παρέδραμον; Εἴθε μὴ ἔζησα τὴν ἡμέραν ἐκείνην, ἢ ἐν νεκροῖς ἐλογίσθην, ἢ καὶ δαιμόνων πέδαις ἐφυλασσόμην, ἢ καὶ πυρετῷ λάβρῳ διεκαιόμην. Πόσους καὶ αὐτήν μοι τὴν σωτηρίαν καὶ τὸ ἔλεος τοῦ Θεοῦ προβαλλομένους καὶ τὸ "οὕτως ἐν μετανοίᾳ ἀποθάνῃς" καὶ τὸ "ἅγιε δέσποτα, ἐλέησον" λέγοντας μηδ' ἀκούειν προσεποιούμην ἢ καὶ ἐπικραινόμην; Πόσα ἐτρύφησα ὁ ἄθλιος λιμῷ τῶν τοῦ Χριστοῦ τηκομένων; Πόσα ἐψευσάμην; Πόσα παρελογισάμην; Πόσα εἰς οὐδὲν ἀνήλωσα; Πόσοις ἁγίοις καὶ σεμνοῖς ἀνδράσιν ὡμίλησά τε καὶ ἐξεδούλευσα μηδὲν τῶν προσόντων αὐτοῖς ἀγαθῶν παρασπάσας;

Πῶς ἐκ μέσου τῶν συγγενῶν καὶ ἀδελφῶν μου μόνος ἐνεκυλίσθην ἐγὼ εἰς τὸν χοιρώδη βίον καὶ βορβορώδη; Εἰ οὖν ἐν λαϊκοῖς, τί μὴ εἴπω ἐν ἐθνικοῖς, ἐπιλήψιμα ταῦτα, πόσῳ μᾶλλον ἐν κληρικοῖς; Εἰ ἐν κληρικοῖς, ἐν ἱερεῦσι τί φήσω; Εἰ ἐν ἱερεῦσι, ἐν ἀρχιερεῦσι πόσῳ πλέον;

Εἴπω δὴ τὸ συμπέρασμα. Εἰ μία μοι καθ' ἑκάστην ἡμέραν καὶ νύκτα λογισθείη ἁμαρτία, τὰς δ' ἄλλας ὁ Θεὸς κατὰ τὸ μέγα ἔλεος αὐτοῦ συγχωρήσει μοι, τὰς τετρακισμυρίας καὶ ὀκτακισχιλίας καὶ ἑκατὸν ὀγδοήκοντα, αἳ χιλιάδες εἰσὶν ὀκτὼ καὶ τεσσαράκοντα, πῶς

---

17 ὃ P: ὡς C ὤφειλε P: ὤφελ( ) C ‖ 17–18 ἐλοιδόρουν C ‖ 18 ἔψαλον P ‖ 20 supplevi: διέτριψα C ‖ 20–21 ὑπέρ . . . ἐμπαθῶς om. C ‖ 21 καὶ ἀμφότερα P: ἑκάτερα C ‖ 22 καὶ . . . καὶ P: ἢ . . . ἢ C ‖ 23 ἐνσεμνυνόμενος C ‖ 24 ἢ² P: καὶ C ‖ 26 ante ἕλκεσι add. ἀνοίκτως C ‖ 27 τῆς Θεοτόκου P: τοῦ Θεοῦ C καὶ om. C ‖ 28 προτείνοντας C ἀσυμπαθῆ καὶ ἀμείλικτον C ‖ 29 μου om. C ‖ 29–30 οὐδ' ἐπεστράφην P: οὐδὲ ἐπεκάμφθην C ‖ 30 ὀξυποδίσας C ‖ 31 καὶ ante ἐν add. C ἢ² P: εἴθε C δαιμόνων PC: fort. δαιμονώντων ‖ 32 μοι P: μου C ‖ 33 προβαλλομένους P: ἐπιβοωμένους C ‖ 36 ἀδελφῶν post Χριστοῦ add. C ‖ 37 δέον post οὐδὲν add. C ἀνάλωσα C ‖ 40–41 ἐξεκυλίσθην C ‖ 41 καὶ βορβορώδη om. C ‖ 42 μὴ εἴπω C: μὲν εἶπον P ‖ 44 πόσῳ πλέον P: τί πλέον εἴπω C ‖ 45 δὴ P: καὶ C ‖ 47 αὐτῷ C χιλίας post τετρακισμυρίας add. P

idle words; or I did what ought not (be done); I heard cursing or I myself cursed; or I sang the psalms indifferently; or I didn't pray at all but spent the whole day loafing instead; or I didn't devote my attention to religious texts; or I spent more time than I should reading profane literature; or I spoke passionately on someone's behalf; or I heatedly defended myself; I either became angry, hit someone, or both; I had my nose in the air or was haughty and conceited and paraded right through the market-place, prancing like my horse, holding my head high, and more or less preening; either I utterly failed to show pity or I did it grudgingly and meanly, which is just as bad.

How many people, covered with oozing sores, have I disdained to notice? How many people have I passed by, even as they called out to God? How many people have I not even turned to when they invoked the name of the Theotokos in supplication to soften my cruel, unsympathetic, hard and stony heart? Heart? It was pure flint, and I briskly went on my way. I wish that I'd never seen that day or that I had been dead or possessed by devils or racked by raging fever. How many people have I pretended not to hear or even become irritated with when they called to me in the name of my own salvation and the Lord's mercy and when they said, "May you thus die repentant" and, "Lord Bishop, have mercy"? How many times have I, wretch that I am, stuffed myself while the people of Christ wasted away with hunger? How many times have I lied? How many times have I equivocated? How much have I frittered away on trifles? How many are the pious and saintly men in whose company and service I have been, yet I failed to take advantage of their virtues?

How is it that I alone, unlike my relatives and friends, have wallowed in a life of filth and swinishness? If these things, then, are reprehensible for the laity, not to mention the heathen, how much more so for the clergy? And if they are reprehensible for the clergy, I hate to think about the bishops. If they are reprehensible for bishops, how much more heinous are they for archbishops?

Let me conclude. If one sin should be tallied for each day and night, and if God, in his infinite mercy, will pardon me the rest, how shall I, wretch that I am, carry on my shoulders the (remaining) four times ten thousand, eight times one thousand, and one hundred eighty, which makes a total of 48,000? "Hewers of

ὁ ἄθλιος κατωμαδὸν οἴσω; "Ξυλοφόρους, ὑδροφόρους," γομοφόρους ποίους προσλήψομαι συνεπικουφίζοντάς μοι βάρος τοσοῦτον; Χωρήσει δ' ὅλως τὸ σῶμά μου, λεπτὴ κόνις, τοσαῦτα κεντήματα, μύρμηκας ἢ ψύλλας ἤ τι λεπτεπιλεπτότερον τοσούτους οἴσειν; Ὦ πῶς διέλθω τὴν στενήν, ὁ παχὺς καὶ γαστροπίων καὶ μηδ' ἐν τῇ πλατείᾳ χωρούμενος; Ὦ πῶς πειραθῶ περᾶσαι; Καὶ σφηνωθήσομαι καὶ τοῖς διελθεῖν μέλλουσιν ἐμποδισμὸς γενήσομαι καὶ καταπατηθήσομαι καὶ καταλοηθήσομαι καὶ ἐξαφανισθήσομαι καὶ ἀπολεσθήσομαι, ὡς ὁ "πιὼν" ἐκεῖνος τὸ "ἁλμυρὸν ὕδωρ."

Ἀλλ' οὐκ ἀπελπιστέον οὐδ' ἀπογνωστέον, ἀλλὰ τῇ ἀβύσσῳ τῆς τοῦ Θεοῦ εὐσπλαγχνίας τὴν ἄβυσσον ἐπιρριπτέον τῶν πολλῶν μου κακῶν καὶ ᾧ τὰς ἀφάτους μυριάδας ἐπίστευσα, τούτῳ καὶ τὸ πολλοστημόριον, τὰς ἀνὰ μίαν φημί, ἐπιρρίψω τε καὶ βοήσω μετὰ ἀναιδείας, μετὰ παρρησίας, μετὰ θράσους· "Ὦ Κύριε, σῶσον δή· ὦ Κύριε, εὐόδωσον δή· ὦ Κύριε, νεῦσον μόνον· ὦ Κύριε, ἄλειψόν με ἐλέῳ· πολὺ γὰρ ἔχεις καὶ ἄφατον τοῦτο δὴ τὸ ἔλεος." Ἀλλὰ καὶ ἐγὼ συμπροθυμηθήσομαι ἔσω ὤσασθαι χωρὶς δισταγμοῦ, κἀκεῖνος συμβοηθήσει μοι καὶ ἀποσφηνωθήσομαι καὶ ἴσως ἐκπεράσω.

τέλος τῶν λα' ἐπιστολῶν τοῦ Συνάδων μετὰ καὶ τῆς διαθήκης αὐτοῦ.

32. Εἰς τὸν πατριάρχην Ἀντιοχείας

Εἴ σοι παραινέσεως εἴπω λόγον, θεομακάριστε δέσποτα, μὴ τολμητίαν οἰηθῇς με καὶ θρασὺν εἶναι, ἀλλ' εἰς νοῦν λαβὼν ὡς εἷς εἰμι τῶν συλλυπουμένων σοι, οἷον ἂν εἴπω, δέξαι μετὰ ἱλαρότητος. Τὸν Σωκράτην οἶδας, ὁ πολὺς ἐν συνέσει, τὸν σοφὸν τὸν Ἕλληνα ἐκεῖνον, ἀποθανεῖν ἀδίκως κατακριθέντα, τά τε ἄλλα ἡ γυνὴ Ξαν-

49 cf. Deut. 29.11 et Josh. 9.27 ‖ 52–54 cf. Matt. 7.13 ‖ 57 cf. Hom., *Od.*, 4.511

50 *ποίους προσλήψομαι* P: *πόσους συνεπιλήψομαι* C ‖ 51 *δὲ* C *λεπτῆς* C ‖ 51–52 *δὲ* post *μύρμηκας* add. C ‖ 52 *οἴσειν* P: *οἴσω* C ‖ 54 *εἰ* ante *πειραθῶ* add. C *σφηνωθήσομαι* Darrouzès: *σφινωθήσομαι* C: *σφηνωθήσεσθαι* P ‖ 55 *ἐμπόδιον* C *γενήσομαι* Darrouzès: *γενήσεσθαι* P: *ἔσομαι* C ‖ 56 *ἢ* post *καταλοηθήσομαι* C ‖ 58 *πάντη* post *ἀπελπιστέον* add. C ‖ 61 *ἀνὰ μίαν* P: *ἁμαρτίας* C ‖ 62 *θάρσους* C ‖ 63 *ὦ . . . νεῦσον μόνον* om. C ‖ 64 *τοῦτο* post *ἔχεις* add. C *τοῦτο δὴ τὸ* P: *τὸ μέγα* C ‖ 65 *συμπροθυμηθήσομαι* Darrouzès: *συμπροθυμήσομαι* C: *σὺν προθυμία θήσομαι* P *ἔσω ὤσασθαι* P: *προσδραμεῖν αὐτῷ* C ‖ 65–66 *βοηθήσει* C ‖ 66 *διεκπεράσω* C

32: 7–9 cf. Diog. Laert., II.35

wood, drawers of water,'' bearers of loads—what sort of people shall I get to lighten so great a burden? Will my body, light as dust, actually be able to endure so many bites and stings, so many ants and fleas, or anything so infinitesimal? How shall I pass through the narrow gate when I'm so fat I can't even get through the wide one? How shall I attempt to pass through? I'll get stuck and form a one-man obstacle course for those about to go through. I'll be trampled and squashed, I'll disappear and be lost, just like that fellow who "swallowed the salt water."

Still, I must not despair or give up. On the contrary, I must throw the abyss of my many imperfections upon the abyss of God's mercy. In him I have confided the countless multitude of my sins; to him I shall also render the fraction (I mean the sins reckoned at the rate of one a day), and to him I shall call for help unashamedly, freely, and boldly: "O Lord, please save me! O Lord, please help me get through! O Lord, just say yes! O Lord, anoint me with the oil of mercy! This mercy of yours is ineffably great!" I, for my part, shall make every effort to squeeze my way in, without faltering, and with a helping hand from him, I shall get unstuck and maybe even pass through.

32. To the Patriarch of Antioch

If I offer you a bit of advice, most blessed lord, don't think that I am impertinent and presumptuous; rather, take into consideration that I am one who shares your sorrow, and accept whatever I am to say with good grace. You are aware, my learned friend, that Socrates, that wise old Hellene, was unjustly condemned to die.

θίππη παρεμυθεῖτο, καὶ δὴ καὶ τοῦτο προσεπεῖπεν ὡς "ἀδίκως ἀποθνήσκεις ὦ Σώκρατες"· ὁ δὲ ὑπολαβὼν ἐν μειδιάματι πάντως "σὺ δὲ ἐβούλου με δικαίως ἀποθανεῖν;" Τοῦτο *οἶδα ὡς καὶ αὐτὸς ἂν εἴποις, εὔθυμος ὢν καὶ εὔελπις καὶ αὐτὸ τὸ ἀδίκως πάσχειν εἰς παραμυθίαν καὶ ψυχαγωγίαν ἔχων.* Εἰ *μή σε οὖν ἡ γείτων, ἣν βλέπεις παρακαθήμενος, ἐκκλησία θράττει καὶ λυπεῖ ὡς χήρα τέ ἐστι καὶ ἔρημος καὶ ἄνανδρος, τοῦ ἱεροῦ καὶ μεγάλου καὶ θαυμασίου καὶ ἀσυγκρίτου ταύτης ἀνδρὸς πρὸς τὸν* Θεὸν *μεταστάντος, καὶ τὸ μὴ ἀντιδίδοσθαι ποιμένας ταῖς τῶν ἐκλιμπανόντων ἀρχιερέων παροικίαις καὶ εἰς οὐδὲν καὶ τὸ μὴ ὂν συνελαύνεσθαι τὴν καθ' ὅλου ἱερωσύνην, οὐδὲν ἐν τοῖς ἰδίοις καὶ τοῖς καθ' ἑαυτόν σε λυπεῖσθαι τέως ἐγὼ συμβουλεύω· ὁ γὰρ στέφανος ἤδη ἐπλάκη σοι ὡς ἀδίκως πάσχοντι καὶ μεγαλοψύχως φέροντι.*

33. Εἰς *τὸν καναστρίσιον*

Οἶδ' *ὡς κατ' ἐμαυτοῦ τὸν λέοντα ἔνυξα καὶ τὸν ἵππον εἰς τὸ πεδίον προεκαλεσάμην, τί γὰρ ἂν εἴποι τις ἕτερον τὴν ἐπιστολὴν ἐκείνην διερχόμενος;* Οὕτω *πολλή, οὕτω καλή, οὕτω σοφή τις ἦν καὶ τῶν χαρίτων πλήρης· καὶ εἰ μὴ ἄπληστος ἦν ἐγὼ ὡς καὶ δευτέρας ἐρᾶν, οὐκ ἂν πρὸς ἑτέραν γραφὴν ἀπεῖδον, ἀλλ' "ἔθηκα ἂν τὴν χεῖρα ἐπὶ τῷ στόματι," δεικνὺς ὡς νενίκημαί τε καὶ ἥττημαι.* Μὴ *οὖν καὶ τῆς δευτέρας φθονήσῃς, εἰδὼς ὡς ναρκᾶν οἱ σοφοὶ λέγουσι τὸν ὄφιν ἅπαξ καλάμῳ τυπτόμενον, κινεῖσθαι δὲ μᾶλλον καὶ ἀποναρκᾶν προσεπιτυπτόμενον.*

32: V 163^{v}.
14 *διὰ* post *καὶ* add. Lambros ‖ 15–16 *παροικίας* V, corr. Darrouzès

---

33: 2–3 *CPG*, I, 191, n. 65 et II, 483, n. 99 ‖ 6–7 cf. Job 39.35 ‖ 8–10 Aelian, *De natura animalium*, I.37

33: V 164^{r}.
2 *οἶδ'* Lambros: *εἶδ'* V: *εἰ δ'* Darrouzès ‖ 9–10 *ἀποναρκοῦν* Darrouzès

Among the various things his wife, Xanthippe, did to comfort him, she said this in particular: "Socrates, you die unjustly." But he replied, no doubt with a smile, "Did you want me to die justly?" I know that this would be your reply too since you are possessed of equanimity and good hope and consider the very act of unjust suffering a source of comfort and consolation. If, then, you are not upset and disturbed by the fact that the neighboring church, which you observe close at hand, is widowed, bereaved, and husbandless because her holy, great, wonderful, and peerless mate has passed on to God; (if you are not disturbed by the fact) that no pastors are being appointed to the dioceses to replace bishops who pass away and that the priesthood is generally dwindling away to nothing, I advise you not to worry over your personal troubles for the time being. A crown has already been woven for you because of your courageous endurance of unjust suffering.

33. To the Canstrisius

I realize that I have goaded a lion against me and that I have called out the horse to the plain. What else could anyone say while reading that letter of yours? It was so long, so nice, so clever and full of charm. If I were not so greedy as to want a second letter as well, I wouldn't dream of writing again but "I would lay mine hand upon my mouth" as a token of your victory and my defeat. So don't begrudge me that second letter, and bear in mind what wise men have to say about the snake: if you hit him once with a reed, he'll go numb; but he'll become all the more active and shake off his numbness if you hit him again.

34. Τοῦ Νικομηδείας εἰς τὸν Συνάδων

Καὶ ὁ λύχνος, εἰ μή τις αὐτὸν τῷ ἐλαίῳ ἐπάρδοι, τάχιστα ἂν πάντως ἀποσβεσθῇ· καὶ τὸ τῆς ἀγάπης φῶς, εἰ μὴ συνεχῶς οἱ φιλοῦντες ἀλλήλοις ὁμιλοῖεν ἢ παρόντες, ἢ ἀπόντες τοῖς γράμμασι, κινδυνεύσοι ἂν ἀπομαρανθῆναι. Ὅπερ ἡμεῖς δεδιότες μή ποτε ἡ μακρὰ ἀπουσία τε καὶ διάστασις καὶ τὸ ἐπὶ τοσοῦτον ἀνομίλητον τὸν τηλικοῦτον τῆς φιλίας ἀποσβέσει πυρσόν, πρὸς τὴν παροῦσαν γραφὴν ὡρμήθημεν, τοὺς τῆς ἀγάπης ἀνασκαλεύοντες ἄνθρακας καὶ τὸ ἐν αὐτοῖς φῶς ἀναζωπυροῦντες καὶ οἱονεὶ πρὸς μετέωρον φλόγα ἀνάπτοντες. Ἰδὲ γὰρ ὅσος ἐρρύη χρόνος καὶ οὐ παρ' ἀλλήλοις ἐφοίτησαν γράμματα, οὐ προσρήσεις φιλικαί, οὐ σύμβολα τῆς ἀγάπης. Μέμφομαι μὲν οὖν ἐμαυτῷ τῆς ἐπὶ τοσούτῳ σιγῆς· αἰτιῶμαι δὲ καὶ τὸν ποθούμενον σὲ ὡς ἐπίσης σιγήσαντα, καὶ ἀξιῶ γράμμασιν ἡμᾶς δεξιώσασθαι φιλικοῖς καὶ δηλῶσαι ὡς ἔχει τὰ σά· ἔχοι δὲ πάντως καλῶς καὶ ὡς εὐκταῖον ἡμῖν. Εἰ γὰρ καὶ "τὸ τῆς ἀγάπης χρῆμα οὐδέποτε ἐκπίπτει" κατὰ τὸν θεῖον Ἀπόστολον, οὐδὲ τόπου διάστασις διακόπτει τὸν πόθον, ἀλλ' ἐν οἷς ἐρρίζωται τοῦτο, θάλλει καὶ αὔξεται καὶ ἀείζωόν ἐστι τὸ τῆς ἀγάπης φυτόν, ἀλλὰ δεῖται πάντως τῆς διὰ τῶν γραμμάτων ἀρδείας καὶ τῆς γλυκείας ἐπιρροῆς τῶν ἐκ ψυχῆς προσιόντων ναμάτων. Ὃ δὴ ποιεῖν μὴ ἐλλίποις ὁ ποθεινότατός μου δεσπότης.

Ἐγὼ μὲν οὖν ἀεί σου τὸ τῆς ἀγάπης εἰλικρινές τε καὶ ἄδολον ᾔδειν ἀκριβῶς· πλέον δέ με πεπληροφόρηκεν ὁ κύρις Κωνσταντῖνος, ὁ θεοστεφὴς βασιλεύς. Αὐτὸς γὰρ ἐντυχών σου πολλάκις τῇ ἱερότητι ἀπήγγειλεν ἡμῖν οἷα πρὸς τὴν αὐτοῦ βασιλείαν περὶ τῆς ἡμετέρας ἐλάλησας οὐθενότητος καὶ ὡς ἐκ ψυχῆς στέργεις ἡμᾶς τῷ περὶ ἡμᾶς φίλτρῳ διακαιόμενος. Τοῦτο μὲν οὖν ἄξιον τῆς σῆς ἱερότητος καὶ πρέπον τῇ ἀγαθῇ σου ψυχῇ· ὁ δὲ τῆς ἀγάπης Κύριος ἀντιμετρήσαι σοι τὸν ὑπὲρ τούτου μισθόν, "ὅτι ἠγάπησας πολὺ" καὶ τὴν τοῦ Χριστοῦ φυλάττειν ἐσπούδασας ἐντολήν, ὡς ἀληθὴς αὐτοῦ μαθητής. Μεμνῆσθαι δὲ ἡμῶν ἐν ταῖς πρὸς Κύριον εὐχαῖς σου μὴ διαλίποις.

34: 15–16 cf. I Cor. 13.8 || 29 cf. Luc. 7.47

34: V 164v.

3 *ἀποσβεσθείη* Lambros || 7 *ἀποσβέσῃ* Darrouzès || 24 *σοι* V, corr. Darrouzès || 29 *ἀντιμετρῆσαί σοι* V, corr. Lambros

34. From the Metropolitan of Nicomedia to the Metropolitan of Synada

Not only would a lamp go out very quickly should someone fail to feed it with oil, but the light of love also is in danger of being snuffed out unless friends are in constant communication, either in person or by letters, if they are separated. Because this is the very thing we feared, that is, that long absence, separation, and lack of communication for so great a period of time would extinguish the flame of our long-standing friendship, we have begun this letter as a means of raking the embers of love and reviving the fire in them and, as it were, stirring it up to a sky-high blaze. Mark how much time has slipped by and no letters have passed between us, no friendly greetings, no tokens of affection. I hold myself responsible for this overlong period of silence; yet I blame you too, my love, for being equally silent, and I think you ought to honor us with a friendly letter and let us know how you are. We hope and pray that all is well. For even if, as the divine Apostle says, "Love never faileth," and even if spatial distance does not dampen desire, but where it has taken root the flower of love shoots up, blossoms, and lives forever; still it certainly must be sprinkled with letters and the sweet outpourings of the waters that spring from the soul. I hope that you, my greatly missed lord, will not fail to do this.

I for my part have always had sure knowledge of the purity and guilelessness of your love; yet the Lord Constantine, the God-crowned emperor, has given me greater assurance of it. For he himself, since he frequently saw your holiness, reported to us in what terms you spoke of our worthlessness to his majesty and how, warm with affection for us, you love us from the bottom of your heart. This is worthy of your holiness and befits your good heart. May the Lord of Love reward you for this "because you have loved much" and because you have endeavored to keep Christ's commandment as his true disciple. Please do not fail to remember us in your prayers to the Lord.

35. Ἀντέγραψεν ὁ Συνάδων

Ἐγώ σε, ὦ θαυμάσιε καὶ σεβάσμιε δέσποτα, ἵν' ἔξω κολακείας καί, ὅ φασιν, ἀπὸ καρδίας καὶ ἀπ' αὐτῆς τῆς ψυχῆς εἴπω γυμνὴν τὴν ἀλήθειαν, καὶ ἐθαύμασα ἐξ ἀρχῆς καὶ ἐσεβάσθην καὶ ἠγάσθην καὶ τῶν πλείστων ἢ καὶ πάντων προέκρινα καὶ προετίμησα καὶ προέθηκα πολλῶν ἕνεκα, τοῦ βίου, τοῦ τρόπου, τοῦ λόγου, τοῦ ἤθους, τῆς ἀληθείας, τῆς γνώσεως, τῆς σοφίας, τῶν ἄλλων καὶ ὁμοῦ τι συμπάντων. Τὰ γὰρ ἔξω καὶ μὴ καθ' ἡμᾶς νῦν ἐάσθω, ὁ θρόνος, ὁ πλοῦτος, ἡ δόξα, ἡ τιμή, τὸ ὕψος, τὸ ἀξίωμα, ἃ καὶ αὐτά σοι καλῶς χρωμένῳ τιμιώτερόν σε ποιεῖ καὶ εἰς αὐτὴν ἄγει τὴν κορυφὴν τῶν καλῶν. Οὐ μέγα οὖν εἰ ταῦτα καὶ πολλὰ ἕτερα ἔχοντά σε εἶπα καλόν· καλὸς γὰρ εἶ καὶ σεμνός—καί μοι μέμνησο τοῦ τῆς ἐπιστολῆς προοιμίου—καὶ σοφὸς καὶ ἀγαθὸς καὶ πρᾶος καὶ ἥμερος καὶ Θεῷ ἐγγίζων καὶ ἀρετῆς ταμιεῖον, ἵν' εἴπω συνελών.

Τὸ οὖν οὕτω σὲ μὲν ἔχειν, ἐμὲ δὲ λέγειν, οὐ χάρις· χάρις γὰρ ἂν ἦν, εἰ πρὸς χάριν ἔλεγον, εἰ ψευδῆ, εἰ κατὰ ἄνθρωπον. Νῦν δ' ἐγὼ καὶ ἀληθῆ εἶπον καὶ λέγων ἐκαυχώμην, καὶ τὰ αὐτὰ εἴπω καὶ πάλιν καὶ πᾶσι· "χείλη μου οὐ μὴ κωλύσω." Τοῦ γὰρ φιλικοῦ ἐλαίου ἅπαξ ἐπιχυθέντος μοι παρὰ σοῦ καὶ ἐξάψαντος, σοφὸν τὸ μὴ σβέννυσθαι καὶ θαυμάσιον οἷον καὶ ὑπὲρ τὸ Μηδικὸν καὶ ὑπὲρ ἐκεῖνο, ὃ τοῖς λουτροῖς τῶν οὐχ ἡμετέρων τις ἐπέχεε καὶ ᾧ ἐπῆδεν, ἃ ἐπῆδέ τε καὶ οἶδεν ἐκεῖνος. Μὴ οὖν τῷ σιγᾶν ἕπεσθαι τὸ μὴ φιλεῖν ὁρίζου ὁ διακριτικώτατος, ὥσπερ οὐδὲ τῷ βοᾶν ἡμεῖς τὸ ἀγαπᾶν. Τούτου ἕνεκα θάρρει, πάτερ ἡμέτερε, καὶ ὡς υἱῷ καὶ ὡς φίλῳ καὶ ὡς εὐγνώμονι καὶ ὡς καλῶς κρίναντι καὶ ὡς ἀληθινῶς ἀγαπήσαντι. Καί σοι λέγω καὶ σὺν Θεῷ λέγω καὶ βεβαιῶ καὶ διατείνομαι καὶ μετ' ἐντάσεως ταῦτα ποιῶ, ὡς καὶ φιλῶ σε καὶ στέργω σε καὶ διακαῶς πρὸς σὲ διάκειμαι καὶ τὸ φίλτρον ἔρωτα εἰπεῖν ἀναγκάζομαι καὶ οὐδ' εἰπεῖν ἔχω ὅσον καὶ βούλομαι, οὕτως με ἡ σὴ ἀρετὴ καὶ τὰ ἐν σοὶ καλὰ διέθηκε. Καί σοι προσεπείπω καὶ τὸ Σοφόκλειον· "Ὦ μακάριε, τοῖς ἄλλοισι πέλας ἵστασο, καθ' ἡμᾶς δ' οὔποτε ἐκρήξει φιλία."

35: 18 Ps. 39.9 ‖ 20 τὸ Μηδικὸν, cf. Plut., *Quaest. conv.*, 681C ‖ 20–21 locum non inveni ‖ 30–32 cf. Soph., *Ajax*, 774–75

35: V 166r.
21 ᾧ Westerink: ὃ V ‖ 27 ἐντάσεως scripsi: ἐνστάσεως V ‖ 31 ἐκρίξει V, corr. Darrouzès

35. The Metropolitan of Synada Replies

To tell the plain truth, marvelous and reverend lord, without flattery and, as they say, straight from my heart and soul, you have from the first been the object of my admiration, respect, and awe. I prefer, honor, and regard you above most, or even all, men for many reasons: your way of life, your character, your intellect, your temperament, your honesty, your erudition, your wisdom, and nearly everything else. For the present, let's leave out your temporal assets and the things outside our control: your see, wealth, prestige, honor, eminence, and position. These things too bring you greater honor and elevate you to the very peak of moral excellence because you put them to excellent use. It is therefore of slight consequence if I called you an excellent man because you have these things and more, for you are excellent and worthy of respect—remember the beginning of my letter—as well as wise, good, gentle, kind, godlike, and, in short, a treasure house of virtue.

That this is the kind of man you are and that I say so is no favor. It would be if I said it with the hope of reciprocation, if it were false, if I were influenced by worldly values. But, as it is, I'm proud to say I told the truth, and I shall say the same things again to everyone: "I shall not refrain my lips." That the fire of our love refuses to go out after I have been kindled by just one pouring of the oil of your friendship is a marvelous and clever thing such as surpasses the properties of both Median oil and that oil that a certain non-Christian poured into the bath and over which he spoke charms, charms which only the man who uttered them knows. Therefore, my highly discerning friend, do not equate silence with hostility, just as we do not confound bombast with affection. For this reason, our father, rely on us as a loyal son and friend, one who is fair in his judgments and true in his affection. I tell you God's own truth when I promise and declare—and I do so emphatically—that I cherish and adore you, that I feel blazing fires of passion for you and I am forced to call my affection love, and even that does not tell the whole of it. This is how your excellent and virtuous qualities have affected me. I shall close with the addition of this line from Sophocles: "Saintly man, concentrate your efforts on the others; the bonds of affection, on my part at least, will never be shattered."

36. Εἰς τὸν Ἐφέσου, διὰ χρυσοβουλλίου

Μέγας ὁ πειρασμός, ἀλλὰ τῇ τοῦ Θεοῦ χάριτι μέγας καὶ σύ, ἀρετῇ πρῶτον, εἶτα καὶ βίῳ καὶ τρόπῳ καὶ χρόνῳ καὶ θρόνῳ καὶ λόγῳ καὶ ἔργῳ καὶ πᾶσιν ὁμοῦ τοῖς ἄλλοις. Κεφαλὴ οὖν καὶ στόμα καὶ λόγος καὶ νοῦς τῆς ὅλης ὢν ἐκκλησίας, ἀντίστηθι γενναιότερον καὶ θερμότερον πρόστηθι καὶ ἀντίπνευσον ῥαγδαιότερον. Τίς ἀντιστήσεταί σου τῇ δόξῃ ἢ τῷ λόγῳ; Τίς τοῖς φρονήμασιν ἢ τοῖς βουλεύμασιν ἐξισωθείη σοι; Ἀρκεῖς ἀντὶ πάντων καὶ μόνος ἢ στῆσαι τὸ κακὸν ἢ αὐτοῦ ἀντίον στῆναι. Ἡμῖν οὖν, πολλὰ βουλευσαμένοις καὶ τῇδε κἀκεῖσε τὸν νοῦν μετακινήσασι, πρὸς σὲ καταφυγεῖν ἔδοξε καὶ πρὸς σὲ ἀποβλέψειν καὶ σοὶ ἐναπερείσασθαι καὶ παρὰ σοῦ τὸ πρακτέον ἐκδιδαχθῆναι. Σὺ γὰρ πατὴρ ἡμῶν καὶ πρὸς σὲ ἀφορῶμεν καὶ σοὶ ἀκολουθήσομεν. Δίδαξον οὖν καὶ δεῖξον ὁδόν, ᾗ χρησόμεθα, σεβασμιώτατε δέσποτα καὶ πάτερ, καὶ βουλὴν βούλευσαι τὴν ἀρίστην καὶ πρόσθες εὐχὴν τοῦ μὴ ἀστοχῆσαι ἕνεκα· πλέον γὰρ ἰσχύσει τῶν πολλῶν καὶ βουλευμάτων ἡμῶν καὶ πράξεων.

37. Εἰς τὸν πρωτονοτάριον

Οἷον εἴπω ἔπος, τοῖον, οἶδα, καὶ ἀκούσω· καὶ τὸ ἀνάπαλιν, οἷον ἀκούσω, τοῖον καὶ εἴπω. Οὐκ ἔγραφον, οὐκ ἔγραφες· τὸ ἐμὸν εἶπα καὶ τὸ σόν· ἐφίλουν, ἐφίλεις, καὶ τοῦτο κοινόν· λαλῶ, λαλήσεις, ἴσον καὶ τοῦτο· καὶ γραφόντι γράψεις, κρεῖττον μέν, θέλοντι δέ μοι καὶ αὐτῷ αὐτό. Τοῖς ἐξισάζουσι τούτοις προσθήσω καὶ τὰ ἴδια. Ἄγροικος ἐγώ, ἀστικὸς σύ· σὺ πολλὰ εἰδώς, ἐγὼ ὀλίγα· πολυμαθὴς σύ, ἐγὼ οὐδὲ τοῦτο. Ἰσάζεις ἐκείνοις, τούτοις διαφέρεις. Ἔχω τι καὶ αὐτὸς τῶν πρώτων, τὸ πρῶτος γράψαι καὶ σὲ πρὸς γραφὴν ἐκκαλέσασθαι·

36: V 167[r].
9 *ἀντίον στῆναι* Lambros: *ἀντὶ στῆναι* V: *ἀντιστῆναι* Darrouzès || 13 *χρησώμεθα* Darrouzès || 14 *βουλεῦσαι* V, corr. Darrouzès

---

37: 2 cf. Hesiod, *Op.*, 721

37: V 167[v].
4 *καὶ* post *ἐφίλουν* add. Lambros

36. To the Metropolitan of Ephesus via Golden Bull

Great is the trial, but by the grace of God you too are great, in virtue, first of all, and secondly in your way of life, character, seniority, throne, words, and deeds, and all else besides. Since, therefore, you are the head, voice, intellect, and mind of the entire Church, put up a more spirited resistance, lead a more passionate defense, and show your opposition with hurricane force. Who will resist your prestige and intellect? Who could be a match for your aims and plans? Single-handed you are worth the lot of them and are capable of either checking the evil or resisting it. We, therefore, who have formed many a resolution and vacillated back and forth, thought it best to look to you for shelter, support, and instruction on what ought to be done. You are our father; we turn to you and will follow you. Direct us, then, and show us what course to take, most reverend lord and father. Give us the best advice and add your prayers so that it may not be in vain. Your prayer will be more effective than the multitude of our plans and actions.

37. To the Protonotarius

I shall undoubtedly hear something very like what I say; conversely, I shall say something very like what I hear. I didn't write, you didn't write; I spoke for myself and for you; I was affectionate, you were affectionate—this too we had in common. I talk, you will talk—this too is reciprocal. If I write, you will write; your letter, to be sure, will be superior, but I gladly accept this. To these points of similarity I shall also add our differences. I am uncultivated; you are urbane. You know a lot; I, little. You are erudite, while I have no claim to this either. You are equal to the former attributes; to the latter you are superior. I also have some claim of my own to be a "first": I was the first to write and prompt you to reply. Yet I realize with

ἀλλ' οἶδα καὶ δέδια τὸ "λοῖσθος ἀνὴρ ἄριστος." Ἐγὼ γοῦν οὐχ ὅσον γράψαι, ἀλλ' ὅσον ἀκροβολίσασθαι καὶ ὡς ζῶ δηλῶσαι ταυτὶ διεχάραξα. Σὺ δέ, εἰ μὲν ἐπαφῇς μοι τὴν γλῶσσαν, ἄφωνον πάντως δείξεις· εἰ δ' ἰσομέτρως ἀντεπιστείλῃς, θρασύτερόν με ἄρα τὸν δειλὸν ἀπεργάσῃ.

38. Εἰς τὸν κῦριν Λέοντα τῆς εἰδικῆς

Καὶ συνήλγησα καὶ συνέκλαυσα καὶ συνεθρήνησα καὶ συνεπένθησα καὶ συνεδάκρυσα καὶ συνῴμωξα καὶ συνεστέναξα ἐπὶ τῇ τελευτῇ τῆς θυγατρός μου· οὕτως γὰρ ἐθέμην εἶναί μοι, ἐπεὶ καὶ σύ, ὡς πιστεύω, ἐγώ. Ἀλλ' ἐπεὶ ὁ Μέγας, καὶ ᾧ ἀντιστῆναι οὐκ ἔνι, καὶ οὗ ἡ βούλησις ἔργον καὶ ὅσον ὑπὲρ ἡμᾶς μᾶλλον οἶδε τὰ καθ' ἡμᾶς, ταύτην ἐμνηστεύσατο καὶ ἑαυτῷ ἡρμόσατο καὶ πρὸς ἑαυτὸν μετέστησεν, ἄπειρον κακῶν, ἄγευστον τῶν τῇδε, ἄθικτον, ἄχραντον, ἀμόλυντον, ἀμίαντον, ἄψαυστον, τοῦτο καὶ ἐμὲ παρηγόρησε καὶ σὲ μὴ θρηνεῖν πεισάτω, ἀλλὰ χαίρειν καὶ εὐφραίνεσθαι, νυμφίου νυμφίον ἀλλαξάμενον κρείττονα· καί, εἰ ἀλγηρὰν τὴν στέρησιν αὐτῆς εἴποι τις, ἀλλ' οὐκ ἀνιαρὰν τὴν μετάστασιν ὡς πολλῶν ἀπηλλαγμένην κακῶν, ἃ ἡμεῖς ἐν τῷ βίῳ εἴδομεν, ἔγωγε φαίην.

Ἀλλὰ τί ἐπᾴδω ταῦτα ὁ μάταιος ἐγὼ τῷ συνετῷ, τῷ σοφῷ, τῷ φρονίμῳ, τῷ ἱκανῷ, τῷ εἰδότι, τῷ ἐπισταμένῳ, τῷ καὶ ἐμὲ καταρτίζοντι καὶ πολλοὺς ἄλλους στηρίζοντι καὶ ἑαυτῷ καὶ τῷ νυμφίῳ παρηγορίᾳ γινομένῳ καὶ παραμυθίᾳ καὶ τὴν δοκοῦσαν συμφορὰν εἰς εὐθυμίαν μεταβάλλοντι; Μᾶλλον αὐτὸς εἰπὲ ἡμῖν καὶ τὰ κρείττονα δίδαξον καὶ τὰς αἰτίας, δι' ἃς ταῦτα γίνεται, γνώρισον καὶ φθέγξαι χαροπόν τι καὶ χαρμόσυνον, ἵν' εἰδῶμέν σε ψυχαγωγοῦντα ἡμᾶς διὰ τῶν γραμμάτων, ἐπείπερ διὰ τῶν πραγμάτων οὐ βλέπομεν. Καὶ σοὶ τί ἂν ἄλλο ἐπευξαίμην ἢ σωτηρίαν ψυχῆς; Χαρίσμασι γὰρ ὁ Θεὸς τοῖς πρώτοις σε κατεκόσμησεν.

---

10 Hom., *Il.*, 23.536 ubi ὥριστος

---

11 ζῶ Darrouzès: ζῶν V || 12 ἐπαφῇς Lambros: ἐπαφεὶς V || 13 ἀντεπιστείλεις V, corr. Lambros

38: V 168^{r}.

1 Κ^υ V: κύριον Lambros τῆς εἰδικῆς V: τὸν εἰδικόν Lambros || 3 συνώμοξα V, corr. Darrouzès || 4 μοι scripsi: σοι V || 6 ὅσον V, fort. ὅς ὢν

some apprehension that "the best man is last." At any rate, as far as I'm concerned, these scratchings are not enough for a proper letter but only for a sniping shot and an indication that I am still among the living. As for you, if you launch a verbal assault against me, you will no doubt render me speechless; but if you reply in kind, you will make your cowardly friend more daring.

38. To Lord Leo, of the Eidice

I shared your grief, weeping, lamentation, sorrow, tears, cries, and groans over the death of my daughter: I felt she was my own as strongly as I believe you and I are identical. Nevertheless, the Great One, whom it is impossible to oppose, whose will is accomplished fact and who, inasmuch as he transcends us, has better knowledge of our concerns, has courted, betrothed, and drawn to himself this girl who was unacquainted with evil and had no taste (yet) of the things of this earth, who was untouched, undefiled, stainless, unsullied, and pure. I took comfort from this; let it persuade you also not to grieve but to rejoice and be glad, because you have received the Divine Bridegroom in return for a mortal one. Further, if anyone should mention that losing her is heartbreaking, I, at least, would counter by saying that her departure is no cause for sadness, because she has won a release from the many troubles we have encountered in this life.

Why am I, trifling creature that I am, conjuring up these phrases to soothe one who is intelligent, wise, thoughtful, capable, knowing, and understanding, who restores me and strengthens countless others, who is a source of comfort and encouragement to both himself and the betrothed, and who transforms an apparent disaster into a cause for joy? You are the one who should speak to us: instruct us in the Higher Wisdom and the reasons for which these things happen; say something bright and cheerful so we may know you are diverting our sorrow through your letters, since we are unable to witness this in your actions. What else could I pray for you than the salvation of your soul? For God has already adorned you with the foremost gifts of grace.

39. Τῷ αὐτῷ

Εἰ μή με πάσης αἰτίας ἀπολύσεις ὁμολογοῦντα παντὶ πταίσματι ἔνοχον γενέσθαι, εἰ μὴ καὶ εὐθὺς τοῦτο ποιήσεις καὶ παραχρῆμα καὶ ταχὺ κατανεύσεις [σ]ὺ καὶ πλεῖον ἢ ἐγὼ θέλω καὶ ὡς τῷ σῷ μᾶλλον ἁρμόζει τρόπῳ, ἅμα τῷ τὴν σφραγῖδα λῦσαι καὶ ἅμα ἄρξασθαι καὶ πρὸ τοῦ διελθεῖν ἕτερόν τι τῆς ἐπιστολῆς, δίκαια μὲν ποιεῖς, ἀσυμπαθῆ δὲ καὶ ἄσπλαγχνα. Τοὺς γὰρ φίλους μετὰ τῶν ἐλαττωμάτων ἔχειν φίλους καὶ αὐτὸς ἀνέγνως. Ἐπεὶ οὖν καὶ ἡμάρτομεν καὶ ἠνομήσαμεν καὶ ἄφιλοί τινες ἐδόξαμεν, ὅπερ μηδέποτε γενέσθαι ηὐξάμεθα, οὕτω καὶ ἐμβραδύναντες, οὕτω καὶ συναπαχθέντες ὡς οὐκ ἔδει, τῆς μὲν προθέσεως ἐκείνης ὁμολογοῦμεν ἐν Θεῷ ὡς οὐκ ἐξέστημεν, τοῦ δὲ ἐπὶ τοσοῦτον μὴ γράψαι χρόνον, εἰ καὶ στρατηγοὺς καὶ βασιλεῖς καὶ ἄλλους εἰς ἀπολογίαν προβαλλόμεθα, ἀλλ' οὖν ἕωλα καὶ ψυχρὰ λέγειν δόξομεν καὶ δέος μὴ τῆς συγχωρήσεως ἀποτύχωμεν, ἀπολογίαν τινὰ καὶ μηχανὴν μηχανώμενοι καὶ τεχναζόμενοι. Δὸς οὖν μεγαλοψύχως καὶ εὐπροαιρέτως τὴν συγχώρησιν καὶ εἰς τὴν προτέραν ἀνακάλεσαι φιλίαν καὶ μήτε ὀνειδίσῃς, μήτε ἐλέγξῃς, μήτε αἰσχύνῃ τινὶ καθυποβάλῃς, εἰδὼς ὡς χρῄζεις καὶ αὐτὸς τῆς τοῦ Θεοῦ συγχωρήσεως, τοῖς αὐτοῖς αἰτιάμασιν ἐμπεριειλημμένος· ἡμῖν γὰρ κρίνειν τὸν ἡμέτερον κριτὴν οὐ λυσιτελὲς κέκριται, κριτοῖς κατά γε τὸ παρὸν οὖσι. Καὶ περὶ τῆς σὺν Θεῷ εὐοδώσεώς σου γνώρισον ἡμῖν ὡς καλῶς τῇ τοῦ Θεοῦ χάριτι ἐξανύεται· ὅπερ καὶ εὐχόμεθα καὶ βεβαίως ἔχομεν. Τὰ σταλέντα ὅτι μικρὰ αὐτόθεν καταφαίνονται, σοὶ δὲ μεγάλα πάντως μετὰ τὴν συγχώρησιν δόξουσιν.

39: P 227r. V 169r.

2 *με* post *αἰτίας* trans. P ‖ 4 *καὶ ταχὺ* om. P [σ]ὺ legi: *μὲν* Darrouzès, om. V *πλεῖον* V: *πλέον* P ‖ 5 *ἅμα*[2] om. P ‖ 7 *ἀσυμπαθὴς δὲ πάντως δόξεις καὶ ἄσπλαγχνος* P *γὰρ* V: *τε* P ‖ 11 *συναπαχθέντες* V: *συνεπαρθέντες* P ‖ 12 *δὲ* om. P ‖ 14 *λέγειν* om. P ‖ 15 *καὶ* post *μὴ* add. P ‖ 15–16 *ἀπολογίαν . . . τεχναζόμενοι* V: *ἀπολογίαν τινὰ μηχανώμεθα* P ‖ 17 post *ἀνακάλεσαι* add. *φιλανθρωπίαν καὶ* P ‖ 19 *χρῄζεις* P: *χρήζω* V

39. To the Same (Lord Leo)

If you will not absolve me from all blame after I assume liability for every transgression, and if you will not do this at once and, as is more in keeping with your character, (if) you will not promptly and speedily grant even more than I desire—immediately upon breaking the seal and beginning to read and before proceeding to another line of my letter—you are well within your rights but unfeeling and heartless. For you too realize that friends accept each other with their faults. Since, then, we have offended, transgressed, and—the very thing we hoped to avoid—given the impression of a lack of friendship on our part because we were detained longer and distracted more than we should have been, we swear before God that we never abandoned our intention of writing; but although we adduce generals, emperors, and others in defense of so lengthy a break in correspondence, our words will still seem stale and cold; and, after composing a makeshift defense out of clever sophistries, there is reason to fear that we shall fail to obtain forgiveness. Grant the pardon magnanimously and generously and restore us to our former friendship. Don't reproach, criticize, or subject us to any embarrassment. Remember that you too are involved in the same sins and are in need of God's forgiveness. For we have decided that it is not in our best interest to pass judgment on our judge inasmuch as we, for the time being at least, are still awaiting a trial. Let us know that your enterprise has reached a happy and successful conclusion with God's grace and help. This is our prayer and we are certain of it. As for the gifts we send, it is obvious at first sight that they are small, but you will surely think them great after forgiving us.

40. Μεθοδίῳ πατρικίῳ

Οὐ τοῦτό με ἐλύπησε, τὸ μὴ εἰσακουσθῆναι, ἀλλ' ἐκεῖν' εὔφρανε τὸ σὲ τοιοῦτον εὑρεῖν προστάτην. Σὰ γὰρ ἦσαν τὰ χρηστὰ πάντα, τὸ κήδεσθαι, τὸ ἐλεεῖν, τὸ ὑπερτίθεσθαι τὰ σωτήρια· τὰ δ' ἄλλα, ὅσα σ' αἰτησαμένῳ μοι χρηστὸν οὐκ ἔσχε τὸ πέρας, ταῖς ἐμαῖς λογίζομαι ἁμαρτίαις. Ἔχω οὖν τό γε ἐπὶ σοί, μεγαλοπρεπέστατε, ὁλοτελῆ τὴν χάριν καὶ εὐχαριστῶ καὶ εὔχομαι τοιοῦτον καὶ σοὶ γενέσθαι τὸν Θεόν, οἷος σὺ ἐμοὶ ἐφάνης. Τοῦ δούλου σου, περὶ οὗ καὶ ὑπέμνησα τὸν ἐνδοξότατόν μου κύριον, τοῦ ἀσηκρῆτις καὶ ἀνθρώπου τῆς εὐτελείας ἡμῶν πρόστηθι, ὡς ἂν καὶ ὑπὲρ αὐτοῦ εὐχαριστήσω σοι.

41. Τῷ αὐτῷ

Σὺ μὲν ἀπαίρεις καὶ χαίρεις καὶ τούτου ἕνεκα χαίρομεν καὶ ἡμεῖς· τὸν γὰρ φύσει σὸν πατέρα, πρὸς ὃν σπεύδεις, θέσει καὶ ἡμεῖς ἔχομεν. Οὕτω γὰρ οὐ μόνον τὸ ἀδελφούς, ἀλλὰ καὶ τὸ φιλαδέλφους ἡμᾶς εἶναι διὰ βίου συντηρηθήσεται. Ἡμεῖς δέ, εἰ καὶ λυπούμεθα ἐπὶ τῷ χωρισμῷ, ἀλλ' οὖν εὐχόμεθα τοῦ καὶ σὲ διασωθῆναι καὶ ἑνωθῆναι τῷ ποθοῦντι καὶ ποθουμένῳ πατρί. Ἐρρωμένος οὖν καὶ χαίρων καὶ εὐθυμῶν τὴν ὁδὸν ἄνυε, τοῦτο εἰδώς, ὡς ἔτρωσάς με καὶ κέντρον ἀγάπης τῇ ψυχῇ ἡμῶν ἐγκατέπηξας μόνην τοῦ δυνηθῆναι καὶ ἐξαιρῆσαι καὶ ἰάσασθαι τὴν αὐτοπρόσωπον συντυχίαν καὶ ὁμιλίαν καὶ χάριν σου.

40: V 170r.

4 fort. *ὑποτίθεσθαι* Westerink || 5 *αἰτησαμένῳ* Westerink: *αἰτιασαμένῳ* V

41: V 170r.

β α

6–7 *διασωθῆναι καὶ ἑνωθῆναι* V, transp. V s.l.

40. To the Patrician Methodius

I was not upset by failing to obtain my request; rather, I took pleasure in finding such an excellent man as yourself to be my champion. For you displayed every act of kindness—concern, compassion, ample protection; as for the other things I asked you but which did not turn out well, I charge them to my own shortcomings. I owe you, my magnanimous friend, complete and wholehearted thanks as far as your efforts are concerned, and I pray that God is as good to you as you have been to me. Take care of your servant, the secretary and man of my humble self, whose cause I have also taken up with my most esteemed lord, so that I may offer thanks on his behalf as well.

41. To the Same (Methodius)

You are happy to be on your way, and for this reason we too are happy, for we consider as our adoptive father your natural father to whom you are rushing. Thus we shall maintain for life our relationship not only as brothers but devoted brothers as well. And though we are unhappy about our separation, at least we can still pray that you arrive safely and are reunited with our loving and beloved father. Complete your journey in good health and spirits and understand that you have wounded me and planted a goad of love in my heart that can be removed and healed only by seeing you face to face and enjoying the pleasure of your company.

42. Εἰς τὸν κριτήν

Πολλὰ καταρῶμαι τοῖς τῆς μετάξης, ὅτι σε ἐπὶ τοσοῦτον χρόνον κατέχουσιν, ἐνδοξότατε καὶ περιφανέστατε κύριε. Ἐκ τούτου ἄδειαν οἱ πονηροὶ καὶ πλεονεκτικοὶ τὴν γνώμην εὑρόντες τὰ ἑαυτῶν ποιοῦσιν. Ὧν εἷς ἐστι καὶ ὁ Διονύσιος, μυρίας λύπας τῷ θείῳ μου τῷ ἐπισκόπῳ ἐπάγων. Ἐκδίκησον οὖν τῷ δικαίῳ πρῶτον, ἔπειτα ἐμοὶ χαριζόμενος τὸν γέροντα καὶ θεῖόν μου, ὡς ἂν παρ' ἐκείνου μὲν εὐχάς, παρ' ἡμῶν δὲ εὐχαριστίας τὰς πρεπούσας κομίσῃ· καὶ τὴν ταχίστην ἐπίσκεψαι ἡμᾶς, ἵνα, ⟨εἰ⟩ μή τι ἄλλο, τέως τὴν ἀγάπην ἀφοσιωσόμεθα, χρόνον πολὺν σωματικῶς μὴ συνελθοῦσαν· τῷ γὰρ πνεύματι καθ' ἑκάστην πείθομαι συνεῖναι καὶ συνομιλεῖν. Ἔρρωσο, τοῖς καλοῖς καὶ δικαίοις καλὰ καὶ δίκαια προστιθείς.

43. Τῷ βασιλεῖ

Ὀχληρὸς μὲν ἴσως δόξω τῇ βασιλείᾳ σου τὰ κατ' ἐμαυτὸν ἀναγγέλλων· ἀλήθειαν δὲ ἐρῶ, καὶ ἱερεὺς ὢν καὶ πρὸς βασιλέα λέγων, ὃν οὐδεὶς ἔλαθεν ἢ λάθοι τῶν ψευδομένων. Ἀντὶ πολλῶν, ὦ δέσποτα, καὶ μεγάλων καὶ αὐτῶν ὡς εἰπεῖν τῶν ἀναγκαιοτάτων καὶ πρώτων τοῦ ζῆν ἀφορμῶν, ἡ δουλική σου μητρόπολις τὸ χρυσοβούλλιον ἔλαβεν. Ἔλαιον γὰρ οὐ γεωργοῦμεν· τοῦτο κοινὸν τοῖς Ἀνατολικοῖς ἔχομεν πᾶσιν· οἶνον ἡ καθ' ἡμᾶς οὐ δίδωσιν, ὑψηλῆς καὶ ταχινῆς λαχοῦσα τῆς θέσεως· ἀντὶ ξύλου τῷ ζαρζάκῳ χρώμεθα, ὅπερ ἐστὶν ἐπιμελείας ἀξιωθεῖσα κόπρος, πρᾶγμα καὶ ἀτιμότατον καὶ δυσωδέστατον· τὰ γὰρ ἄλλα ὅσα νοσοῦσιν ἢ ὑγιαίνουσίν εἰσιν ἐπιτήδεια ἀπὸ τοῦ Θρακησίου καὶ τῆς Ἀτταλείας καὶ αὐτῆς τῆς βασιλευούσης ἐρανιζόμεθα. Ἀντὶ πάντων τούτων καὶ ἄλλων, ὧν ἐν χρείᾳ καθίσταται ὁ πολλοὺς ὑποδεχόμενος, ἄνθρωπος καὶ αὐτὸς ὤν, ἔτι δὲ καὶ τῆς τῶν ψαλλόντων καὶ εὐχομένων ῥόγας καὶ λοιπῶν τῶν ἐξυπηρετουμένων, τοῦ μακαριωτάτου σου πατρὸς καὶ βασιλέως

42: V 170v.
9 *εἰ* add. Lambros || 10 *ἀφοσιωσώμεθα* Lambros || 12 *τοῖς* Lambros: *τῶν* V

43: V 170v.
7 *Ἔλαιον* Lambros: *ἔλεον* V || 9 *ταχινῆς* V: *τραχείας* Robert || 12 *θρακίστη καὶ τῆς ἀταλίας* V, corr. Lambros

42. To the Judge

I roundly curse those "silk people" for occupying so much of your time, most honorable and eminent lord. As a result of this, nasty and greedy individuals have taken advantage and are going about their business with impunity. There is one of them, Dionysius, for example, who inflicts on my uncle the bishop ten thousand annoyances. Therefore, avenge my aged uncle as a favor to the law first and then as a personal favor to me so that you may receive prayers from him and due thanks from us. Visit us as soon as you can so that we may, if nothing else, satisfy for a while our love which for a long time has been deprived of physical union; for I believe that I enjoy the company and conversation of your spirit every day. Farewell and add to the good and just that which is good and just.

43. To the Emperor

Perhaps I shall seem a nuisance to your majesty for reporting on my personal affairs; still, I shall tell the truth both because I am a priest and because I am addressing the emperor, whom no liar has or could deceive. Instead of many important items, Your Highness, including, as it were, the very necessities and staples essential to life, your subject metropolis has received a golden bull. You see, we do not produce olive oil; this is something we have in common with all the residents of the Anatolikon theme. Our land does not yield wine because of the high altitude and the short growing season. Instead of wood, we use "zarzakon," which is really dung that has been processed, a thoroughly disgusting and smelly business. All the other requisites for the healthy or infirm we solicit from the Thracesion theme, from Attaleia, and from the capital itself. We adduce the golden bull of your most blessed father the emperor in compensation for all these things and more—the stipends, for example, of those who attend to the psalms and prayers and the rest of those who serve in an auxiliary capacity—in need of which stands one who, besides being human himself, has to extend hospitality to many. Use discretion in judging me, and

χρυσοβούλλιον ἐπιφερόμεθα. Κρῖνον οὖν με μετὰ διακρίσεως καὶ μὴ συγκρίνῃς τοῖς πάντα ἔχουσιν, ἃ οὐκ ἔχομεν, μηδὲ ὁ μέγας σου νοῦς καὶ βασιλικώτατος καὶ διακριτικώτατος ἀλόγως ζῆν ἐάσῃ με κριθῇ τρεφόμενον καὶ χόρτῳ καὶ ἀχύροις· οὐδὲ γὰρ σιτοφόρος ἡ τῶν Συνάδων χώρα, ἀλλὰ κριθοφόρος μόνον. Ταῦτ' οὖν ἀληθῆ λέγω· ἀξιῶ τὴν βασιλείαν σου καὶ ἐρευνηθῆναι. Εἰ δέ μέ τινες λέγουσι πλούσιον καὶ περιφανῆ τὴν μητρόπολιν, ἐκεῖνοι μὲν ἃ οὐκ οἴδασι λεγέτωσαν καὶ τὴν ἁπλότητα διαβαλλέτωσαν, ἐγὼ δὲ συμμετρήσασθαι ἀξιῶ καὶ τὸν πλοῦτόν μου καὶ τὰ χρέη μου.

44. Εἰς τὸν γενικόν

"Ἔκραξα καὶ οὐκ ἤκουσας"· ἔγραψα καὶ οὐκ ἀντέγραψας· ἐκάλεσά σε εἰς βοήθειαν καὶ οὐκ ἐπεστράφης μοι. Ἔπραξας ἄρα ἐπ' ἐμοὶ τὰ μὴ προσόντα τῇ φύσει σου. Εἰ μὲν ἀποτυγχάνειν με διδάσκων καὶ μὴ λυπεῖσθαι, εὐγενῶς καὶ σοφῶς. Τοῦτο καὶ Διογένης· τοὺς γὰρ ἀνδριάντας ἐκεῖνος ᾔτει προσερχόμενος, καὶ τὴν αἰτίαν ἐρωτώμενος, ἀποτυγχάνειν ἔλεγε μελετᾶν. Εἰ δ' ὡς εὐτελῆ με περιεφρόνησας, ἴσθι τῆς αὐτῆς ἁμαρτίας εἶναι καὶ τὸ διδόναι οἷς οὐ δεῖ καὶ τὸ μὴ διδόναι οἷς δεῖ. Γενικῶς οὖν τὰ πράγματα κυβερνῶν καὶ πολλοῖς ἐπικουρῶν, ὡς ἀκούω—οὐ γὰρ οἶδα τοῦτο πείρᾳ—ἢ κατάνευσον καὶ ἐμοὶ σῆς δόξης ἕνεκεν, ἢ ἀπόειπε, ἵνα μὴ δι' ὄχλου σοι ἔτι γένωμαι κινῶν πρὸς τοῦτο καὶ φίλους.

45. Ἄλλη

Οὐ καλῶς ἐποίουν ἐγὼ ὁ μάταιος μὴ γράφων τῷ δεσπότῃ μου, μηδὲ τὰ κατ' ἐμαυτὸν ἀνατιθείς σοι καὶ τὰς θεοπειθεῖς εὐχάς σου εἰς βοήθειαν ἐκκαλούμενος. Ἀλλὰ νῦν καὶ γράφω καὶ συγγνώμην αἰτῶ

---

24 διαβαλέτωσαν V, corr. Lambros

44: 2 cf. Job 30.20 || 5 ff. Diog. Laert., VI.49

44: V 172r.
3 μοι V: μου Lambros

45: P 227r. V 172v.
2 οὐ . . . μάταιος P: κακῶς ἐγὼ ὁ μάταιος ἐποίουν V

do not compare me to those who have everything, which we do not, and do not let your great, most royal, and discriminating mind allow me to live like an animal, feeding on barley, hay, and chaff. For the farmland around Synada doesn't even yield wheat, but only barley. This, then, is the truth of the matter; I ask your majesty, if necessary, to have it checked. And if some people say that I am rich and that the metropolis is famous, let them—they don't know what they're talking about—and let them attack my bluntness. I, on the other hand, believe that my assets ought to be measured against my liabilities.

44. To the Genicus

"I cried out and thou didst not hear." I wrote and you did not write back. I summoned you to my aid and you paid no attention to me. Your behavior toward me, as it seems, was not in character. If, on the one hand, you were trying to teach me how to be refused and not become upset, your conduct was noble and wise. Diogenes did this too, for he used to go up to statues and beg alms. When he was asked why, he replied that he was getting practice in being refused. Yet if, on the other hand, you looked down on me as a worthless fellow, take note that giving to those who don't deserve it is just as wrong as not giving to those who do. Since, then, you are managing state affairs on a large scale and providing assistance to many—so I hear, for I don't speak from personal experience—either give your consent to me too for the sake of your reputation, or refuse so that I won't pester you anymore by inciting even my friends to meddle on my behalf.

45. Another (Letter)

Good-for-nothing that I am, I behaved badly because I repeatedly failed to write (to you) my lord and recommend my affairs to you and call upon the aid of your God-persuading prayers. But now as I write, I beg your forgiveness and at the

καὶ ἐρρῶσθαί σε εὔχομαι καὶ ἐν ἀλυπίᾳ διάγειν καὶ εὐθυμίᾳ. Εἰ δὲ *δεῖ τι καὶ παρρησιασάμενον χαριεντίσασθαι, οὐδὲ αὐτός, ὦ μακάριε δέσποτα, πολλὰ καὶ συνεχῆ ἡμῖν ἔγραψας, καὶ οὐκ οἶδ᾽ ὅπως, ὡς νιφάδας ἐπιστολῶν πέμψας, οὕτως καὶ ὠνείδισας καὶ σοβαρῶς καὶ μέγα φρονῶν ἡμῶν καθήψω, δικαίως μέν, καὶ αὐτὸς δὲ σχεδὸν τῷ αὐτῷ ἐνεχόμενος κρίματι.* Τὴν *οὖν ἐπιτίμησιν, ἵν᾽ ἀληθῶς εἴπω, πατρικῶς καὶ ἀπὸ διαθέσεως χρηστῆς γενομένην, καὶ ἠσπασάμεθα καὶ ἀπεδεξάμεθα.* Παρακαλοῦμεν *δὲ καὶ ἔτι τοῦτο ποιεῖν σε καὶ συνεχῶς γράφειν καὶ πρὸς τὰ καλὰ ἡμᾶς διεγείρειν, πρὸ δὲ πάντων εὐχαῖς ἡμᾶς στηρίζειν· πολλῶν γὰρ τούτων καὶ μάλιστα οἵων τῶν σῶν δεόμεθά τε καὶ χρήζομεν.* Οἱ *πρίσται, ὡς ἐκέλευσας καὶ ὡς ὑπεσχόμεθα, ἐστάλησαν· οὐκ οἶδα δὲ εἰ ἀρέσουσι τῇ ὑπερφυεῖ σου χρηστότητι.*

46. Εἰς *τὸν καστρίσιον*

Καὶ *σὺ καλός τις ἦσθα καὶ σοφὸς καὶ ἀρετὴν ἄμαχος· καὶ ἡμεῖς ᾔδειμεν τοῦτο καὶ καιρὸν ἐζητοῦμεν, ὥστε καὶ τὴν πρόθεσιν ἐνδείξασθαι καὶ τὰ προσόντα σοι μαρτυρῆσαι· καὶ ὁ κουβουκλείσιος νῦν ἐλθὼν πολλὰ τούτοις ὅμοια προσέθηκε, μέγαν σε ποιῶν τῷ λόγῳ καὶ ὅσος εἶ ἐκδιηγούμενος· καὶ ὁ ἀδελφὸς ὑπεξῆρέ σε τῶν λοιπῶν καὶ ὑπερῆρέ σε τῶν πολλῶν καὶ προέθηκε πάντων· καὶ νῦν σὺ παρ᾽ ἡμῖν, ἵνα κυκλικῶς καθ᾽ ὑμᾶς εἴπω τοὺς ῥήτορας, καλός τις εἶ καὶ σοφὸς καὶ ἀρετὴν ἄμαχος.* Τοιοῦτος *οὖν ὤν, μέμνησο καὶ ἡμῶν, ἀλλὰ καὶ γράφε καὶ μέμνησο.*

---

7 *δέσποτα* om. V ‖ 9–10 *καὶ αὐτὸς σχεδὸν τῷ αὐτῷ* P (om. δὲ): *τῷ αὐτῷ δὲ σχεδὸν καὶ αὐτὸς* V ‖ 10 *ἵν᾽* P: *ἣν* V ‖ 13 *δὲ* om. V ‖ 15–17 *οἱ πρίσται . . . χρηστότητι* om. V

46: V 173r.

4 *κουβου(κλείσιος)* V: Κουβούσης Lambros ‖ 7 *προσέθηκε* V, corr. Darrouzès ‖ 8 *ὑμᾶς* Westerink: *ἡμᾶς* V

same time pray that you are in good health and enjoying a carefree and happy existence. Yet if one should temper candor with humor, not even you yourself, my dear lord, wrote abundantly or frequently to us; and I fail to understand how you, as though you were the author of an epistolary blizzard, could have scolded us so and reproached us in a high-handed and imperious manner—justifiably, to be sure, but you too are subject to the same verdict. We therefore embrace and accept your censure—the term is accurate—because it sprang from paternal and kindhearted sentiments. We urge you to do this again and to write us often and spur us toward the good but above all to fortify us with your prayers, for we need plenty of those and especially such as yours. The cutters have been sent as you requested and we promised, but I don't know whether your incomparable excellency will find them satisfactory.

46. To the Canstrisius

Not only were you a wise and surpassingly virtuous gentleman, but we, too, knew this and were constantly on the lookout for an opportunity to make our feelings public and to testify to your character. In addition, the cubuclisius just came and added a multitude of qualities very like these; he used his eloquence to glorify you and described in detail what an outstanding person you are. Further, my brother set you apart from the rest, exalted you above the crowd, and preferred you to everyone. Moreover, you now, in our judgment—to revert to my starting point in the manner of you orators—are a wise and surpassingly virtuous gentleman. So, being such an excellent fellow, think of us, too; rather, write often *and* think of us.

47. Εἰς τὸν χαρτοφύλακα

Οὐκ ἔγραφον οὕτως συμβὰν καὶ μὴ δεξαμένου ἀρχὴν τοῦ πράγματος, ἐφίλουν δὲ ἄρα καὶ ἀγράφως, ὅπερ οἶδα καὶ ἄλλους ποιεῖν· καὶ τὴν ἀρετήν, ὅση σοι πολλὴ περίεστιν, ἡδούμην καὶ τὸ ἦθος ἐσεβαζόμην καὶ ἡ γνῶσις ἐξέπληττέ με καὶ ἡ φιλικὴ διάθεσις ἐφείλκετό με καὶ τὸ γειτονεῖν ὑπέσυρέ με καὶ κατ᾿ αὐτοῦ τοῦ πρανοῦς. Οὕτω σὺ πολλὰς ἔχεις τὰς ἴυγγας καὶ θέλγεις ὁρώμενος καὶ κατακηλεῖς ἀκουόμενος καὶ προσλαλῶν ἡδὺς εἶ καὶ συνομιλῶν χαριέστερος. Ταῦτα ἡ πεῖρα καὶ ἡ γραφὴ τοῦ ἀδελφοῦ καὶ εὐχαριστία προσμαρτυρεῖ· καί σοι δοίη τὸν μισθὸν ὁ Θεὸς ἀντισηκώσας, ὅτι καὶ τὸ τῆς δυστομίας βάρος αὐτῷ ἐπελαφρίζεις ἢ καὶ παντελῶς ἀφαιρεῖς καὶ εὐεργετεῖς προσεπιδαψιλευόμενος, καὶ ἡμῖν ταῦτα ποιῶν χαρίζῃ τὰ μέγιστα. Ἔρρωσο τοιοῦτος ὢν καὶ τιμηθεὶς ὑπὸ Θεοῦ τιμὴν τὴν ἀνωτάτω καὶ μακαριωτάτην.

48. Τῷ αὐτῷ

Ἡμεῖς οὐδέποτέ σου ἐπελαθόμεθα, κάλλιστε ἀνθρώπων, ἀλλ᾿ εἰς νοῦν σε ἔχομεν καὶ τῶν ἀπείρων σου καλῶν ἐν διηνεκεῖ ἐσμεν μνήμῃ. Ἀλλ᾿ οὕτω συμβὰν ὑπὸ τῆς ἀφυΐας ἡμῶν οὐκ ἐγράφομεν· οὐ μὴν διὰ τοῦτο καὶ τοῦ φιλεῖν ἀφιστάμεθα, ἀλλὰ πλέον διὰ τοῦτο καὶ ἡδούμεθα καὶ ἠγαπῶμέν σε. Νῦν δὲ πρῶτος καὶ γράψας καὶ πράξας καὶ πέμψας τὰ συνήθη δῶρα, πρῶτος καὶ εἰς φιλίαν, πρῶτος καὶ εἰς εὐεργεσίαν παρ᾿ ἡμῶν ἀναγραφήσῃ τε καὶ ἀναγορευθήσῃ. Τὴν οὖν δίοδον, ὡς ἐκέλευσας, καὶ γνωρίσομέν σοι καὶ ἴδωμέν σε, τῆς τε θέας καὶ ὁμιλίας σου καὶ τῶν εὐχῶν σου γλιχόμενοι. Τὰς ῥοιὰς ἀπολαβόντες, ἐπιρριπτάριόν σοι ἀπεστείλαμεν, οὐχ ὅμοια ποιοῦντες, ποῦ γὰρ τὰ δεύτερα τοῖς πρώτοις ἴσα; Φίλα δὲ καὶ τῇ σῇ ἀγάπῃ μὴ ἀπαρέσκοντα.

47: V 173ᵛ.

12 *προεπιδαψιλευόμενος* V, corr. Darrouzès || 13 *ποιῶν* Westerink: *ποῖ* V: *πῃ* Lambros

---

48: V 174ʳ.

47. To the Chartophylax

It so happened that I didn't write—I didn't even get started; yet of course I cared for you even without writing, which I understand is the experience of others as well. I never ceased to feel regard for your immense integrity and respect for your character; the range of your knowledge astounded me; your amiable disposition attracted me and your being near charmed me head over heels. Such is the force of your many charms: you are enchanting to behold and bewitching to hear; in conversation you are pleasant; in company, even more delightful. My (own?) brother's personal experience, letter, and gratitude corroborate this. May God in compensation give you your reward for lightening the burden of his speech impediment or even removing it altogether and for lavishing upon him additional benefactions. In doing these things, you show the greatest kindness to me, too. Farewell to you who are so good and who have received from God the highest and most blessed honor.

48. To the Same (the Chartophylax)

We have never forgotten you, excellent sir, but we keep you in our thoughts and are ever mindful of your immeasurable virtue. Yet, as it turned out, our own incompetence was responsible for our not writing. We certainly do not for this reason also cease to care about you; on the contrary, it was because of this that we loved and respected you more. But now, since you were the first one to act by writing and sending the usual presents, you shall be duly registered and proclaimed by us to be first in friendship as well as first in beneficence. Therefore we shall let you know when we pass through, as you requested, and we shall see you; we are eager for the sight of you as well as for your conversation and prayers. We received the pomegranates and sent you a cowl in return—not an equal exchange, for how can a subsequent (gift) equal the original? Still, my intentions were kind and not displeasing to your affection.

49. Τῷ αὐτῷ

Ἐγὼ τὴν εἰς τὸ Δορύλαιον ὑποστροφὴν οὐκ ἐψευσάμην, φίλε καὶ ἀδελφὲ ποθούμενε, ἀλλ' ἐψεύσθην τὴν σὴν συνάντησιν, εἴτε τῆς ἐμῆς ἀργίας ἕνεκα, εἴτε τῆς σῆς ταχυτῆτος, οὐκ οἶδα, σὺ δ' ἂν εἰδείης ὁ μὴ βραδύνας, ἀλλὰ τοῦ δέοντος πλέον ταχύνας. Τούτου οὖν ἕνεκα καὶ ὥστε τοῖς αὐτοῖς μὴ περιπεσεῖν, τὸ πότε συντύχωμεν οὐκ ἐδήλωσα· ἔσται δὲ σὺν Θεῷ ταχύ, αὐτοῦ τούτου εὐδοκοῦντος καὶ πράττοντος. Ἔρρωσο εὐθυμῶν, εὐεκτῶν καὶ εὐοδούμενος.

50. Ἄλλη

Τὰ μὲν σὰ περὶ ἡμᾶς ἄμεμπτα καὶ πάντῃ ἀσύγκριτα. Γέρων γὰρ εἶ καὶ τῷ χρόνῳ καὶ τῷ τρόπῳ, καὶ εἰς πατρὸς ἔφθασας τάξιν καὶ θείου καὶ προνοητοῦ καὶ κηδεμόνος. Τὰ δ' ἐμὰ περὶ σέ, ἵν' αὐτὸς ἐμαυτοῦ κατηγορήσω, ἀγνώμονος, ἀμνήμονος, ἀπροαιρέτου, ἀσυνειδήτου, ἀχαρίστου καὶ ὅπερ ἂν ἕτερον εἴποις. "Μὴ οὖν εἰς κρίσιν ἔλθῃς μεθ' ἡμῶν, ὅτι οὐ δικαιωθησόμεθα ἐνώπιόν σου," ἀλλ' ἔχου μὲν καὶ σὺ τῆς αὐτῆς προαιρέσεως καὶ διαθέσεως, ἥ σε καὶ κοσμεῖ καὶ κρείττονα δείκνυσιν, ἡμῖν δὲ συγγίνωσκε ὡς οὐ κακίᾳ μᾶλλον ἢ ἀνοίᾳ πταίουσι. Σὺ οὖν ἐν ταῖς εὐχαῖς μέμνησό τινος Λέοντος καὶ ἔρρωσο.

49: V 174v.
6 *συντύχομεν* V, corr. Lambros || 7 fort. *τοῦτο*

50: 6–7 cf. Ps. 142.2

50: V 174v.
10 *ἢ ἀνοίᾳ* coni. Westerink: *οἱ ἄνοι̅* (i.e., *ἄνθρωποι*) V

49. To the Same (the Chartophylax)

I didn't lie about returning to Dorylaeum, my dearly beloved brother; I was, however, mistaken about meeting you. Whether it was due to my sloth or your haste, I don't know, but you might, since you weren't late but, on the contrary, were earlier than you should have been. For this reason, then, and so that the same thing doesn't happen again, I have left open the date when we are to meet. But it will be soon, God willing and if he himself consents and brings it about. Good-bye and have a good trip in good spirits and good health.

50. Another (Letter)

Your behavior toward us was faultless and absolutely peerless since you are mature both in years and in character and have attained the status of both father and uncle, protector and guardian. My behavior toward you, on the other hand—to indict myself personally—was insensitive, thoughtless, irresponsible, inconsiderate, ungrateful, and whatever else you care to add. "Therefore enter not into judgement with us; for in thy sight we shall not be justified," but keep the same disposition and temperament that ornament you and show off your superiority, and forgive us on the grounds that we blunder not from malice but rather from thoughtlessness. So remember a certain Leo in your prayers and farewell.

51. Εἰς Νικήταν τὸν τοῦ Ἀθηνῶν ἀδελφόν

Οὐκέτι τὴν βασιλεύουσαν πόλιν ἰδεῖν ἐθέλω, οὐκέτι τὴν προκαθεζομένην καὶ πλεονεκτοῦσαν· οἱ γὰρ σοφοί με ταύτης ἐν Πύλαις ἐξεδέξαντο. Σοφοὺς γὰρ ἐγὼ πληθυντικῶς καλῶ τὸν ἕνα Νικήταν, τὸν πολυρρήμονα, τὸν πολυγνώμονα, τὸν ἔνθουν, τὸν ἔμμουσον, τὸν πολλὰ λέγειν, τὸν πολλὰ γράφειν εἰδότα, τὸν σιωπῶντα μηδέποτε, τὸν λαλοῦντα {μηδὲ} πάντοτε, τὸν ἀηδόνα, τὸν χελιδόνα ὄντα, τὸν ἐν χειμῶνι τέττιγα, τὸν πρῶτον ἢ δεύτερον τῆς σοφῆς συμμορίας. Ποῦ δέ σοι τὸ κάλλος ἐκεῖνο, ἵνα καὶ πρὸς σὲ ἀποστρέψω τὸν λόγον, ὦ θαυμάσιε; Ποῦ ἡ συνθήκη ἐπινενόηται; Ποῦ τὸ καινοπρεπὲς τοῦ λόγου, ποῦ τὸ ἀνθηρὸν ἐξεῦρες τῆς λέξεως; Ποῦ τὸ τῶν νοημάτων ἐπάλληλον; Ἦ που οὐ τὴν ἡμετέραν ἐβάδισας, τὴν συνήθη καὶ τετριμμένην, ἀλλά τινα ἑτέραν, ἀτριβῆ καὶ ἀπόρευτον· καί σε Ἀναξιμένης ὁ ποτὲ τῶν λόγων ἀπολαύων τῶν νῦν ὑπερῆρε καὶ ὑπὲρ ἡμᾶς ἐσόφισε καὶ θαυμάζεσθαι ὁσημέραι πεποίηκεν. Ἡμεῖς μὲν οὖν μὴ ἐφικνεῖσθαι τῶν σῶν λόγων δυνάμενοι, χαμαιπετεῖς ὄντες καὶ χαμαίζηλοι καὶ αὐτὴν τὴν οἴκησιν ὑποβεβηκυῖαν ἔχοντες καὶ οἷον εἰπεῖν γήϊνοι καὶ ἀνθρώπινοι, ταπεινά σοι καὶ προσλαλοῦμεν καὶ προσφθεγγόμεθα καὶ ἀγροικότερον ἐπιστέλλομεν. Σὺ δὲ ἡμῖν τὰ συνήθη ποιεῖν μὴ ἐλλείποις ἄνωθεν καὶ ἀπὸ ὕψους ἐποικοδομῶν, ἀποβλέπων, φρονῶν, λαλῶν, γράφων, πράττων, ἐπιστέλλων καὶ διαλεγόμενος.

52. Τῷ αὐτῷ

Εἶδον διὰ γραφῆς τὴν σεβασμίαν ἐμοὶ καὶ τριπόθητον κεφαλήν σου, εἶδον τὸν προσηνῆ καὶ ἥμερον χαρακτῆρα τῆς θεσπεσίας σου ὄψεως, σεβασμιώτατε δέσποτα· εἶδον ὅσα δι' εὐχῆς εἶχον. Ἐγὼ γὰρ διηνεκῶς ἐν τῇ ψυχῇ μου περιφέρων σε καὶ ἀπομνημονεύων τῆς κεχαριτωμένης ὁμιλίας σου, ἔδοξα διὰ τῆς γραφῆς αὐτόν σε καὶ

51: V 175r.

3 Πύλαις Lambros: *πάλαις* V || 7 delevi || 9 *δέ σοι* Westerink: *δέοι* V || 12 Ἦ *που οὐ* scripsi: *ἤ που σὺ* V: *οὔ που σὺ* Lambros || 16 *διὰ τὸ* post *οὖν* add. Lambros *τῆς* post *ἐφικνεῖσθαι* add. Lambros *δυνάμενοι* Darrouzès: *δυνάμεως* V || 17 *ὑποβεβηκυῖαν* scripsi: *ὑπερβεβηκυῖαν* V

52: V 176r.

51. To Nicetas, Brother of the Metropolitan of Athens

I no longer wish to visit the imperial city, no longer the capital and preeminent among cities; for her intelligentsia has received me at Pylae. I use the plural "intelligentsia" to indicate the singular Nicetas, the loquacious, the polymath, the one inspired by God and the Muses, the one who knows how to speak and write at length, the never silent, the always talking, the nightingale, the swallow, the cicada in winter—he's at the top of his class. But to turn the conversation to the second person, where did you get that elegance, admirable sir? Where did you conceive that style? Where did you find that originality of expression, that flowery diction? Where the flow of ideas? You certainly did not travel our road, the familiar and well-worn, but instead (took) another route, fresh and unexplored: it was the (rhetoric of) Anaximenes, who once enjoyed the fruits of literary accomplishment, that elevated you above your contemporaries, trained you better than ourselves, and made you an object of daily marvel. We, then, since we are unable to achieve your eloquence because we are earthborn and earthbound, because our very domicile is inferior, and, because we are, as it were, a terrestrial and human creature, address and speak to you in our lowly way and send you a rather unsophisticated letter. But as for you, continue to behave toward us in your usual elevated and celestial manner, edifying, regarding, thinking, talking, writing, acting, communicating, and conversing with us.

52. To the Same (Nicetas)

I saw in your letter the person I revere and love, I saw the gentle and kindly expression of your divine face, most reverend lord; I saw everything I prayed for. Since I always keep you near my heart and am ever mindful of your delightful company, I believed that through your letter I not only saw and embraced you in person

ἰδεῖν καὶ προσπτύξασθαι καὶ συλλαλῆσαί σοι καὶ ἐνωτισθῆναί σου τῆς γλυκυτάτης φωνῆς. Οὕτως ἐγὼ περὶ σοῦ καὶ φρονῶ καὶ λαλῶ καὶ λογίζομαι καὶ οὕτως ἐξέχομαι τοῦ χρηστοῦ καὶ καλοῦ μου δεσπότου. Ὁ ἀντιδικῶν καὶ ὁ ἀνθιστάμενος τῷ ἀληθινῷ σου τρόπῳ οὕτω διασύρεται ὡς ἂν αὐτὸ ηὔξω καὶ ἠθέλησας. Οἱ γὰρ ἐντυχόντες σοὶ καὶ ἐκείνῳ, σὲ μὲν ὑπερεπαινοῦσι καὶ ὑπεραίρουσι πολλῶν ἢ πάντων ἕνεκα, ἐκεῖνον δὲ ἐκ τοῦ ἐναντίου καὶ ψέγουσι καὶ διασύρουσιν. Ἐμὲ δὲ ἴσθι τοῖς ἐπαινοῦσι προσκείμενον καὶ ⟨δι'⟩ εὐφημίας ἄγοντά σε, τὸν πάσῃ ἀρετῇ κεκοσμημένον. Οἶδα δὲ ὅτι καὶ ὑπερτερήσεις τούτου καὶ ἀσθενῆ αὐτὸν ἀποδείξεις καὶ ἀνελεύθερον, ὡς τῇ ἀληθείᾳ ἀνθιστάμενον καὶ τῷ ψεύδει συνηγοροῦντα. Ἴδοιμί σε καὶ ὀφθαλμοῖς ἑστῶσι, τὸ ἐγκαλλώπισμά μου, τὸν πάσης παρηγορίας ἔμπλεων.

53. Ἄλλη

Τῆς βασιλικῆς εὐνοίας κατ' εὐχὰς ἡμῶν δοθείσης ὑμῖν, πατέρες καὶ ἀδελφοὶ ἱερώτατοι, τίνος ἕνεκεν οὐκ ἐμνήσθητε ἡμῶν, ἀλλὰ τέλειον ἐξελάθεσθε τῆς ἀδελφικῆς συμπνοίας καὶ ὁμονοίας, καὶ ταῦτα διὰ πολλῆς πείρας ἐλθόντες καὶ πάσῃ τριβῇ ἐγγυμνασθέντες καὶ νέα καὶ παλαιὰ ἰδόντες τε καὶ ἀκούσαντες; Οὐχὶ πλέον αἱ δύο χεῖρες τῆς μιᾶς πράττουσι καὶ οἱ ὀφθαλμοὶ καὶ τὰ ὦτα καὶ αὐτοὶ οἱ πόδες; Οὐχὶ καὶ οἱ τῶν ᾀδόντων χοροὶ καὶ ἡ περὶ ψαλμοὺς καὶ φόρμιγγας ἁρμονία διὰ πολυφώνων ἢ ἀντιφώνων τὸ σύμφωνον ἔχουσιν; Οὐχ ὁ Πολυδεύκης, τὸ παλαιὸν ἐκεῖνο διήγημα, τὸ θεὸς μὴ λαβὼν τὸ ἡμίθεος σὺν τῷ ἀδελφῷ ἔλαβεν; Τί δαὶ καὶ ὁ Ῥωμαίων Λεύκολλος· οὐχὶ τὸν ἑαυτοῦ παρεὶς καιρόν, τὸν τοῦ ἀδελφοῦ περιέμεινεν, ἵνα μὴ μόνος ἀλλὰ σὺν τούτῳ ἄρξῃ; Οὐχὶ καὶ οἱ εὐγενέστατοι καὶ σεβαστοὶ βασιλεῖς νῦν ἅμα συνεισῆλθον, τὸν ἀδελφικὸν κἀν τούτῳ σῴζοντες τρόπον; Οὕτω καλὰ τὰ τῆς προτροπῆς καὶ ἐπαγωγὰ καὶ ὁλκὰ πρόκεινται, καὶ τὸ μυθικὸν καὶ τὸ ἱστορικὸν καὶ τὸ νῦν ὁρώμενον. Ἀλλ' οὐχ ἡμεῖς τοιοῦτοι ὅσα ἡμᾶς εἰδέναι, ἴσως δὲ καὶ τοιοῦτοι ὅσα ἡμᾶς μὴ εἰδέναι.

---

14 add. Lambros   εὐφημίας V: εὐφημίαις Darrouzès

53: 6–8 cf. Plutarch, *De fraterno amore*, 478D ‖ 10–13 cf. Plutarch, *ibid.*, 484D–E

53: V 176v.
17 ἡμεῖς V: fort. ὑμεῖς

but that I also spoke to you and heard the sweet sound of your voice. This is how I think about you, speak about you, and regard you; this is how attached I am to you, my good and excellent lord. Your adversary, who denies your true character, is being derided in just the way you would hope for and desire. After people have met you and him, it is you they praise and extol to the skies for many or, rather, every reason, while your detractor is the object of their censure and ridicule. Know that I side with those who praise you and that I speak well of you who are enriched with every virtue. Besides, I know that you will overshadow this man and expose him for the petty and illiberal creature he is, inasmuch as he opposes the truth and sides with the false. I hope to set eyes on you in the flesh, my jewel who are an abundant source of comfort.

53. Another (Letter)

Although the imperial goodwill has been granted to you as we had prayed, most pious fathers and brethren, why is it that you have not remembered us but instead have completely forgotten fraternal concord and harmony? And this despite the fact that you have been through many a trial, have been schooled in every hardship, and have seen and heard things from both the immediate and distant past. Is it not true that two hands accomplish more than one, and also eyes, ears, and even feet? Is it not true that the choirs of singers and the music for psalms and lyres have harmony, be it polyphonous or antiphonal? Did not Polydeuces, that ancient legend, reject the title "god" to share that of "demigod" with his brother? And what about the Romans' Lucullus? Did he not let his own opportunity slip by and wait for his brother's, so that he could rule, not alone, but with him? Did not our most noble and august emperors just now enter together, preserving fraternal behavior even in this? Thus set before you as an incentive are inviting and attractive examples that embrace the mythic, historic, and recent past. We, however, are not so noble, as far as we know; yet perhaps we are, without our being aware of it.

Οἱ μὲν οὖν σοφοὶ ὡρίσαντο, "ἑνὸς ἀτόπου δοθέντος, πολλὰ τὰ ἄτοπα ἕψεσθαι," ἡμεῖς δὲ καὶ συμβὰν τοῦτο εἴδομεν καὶ εἰς τέλος ἐκβάν. Περιεφρονήθη τις τῶν ἀρχιερέων, ὡς οὐκ ὤφειλεν, ἐν ταῖς ἐκκλησιαστικαῖς ψήφοις, ἐκινήθη τοῦτο καὶ μέχρι δυάδος καὶ ἕως αὐτῆς ἀνέβη τῆς τριάδος· νῦν δὲ καὶ περαιτέρω πρόεισιν. Ἐγὼ δὲ καὶ παιδάριον ἦν ἔτι· μέμνημαι γάρ, καὶ τὸν ἀντιλέγοντα εἶδον, καὶ πόσοις ἀντέλεγεν ὁ εἷς, καὶ ὁ τίς, καὶ ἐπὶ πόσων, καὶ διὰ τίνα, καὶ μὴ παρορώμενον. Ἐσχίσθησάν ποτε καὶ οἱ ἀρχιερεῖς βασιλικῷ τόμῳ καὶ δόγματι, καὶ τὸ κακὸν ἄρρηκτον ἔμεινεν, ἕως ἐσχίσθη καὶ αὐτὸς ὁ σχίσας.

Πολλὰ τοιαῦτα ἂν εἶπον, εἰ πρὸς μὴ εἰδότας εἶπον· νῦν δὲ ὁ ἔξω πολλῶν τοῖς ἔσω διαλεγόμενος, πολλὰ ἂν κράξειεν καὶ ὑπερφωνήσειεν ὥστε ἀκουσθῆναι. Ἀλλ' ἔσται καὶ ἡμῖν τοῦτο δὴ τὸ πολίτευμα, καὶ τὸ καθ' ἡμῶν νῦν εἰσαγόμενον ὑπὲρ ἡμῶν ποτε γενήσεται, καὶ ὁ νόμος, ὃν αὐτοὶ γράψετε, τὸ κῦρος παρ' ἡμῶν δέξηται. Πατριάρχης μέλλει δοθῆναι τῇ οἰκουμένῃ· οὕτω γὰρ αὐτὸν οἰκουμενικὸν πάντως καλέσετε—καὶ πατριαρχῶν ὁ πρῶτος (τί γὰρ εἰ δεύτερος, τοῦ πρώτου ὄντος ἀφανείᾳ τετιμημένου καὶ μόνῳ σεμνυνομένου τῷ ὀνόματι;) καὶ τῶν ἀδελφῶν ἄνευ, πολλῶν ὄντων καὶ μεγάλων, δέξεσθε τοῦτον ἢ καὶ ἐκλέξεσθε καὶ χειροτονήσετε καὶ εὐφημήσετε. Καὶ ὥσπερ οἱ τὴν Ἀσίαν ποτὲ κατοικοῦντες καὶ ἄκοντες ἑνὶ δεδουλεύκασιν ἀνθρώπῳ διὰ τὸ μὴ δυνηθῆναι μίαν εἰπεῖν, τὴν οὔ, συλλαβήν, οὕτω καὶ ὑμεῖς κύψαντες φρίξετε καὶ σιωπήσετε καὶ τὴν ἐλευθερίαν εἰς ἀνελευθερίαν μετατρέψετε καὶ οὐδ' ἐν παρόδῳ ἢ παρέργῳ τῶν ἀδελφῶν μεμνήσεσθε, ἀλλὰ τοὺς μὲν ἐξελαυνομένους ὁρῶντες, ὅτι μὴ καθαροῖς, ὡς ἔοικε, τοῖς ποσὶ τὸ ἅγιον ἐπάτησαν ἔδαφος, τοὺς δὲ πλησίον που κρυπτομένους καὶ λανθάνοντας, ἵνα μὴ ταὐτὰ {τοῖς} αὐτοῖς πάθωσι, κάθησθε, δεσπόται καὶ πατέρες, σεμνοί, σιωπηλοί, αἰδέσιμοι, ἄφωνοι, ἄναυδοι, θείου μὲν Πνεύματος ἀπόζοντες, μηδὲν δὲ τολμῶντες παρρησίας καὶ ἀληθείας εἰπεῖν πλῆρες. Μὴ ὑμεῖς γε τοιοῦτοι γένοισθε μηδὲ τῇ σιωπῇ τὸ εὐδόκιμον κτήσοισθε. Αἱρήσασθε λαλῆσαι μᾶλλον καὶ συνεξελθεῖν καὶ συγκαμεῖν ἡμῖν ἢ σιωπῆσαι καὶ ἐνδοτέρω χωρῆσαι.

Αἰδοῦμαι, πατέρες καὶ ἀδελφοὶ ἅγιοι, τὸ ἐπελθόν μοι νῦν εἰπεῖν, ἀλλὰ τοῖς τοῦ Θεοῦ ἀρχιερεῦσι λέγων ἐκλαλήσω καὶ τοῦτο·

19–20 cf. Aristotle, *Physica*, I.2, 185a 11–12 || 22–23 cf. Greg. Naz. *Or.* 29.2

---

22 *τοῦτο* Westerink: *τοῦ* V: *τις* Lambros || 33 *δέξεται* Lambros || 42 *οὐδὲν παρ' ὁδῷ ἢ παρ' ἔργῳ* V, corr. Westerink || 44 *ἐπάτησας* V, corr. Lambros || 45 delevi || 48 *ἡμεῖς* V, corr. Lambros || 50 *ἡμεῖν* V, corr. Lambros || 51 *ἐνδοτέρῳ* V, correxi ||

Now the sages have determined that when one absurdity has been granted, many will follow; we, on the other hand, have seen this happen in actual fact. One of the bishops was slighted in the ecclesiastical vote, though he ought not to have been; this increased to two and climbed to the number of the Trinity itself. Now it is going even farther. I was still a child, for I remember that I saw the man who spoke in opposition, how many that one man opposed, who he was, before how large a gathering (he spoke), what his reasons were, and how he was not ignored. Even the bishops were once divided by imperial ordinance and decree, and the unfortunate situation continued without a break until even the source of division was himself divided.

I would mention a number of similar incidents were I addressing uninformed men; as it is, when communicating with "insiders" the man shut off from the majority should shout and bellow at the top of his lungs so as to be heard. Well, this, you may be sure, will be our policy; the motion that is presently being introduced against us will one day be in our interest and the law that you yourselves are going to draft will acquire validity from us. A patriarch is going to be given to the Oikoumene (for thus you will call him, at any rate, oecumenical) and the first of patriarchs—what does it matter if he is second, when the one who is really first has been rewarded with obscurity and can boast of the name only?—and it will be without the consent of many important brethren that you accept this man, or even elect, appoint, and acclaim him. And just as the former inhabitants of Asia unwillingly became enslaved to a single man because they were unable to pronounce a single syllable, "no," so you too will cower and cringe, keep silent, change freedom into servitude, and show no consideration for your brothers, not even in passing or as an afterthought; on the contrary, as you see some of them driven out, apparently because they trod holy ground with impure feet, and others secretly hidden somewhere nearby so that they don't suffer the same fate as these, you are seated, lords and fathers, venerable, silent, august, voiceless, speechless, redolent of the Holy Spirit yet daring to speak not a word that smacks of candor or truth. It is my hope that you at least will not behave in this way nor acquire honor through your silence. Prefer to speak up, come outside and toil with us instead of keeping quiet and retreating farther inside.

I am ashamed, holy fathers and brethren, to say what is now on my mind, but though I address God's bishops I may as well blurt this out too. Perhaps even in the

ἴσως κἀν τούτῳ σιωπήσετε. Ἤκουον δὴ περιᾳδόμενον τοῦτο δὴ τὸ δημῶδες ὡς ὁ ἔσω τόπον οὐ ποιεῖ τῷ ἔξω. Ἐνόμιζον ἐπὶ βαλανείου τοῦτο λέγεσθαι καὶ θεάτρου, ἐπὶ δὲ ἀρχιερέων οὐκ ἂν προσεδόκησα ἢ ἐκκλησίας· νῦν δὲ δέδοικα μὴ καὶ λάλημα τοῦτο γένηται ὡς ἐφ' ἡμῶν τε καὶ ὑφ' ὑμῶν πληρωθέν. Τί δαὶ καὶ εἰ διὰ θεραπείαν σώματος ἔμελλέ τις εἰσελθεῖν καὶ τυχεῖν ἐπισκέψεως; Τί δαὶ καὶ εἰ τῶν ἐκκλησιῶν ἕνεκα καὶ τῶν ἁγίων; Τί δαὶ καὶ εἰ διὰ χρείαν ἄλλην, οἷα πολλὰ τὰ περιστατικὰ τυγχάνει, ἢ συγγενοῦς ἐπίσκεψις, ἢ κτήματος περιποίησις; Εἰ δὲ καὶ ἀδικούμενός τις ἢ ἐπηρεαζόμενος προσέλθοι, τί τῷ τοιούτῳ γενήσεται, ἀποκλειομένῳ καὶ ἐξωθουμένῳ καὶ ἐκδιωκομένῳ παρ' ὧν ἥκιστα ἐχρῆν, παρ' ὧν ἔδει μᾶλλον καὶ συγκροτεῖσθαι καὶ βοηθεῖσθαι καὶ διεκδικεῖσθαι; Ἑβραίοις τοῦτο ἔγνωμεν ἀπὸ τῆς ἱστορίας πάλαι διατεταγμένον, τὸ μὴ πελάζειν Ἱεροσολύμοις, ἀλλ' ἀπὸ τριῶν ἵστασθαι ἢ καὶ ἓξ μιλίων, ἀλλ' ὡς στασιώδεσιν, ὡς θερμουργοῖς καὶ τολμηροῖς καὶ πολλάκις ἐπιχειρήσασι τὴν ἀεὶ κεισομένην ἀναστῆναι πόλιν. Ἡμῖν δὲ ἡ αἰτία ἄδηλος καὶ ἡ αἰσχύνη ἄρρηκτος.

Μὴ οὖν ἀνάσχησθε, πατέρες ἅγιοι καὶ συλλειτουργοί ποτε χρηματίσαντες, τὸ τοιοῦτο γενέσθαι κακὸν καὶ μὴ νομὴν λαβεῖν τὴν καὶ καθ' ὑμῶν αὐτῶν, ἀλλὰ καὶ παρρησίᾳ χρήσασθε καὶ δεήσει καὶ ἀξιώσει καὶ παρακλήσει καὶ κλίσει γονάτων, ὥστε τὴν βασιλικὴν καὶ ἡμῖν δοθῆναι εὐμένειαν καὶ τὸ τῆς εἰσελεύσεως ἐνδόσιμον καὶ πράγματι τυπωθῆναι καὶ γράμματι, εἰ δὲ μηδὲν ἄλλο, τοῦτο γοῦν ἔχοντι· "Βασιλεὺς ὁ μέγας, τοῖς ἀρχιερεῦσιν· εἰσέλθατε." Ἴστε γὰρ ὡς, εἰ μὴ τοῦτο γένηται, ἢ ἕτερόν τι θεσμῶν ἔξω ἐκκλησιαστικῶν γένηται παρ' ὑμῶν, τῆς μηδ' ἐντελοῦς συνόδου, ἡμεῖς μὲν οὖν θυσιαστήριον ἕτερον οὐ στήσομεν, οὐδ' ἰδίᾳ καὶ χωρὶς συναγάγωμεν· μαρτυρόμεθα δὲ ὑμῖν καὶ προλέγομεν ὡς οὐκ ἐν δίκῃ τὰ γινόμενα γίνεται, ἀδελφῶν τοσούτων ἢ καὶ μακρῷ πλειόνων παρεωραμένων τε καὶ οὐδ' ὅσον νῦν ἐμπαζομένων. Ταῦτα καὶ τὰ τοιαῦτα οἱ ἔξω εἴποιεν ἄν· ἐγὼ δὲ εἴρηκα.

65–67 cf. Eusebius, *Historia Ecclesiastica*, IV. 6. 3

63–64 *ἐκδιωκωμένῳ* V, corr. Lambros ‖ 68 *θεμουργοῖς* V, corr. Lambros ‖ 69 *πόλιν* Lambros: *πάλην* V ‖ 78 *τι* Lambros: *τις* V ‖ 79 *ὑμῶν* Darrouzès: *ἡμῶν* V ‖ 81 *ὑμῖν* Lambros: *ἡμῖν* V ‖ 83 *ἐμπαιζομένων* Lambros

face of this you will be silent. This is the very thing I kept hearing commonly bandied about: the man inside does not make room for the one outside. I thought this was an expression used at the baths and the theater. I would never have expected it of bishops or of a church. As it is, I am afraid that this saying is true, given currency, as it were, with respect to ourselves by you. What if someone, in order to receive medical attention, were to come in and obtain a visit? What if he were to do it for the sake of the churches and the saints? What if for other business, such as the many pressing concerns that arise, whether visiting a relative or acquiring property? But if even a victim of injustice or abuse were to approach, what will become of such a man when he is excluded, pushed out, and chased away by those who least ought to do so, by those who should instead support, help, and champion him? From history we know that the Hebrews were long ago subject to this order, that they not approach Jerusalem but stay three or even six miles off; but then this was on the grounds that they were seditious, hotheaded, reckless, and had on many occasions attempted to rebuild the city that was to lie in ruins forever. In our case, however, the reason is obscure and the disgrace unmitigated.

Therefore, holy fathers who were once called fellow ministers, do not allow such a calamity to occur and do not allow the contagion to spread. It is one from which not even you yourselves are immune. Instead, speak out openly, entreat, appeal, and implore on bended knee that the imperial goodwill be granted to us too, and that the signal for entry be ordained by actual fact as well as by document, containing this at least, if nothing else: "His Imperial Majesty to the bishops: Enter." For understand that, if this does not happen, or if you, the incomplete synod, do something else in violation of ecclesiastical canons, we shall not, on this account, set up a rival altar nor shall we meet in a private and separate assembly; we do, however, serve notice and warn you that what is going on is not right, when so many brethren—indeed, by far the majority—have been slighted and are not even now receiving your attention. The people outside might make these and similar remarks. I, at any rate, have done so.

54. Ἄλλη

Ἄλλα μέν, ἐξ οἰκείων ὁρμηθεὶς ἠθῶν καὶ τῆς λαχούσης με, ἐπ' ἄλλαις ἐλπίσιν ἐμελέτησά τε καὶ ἐφρόντισα· ἕτερα δὲ νῦν ἐφ' ἑτέροις, ἅ μοι παραδόξως ἀπήντησε, καὶ γράφειν καὶ λέγειν μεθαρμόζομαι. Τίνα δ' *ἦν ἑκάτερα;* Ἐγὼ *καὶ ταῦτα καὶ ἐκεῖνα δηλώσω.*

Ἤλπισα καὶ ὠνειροπόλησα πάντως διὰ χρόνου πολλοῦ κατιὼν ἰδεῖν τὰ τιμιώτατα· βασιλεὺς δ' ἦν τούτων τὸ μέγιστον, καὶ βασιλεὺς μετὰ λαμπρᾶς ἐπανιὼν τῆς νίκης καὶ οἵας οὐκ ἄλλος, χρόνῳ μέν, ὃν πολὺν ἐταλαιπώρησεν ὥσθ' ὁλοσχερῆ τὴν νίκην ἄρασθαι, ποθεινὸς καὶ ἐπέραστος, ἔργῳ δὲ λαμπρὸς καὶ ἐπίσημος καὶ Σκυθικὸς *ὥσπερ δὴ καὶ* Ἀνταρκτικὸς *καλεῖσθαι μὴ ἀπαξιῶν.* Σὺν *αὐτῷ καὶ τὸν ναὸν ηὐχόμην ἰδεῖν τοῦ* Θεοῦ, *τὸ μέγα τῆς μεγάλης* Σοφίας *τέμενος, ὃν εἴποι μὲν ἕτερος, ἥμισυ, λέγων ἀνῳκοδόμησεν, ἐγὼ δέ φημι ὅλον καὶ πᾶν ὁ βασιλεὺς ᾠκοδόμησεν.* Οὐκ *ἔξω δὲ ταῦτα πάντως ὠσσόμην ἀλλὰ τῆς πόλεως ⟨ἔσω⟩.* Τοὺς *δ' ἐν τέλει καὶ συνόδῳ, τί χρὴ λέγειν ὡς ἤδη καὶ ἔβλεπον καὶ τοῖς ἄλλοις ναοῖς μικροῦ προσηυχόμην ἐμφὺς καὶ τοὺς φίλους ἠσπαζόμην ὑπαντῶν;* Καί *που καὶ ⟨περὶ⟩ πατριάρχου τι καὶ αὐτὸς ἐδόκουν λέγειν, ὡς ὁ βασιλεὺς τὸ κῦρος ἔχει κἂν τούτῳ, καὶ ὃν ἐκεῖνος αἱρήσοιτο καὶ προκρίνειε, προσκυνητέος οὗτος καὶ χειροτονητέος ἐκ προσκυνητοῦ καὶ αὐτοκράτορος.*

Ἦν ἄρα καὶ ἄλλα τὰ τὴν ὁρμὴν κατεπείγοντα καλὰ καὶ ποθεινά, ὡς ἐμοὶ τότε ἐφαίνετο. Τούτοις *τὸν νοῦν ἔτρεφον καὶ τῷ δοκεῖν ἐπλούτουν καί τις φανήσεσθαι προσεδόκουν τὸν πανηγυρικὸν πλέκων, τὸν ἐγκωμιαστικὸν γράφων, τὸν ἐπιβατήριον λέγων καὶ τὸν ἐπινίκιον, ἴσως καὶ τὸν ἐπὶ καταστάσει τῆς* Ἐκκλησίας *εὐχαριστήριον.* Ἀλλ' *ἐφθόνησέ μοί τις, οὐκ οἶδ' ὅπως εἴπω, δαίμων ἢ τύχη—εἴτε πλῆθος ἐπέβρισεν ἁμαρτιῶν εἴτε τι ἕτερον, ἀγνοῶ τοῦτο—καὶ μεχρὶ* Πυλῶν *ἔστησε ταῦτα, λυπρῷ χωρίῳ καὶ ἐξωτέρῳ, πτωχῷ γὰρ οὐ λέγω, μηδ' αὐτὰ τὰ μέτρια ἢ τὰ ἀναγκαῖα κεκτημένῳ, ἓν ἀστεῖον ἔχοντι πάντως καὶ περισπούδαστον, τὸ χοίρους καὶ ὄνους, βόας τε καὶ ἵππους καὶ πρόβατα τοὺς ἐν αὐτῷ κατοικοῦντας μεθ' ὅσης οὐκ ἂν εἴποι τις ἐπιμελείας ἐκδέχεσθαι καὶ διαπερᾶν καὶ τῇ βασιλίδι παραπέμπειν τὰ θρέμματα, ἐπέχειν δ' ἡμᾶς τοὺς ἀνθρώπους καὶ μὴ προσδέχεσθαι ὡς ἀποτρόπαιά τινα καὶ μύση μιαρά τε καὶ ἐναγῆ καὶ ἀφυβρίσματα.*

54: V 180v.

15 *ὠσσόμην* V: *ὀσσόμην* Darrouzès ‖ 16 addidi: *ἀλλ' ⟨ἐντὸς⟩* Lambros ‖ 18 add: Westerink ‖ 23 *ἔτρεφον* Lambros: *ἔστρεφον* V *τῷ* ex *τὸ* V ‖ 24 *προσεδόκων* Lambros

54. Another (Letter)

When I set out from my own territory and appointed see, I had other expectations and accordingly devoted my thoughts and attention to other matters. However, now that I am unexpectedly faced with a different set of circumstances, I am adopting different subjects for my correspondence and discourse. What was each of these two situations? I shall disclose the former as well as the latter.

As I made my way back (to the capital) after a long lapse of time, I hoped and dreamed that I might see the things that are most precious (to me). The emperor was the greatest of these, the emperor who was returning from a brilliant and incomparable victory; who was missed and longed for because of the long time he labored in adversity in order to secure the complete victory; who, because of his achievement, was brilliant and celebrated and did not disdain the appellations "Scythicus" and, if I may say so, "Antarcticus." It was with him that I hoped to behold the church of God, the great sanctuary of the great Wisdom, which another man would say he partially restored, whereas I assert the emperor built the whole, entire thing. I thought I saw these things, not from outside the city but within it. Do I need to add that I actually saw the officials and participants in the synod, that I nearly stood rooted in worship in the other churches, that I met and embraced my friends? I even imagined myself making some remarks about a patriarch, to the effect that the emperor has authority in this too and that we must venerate and consecrate the man whom he should choose and prefer because it is the choice of our venerable autocrator.

There were other considerations speeding me on my way which were, as they seemed to me at the time, desirable and good. These were the things that fed my thoughts and I was the richer for my dreaming; I supposed that I would appear to be a person of some consequence, composing the panegyric, writing the encomium, delivering the welcome and victory speeches, perhaps even the homily of thanksgiving on the restoration of the church. But out of spite something denied me, I don't know whether to call it chance or fate; whether a multitude of sins bore down on me or something else, I don't know. In any case, these malignant forces brought me to an abrupt halt when I had made it as far as Pylae, a miserable and remote little place—not to say beggarly and deprived—since it doesn't even possess the barest necessities for human existence; it does have, at any rate, a single attractive feature: its inhabitants accept delivery of pigs, asses, cattle, horses, and sheep with indescribable zeal and then transport and conduct these creatures to the capital; us humans, however, they detain and declare personae non gratae as though we were evil incarnate, lowdown, filthy trash, and moral degenerates.

Μεταλλαττόμενος οὖν παλινῳδίαν ᾄδω καὶ κλαίων ἤδη γράφω τὸν συντακτήριον, εἰ καὶ μὴ πρὸς παρόντας ἢ ἀκούοντας, ὥσπερ αὐτοῦ νόμος, ἀλλ' οὓς οὐκ εἶδον καὶ ὧν τῆς φωνῆς οὐκ ἤκουσα καὶ οἵ με οὐκ ἔβλεψαν. Καὶ σοὶ μὲν λέγω, Χαίροις, ὦ βασιλεῦ, καὶ βασιλεῦ κράτιστε καὶ μέγιστε καὶ κάλλιστε, μεθ' ὅσων αὐτὸς βούλει καὶ οἵων· ἔρροιεν δ' οἱ ἀντικείμενοί σοι καὶ τῇ ζωῇ σου μὴ ἐπευχόμενοι, ὅσοι τε καὶ οἷοι. Συγχαιρέτω σοι καὶ ὁ ἀδελφὸς καὶ βασιλεύς, ὁ ἐπιτερπόμενός σοι καὶ ἐπιτέρπων σοι, ὁ φυλασσόμενος καὶ φυλάσσων σε, ὁ συμβασιλεύων σοι καὶ συμπροσκυνούμενος. Συγχαιρέτω σοι καὶ τῶν ἐν τέλει, ὅσον καταθύμιον καὶ ὅσον δραστήριόν ἐστι πρὸς ὑπουργίαν σοι καὶ ὅσους αὐτὸς διορατικώτατος ὢν ἀξίους κρίνεις τοῦ χαίρειν. Σκύθην δὲ ἄνθρωπον "μηδ' ὅντινα γαστέρι μήτηρ κοῦρον ἐόντα φέροι" λίποις, ἀλλ' ἅμα πάντας ἐξαπολέσειάς τε καὶ ἀϊστώσειας. Χαίρετε, ναοὶ καὶ οἶκοι σεβάσμιοι Κυρίου πρῶτον, εἶθ' οἱ λοιποὶ αὐτῆς τε τῆς πανάγνου Μητρὸς καὶ τῶν Ἁγίων αὐτοῦ πάντων. Ὄψεσθαι γὰρ ἔτι ὑμᾶς ἀπήλπισα καὶ ἀπεκαραδόκησα. Χαίρετε, φίλοι, οὓς προσεδόκησα μὲν ἰδεῖν καὶ προσπτύξασθαι, οὐκ ἐγένετο δέ μοι, διὰ τί οὐκ οἶδα, οὐδὲ συνεχωρήθη, τίνος ἀγνοῶ ἕνεκεν, οὔτε προσιδεῖν οὐθ' ὅλως περιπλακῆναι. Ἡμεῖς δὲ παλίνορσοι, συννοίας πλήρεις καὶ κατηφείας, σκυθρωποὶ μὲν ὀφθῆναι, ταπεινοὶ δ' ὁραθῆναι, νεκροὶ μικροῦ καὶ ἄφωνοι, τοὺς ὑπαντῶντας ἐκτρεπόμενοι, τοὺς προσλαλοῦντας παρερχόμενοι, τισὶν ὅλως μὴ ἐπιστρεφόμενοι τὴν ὀπίσω ἄπιμεν, οὐδὲ πυκνὰ μάλα ἢ οὐδ' ὅλως ἐντροπαλιζόμενοι. Πρὸς τίνα γὰρ ἐπιστραφείημεν οὐδ' ὅσον κτήνεσι τοῖς διὰ σπουδῆς περῶσιν ἀπεικαζόμενοι; Ἐγὼ δὲ ὁ μάταιος οἶδα τότε δεινοπαθήσας ὡς καὶ ηὐξάμην συναποθανεῖν αὐτοῖς καὶ συσφαγῆναι, μόνον εἰ διαπεράσαιμι καὶ τὴν ἁγίαν καὶ προσκυνητὴν ἴδοιμι πόλιν.

Ἓν ἔτι προσθεὶς καταπαύσω τὸν λόγον. Τοὺς συνθύτας, ἐπεί σε ὑπὲρ ἡμῶν οὐκ ἐξεδυσώπησαν ἢ ἐξελιπάρησαν, δέσποτα, ἀλλὰ μόνοι τῷ μεγάλῳ θεάματι, τῇ ὄψει σου, ἐνετρύφησαν καὶ τοῖς τρόποις σου ἐνετέρφθησαν καὶ ταῖς προσκλήσεσι καὶ ταῖς προελεύσεσί σου ἐνωράθησαν καὶ τῇ εἰς τὸν μέγαν τοῦ Θεοῦ ναὸν ἐλεύσει σου συν-

---

54: 48–49 Hom., *Il.*, 6.58–59 ‖ 59–60 cf. Hom., *Il.*, 6.496

---

37 *μεταλλαττόμενος* Darrouzès: *μεταλλόμενος* V ‖ 40 *οἵ με* V s.l.: *οἶμαι* a. corr. ‖ 44 *σοι*[2] V: *σε* Darrouzès ‖ 51 *εἴθ* V, corr. Lambros ‖ 62 *τότε* Lambros: *πότε* V ‖ 68 *προελεύσεσί* Lambros: *προελεύσαις* V: *προσελεύσεσί* Darrouzès ‖ 69 *ἐνωράθησαν* V: fort. *ἐνωραΐσθησαν* Darrouzès

I therefore change my tune to a palinode and am now tearfully composing my valedictory, although not for an actual audience, as is the normal practice, but for people whom I have not seen, whose voices I have not heard, and who have not seen me. And now it is to you that I speak. Farewell, my Emperor, who are exceedingly mighty, great, and good, along with all those who are such as to find favor with you. As for those opponents of yours, who fail to pray for your life, to hell with them, all of them, whoever they may be. Along with you, farewell to your brother emperor, who gives and takes pleasure in you, who protects and is protected by you, and who shares in your rule and veneration. Along with you, farewell to that portion of the bureaucracy that renders you satisfactory and efficient service and everyone whom you yourself, perceptive judge of character that you are, deem worthy of the greeting. Don't, however, spare a single Bulgarian, "not even the little boy his mother carries in her womb," but annihilate and destroy them all together. Farewell first of all to you, churches and venerable houses of the Lord, and then to the remaining churches dedicated to his all-holy Mother and all his saints. For I have abandoned all hope, and despair that I will ever see you again. Farewell, friends. I don't know why I was cheated of my hopes of seeing and embracing you; nor do I understand the reason I was denied permission to look at you and give you the least bit of a hug. We retreat, fraught with worry and dejection, a sad and pitiful sight, half-dead and mute, ducking out of the way when we see people coming and slinking past if anyone calls out to us; we take to our heels without giving the slightest acknowledgment to anyone nor do we keep turning around again and again; in fact, we never glance back at all. For whom could we look in the eye when even dumb animals take precedence over us in express transport to the capital? And I, worthless creature that I am, was so acutely aware of my misery at the time that I even went so far as to pray that I might be slaughtered and die along with them, if only I might gain passage and see the holy and venerable city.

I will conclude my remarks after making one additional point. It concerns my fellow ministers. Since they have failed to move you, my lord, by shame or entreaty on my behalf, but instead have reveled all by themselves in your face, that magnificent sight, and have luxuriated in your charming personality; since they have been conspicuously present at your receptions and your (imperial) processions; since they form the entourage when you make your entrance into the great church of God; and

εχόρευσαν καὶ συνανεκλίθησαν καὶ συνειστιάθησάν σοι, ἀντικαταλλάξαις ἤδη ἡμῶν ὥσθ' ἡμᾶς μὲν ἔσω, ἐκείνους δὲ ἔξω γενέσθαι—τοῦτο δὴ τὸ ἴσον καὶ μηδενὶ βαρύ—καὶ ἀποκαταστήσαις ταῖς ἐκκλησίαις αὐτῶν. Τοῦτο ἡμεῖς οἱ ἔξω πρεσβεύομεν, μηδὲν αὐτοῖς μνησικακοῦντες τῆς παροράσεως καὶ τοῦ μισαδέλφου τρόπου. Ἑξαμήνου γὰρ πλέον τῶν ἐκκλησιῶν ἀποδημεῖν ὁ κανών, ὃν αὐτὸς τηρεῖς, ὦ βασιλεῦ, οὐ δίδωσιν. Ἡμᾶς δὲ πρὸς μικρὸν ἀξιώσεις ἢ τῆς θέας σου τυχεῖν, τὸ πρῶτον καὶ δι' ὃ σπεύδομεν, ἤ, τό γε δεύτερον, ἰδεῖν τοὺς ἰδόντας σε καὶ μαθεῖν παρ' αὐτῶν πῶς εἰσῆλθες, πῶς διῆλθες, πῶς πάλιν ἐξῆλθες, τὰ θαυμάσια, τὰς κοσμικὰς φροντίδας ἐπὶ τῶν ὤμων φέρων, τὰς πολεμικὰς ἐπὶ τῶν χειρῶν, τὰς πολιτικὰς ἐπὶ στόματος.

Ταῦτα ἡμεῖς ἀξιοῦμεν, ταῦτα καὶ αὐτὸς ποιήσεις, γλυκύτατε δέσποτα, καὶ ἐπὶ μακρὸν βιώσαις καὶ τὸν κόσμον ὀρθώσαις, οὐκ ἐπὶ γόνυ, ἀλλ' ἐπὶ στόμα πεσόντα οὐδ' ὕπτιον, ἀλλ' ὡς εἰπεῖν πρηνῆ κείμενον.

70–71 ἀντικαλλάξαις V, corr. Lambros || 71 ἤδη Darrouzès: ἢ δι' V

since they have dined with you and enjoyed your hospitality, you should now exchange them for us, so that we are within and they are without—this is really the fair thing and easy for everyone to accept—and send them back to their own churches. This is what we advocate from the outside nor are we motivated by any hard feelings on our part for their neglect and unbrotherly behavior. For the canon that you yourself preserve, Your Majesty, does not permit an absence from one's see in excess of six months. May we receive from you the privilege either of gaining a brief glimpse of you (our first choice and the reason for our impatience) or (our second choice) of seeing those who have seen you and of learning from them the particulars of your entrance, the actual procession, and again your exit—the marvelous experience of seeing you who bear the cares of the world on your shoulders, the cares of war in your hands, and the cares of state on your lips.

We believe we are justified in making these requests and you yourself will do as we ask, sweetest lord. May you enjoy a long life and may you help the world to its feet. It has fallen not to its knees but on its face; it lies not recumbent but, as it were, utterly prostrate.

COMMENTARY

1.

The rank of ostiarius was not purely honorific but included an active role in court ceremonial—e.g., the ushering and introduction of visitors to the palace—which brought the holder of this title into frequent contact with the emperor(s).[1] Cf. Ep. 6.13–15. Leo's addressee is probably the nephew of the eunuch protovestiarius Leo who commanded the imperial forces during the revolt of Bardas Sclerus,[2] and he (John) also figures in the correspondence of Nicephorus Uranus.[3] The rank of ostiarius, like the office of protovestiarius, was peculiar to eunuchs.[4] For this reason it is more likely that the relationship between John and Leo, which is unspecified in the text, is that of nephew and uncle than son and father.[5] Cf. also Ep. 6.

Schramm dates this letter to May 998, since in early May there was a "reich besuchtes Konzil."[6] He thinks that Philagathus was condemned at this time. This seems to be too late. The Western sources imply that the Philagathus affair was concluded before Easter (April 17) and certainly before the capture of Crescentius (April 29).[7] Further, it seems hard to believe that Gregory would have waited two whole months to get rid of the inconsequential Philagathus or that he would have had any trouble in rounding up a quorum of bishops for an ad hoc council during the Easter season at Rome. I am inclined to date the letter a month or so earlier than Schramm, i.e., in late March or early April.

10 ff. The accounts of Leo and the Western writers are in complete agreement on what happened to Philagathus. For this episode, the Latin sources are supplemented by the Greek *Vita Sancti Nili*.[8] The sequence of events, as pieced together from these various accounts, indicates that the deposition of Philagathus falls into two parts. In late February, Philagathus was captured at some distance from Rome by the soldiers of Otto III and mutilated. He was then returned to Rome and incarcerated. It is at this point that St. Nilus stepped in and attempted to intercede on behalf of his compatriot. He did not meet with success: Gregory V was not yet satisfied that justice had been done, and at his instigation Philagathus was condemned by the Church and stripped of his ecclesiastical garb. (According

to the *Chronicon Venetum*, MGH *SS*, VII, 31, the donkey ride followed rather than preceded the ecclesiastical deposition.)

[1]N. Oikonomides, *Les listes de préséance byzantines des IXe et Xe siècles* (Paris, 1972), 300.

[2]R. Guilland, *Recherches sur les institutions byzantines*, I (Berlin–Amsterdam, 1967), 220 and note 77; Scylitzes, *Synopsis Historiarum*, ed. J. Thurn, *Corpus Fontium Historiae Byzantinae* (Berlin, 1973), 320 (= Cedrenus, II, 424, Bonn ed.).

[3]Darrouzès, *Epistoliers*, V. 20, 25, 38, 43, 49, and 50.

[4]Oikonomides, *Listes*, 300; Guilland, *Recherches*, I, 216 and 288.

[5]The latter view is held by Guilland, *Recherches*, I, 288, and Darrouzès, *Epistoliers*, 165.

[6]Schramm, "Briefe," 93–94 and note 1.

[7]*Annales Quedlinburgenses*, ed. G. H. Pertz, MGH *SS*, III (Hanover, 1839; reprint, Stuttgart-New York, 1963), 74; *Annales Hildesheimenses*, *ibid.*, 91; *Ioannis Chronicon Venetum*, ed. G. H. Pertz, MGH *SS*, VII (Hanover, 1846; reprint, Stuttgart–New York, 1963), 31.

[8]The relevant portion of the *Vita* has been excerpted and appears in MGH *SS*, IV, ed. G. H. Pertz (Hanover, 1841; reprint, Stuttgart–New York, 1963), 616–18.

2.

This letter was written in the fall of 998, apparently from Byzantine southern Italy. Nothing more is known of the magister Michael to whom Leo entrusted his personal affairs during his absence.

16–18 August 997–January 998.

19 Leo is probably referring to the deposition of Philagathus, which took place in the spring of 998.

20–21 Leo's role in the Philagathus affair evidently escaped detection by the Ottonian court.

22 The legate of greater stature is the prince-bishop of Milan, Arnulf. Leo waited for him at Hidrous (Otranto) in September 998; see Ep. 3.

3.

This letter is contemporary with the preceding and was written in the fall of 998 from southern Italy.

Two brothers named Hagiozacharites (Theodore and Nicetas) deserted Bardas Sclerus for the imperial forces led by Leo the Protovestiarius. They were captured (along with Leo) and blinded after the defeat at Ragea in the fall of 977.[1]

2–3 The allusion is to Job 29.23: *ὥσπερ γῆ διψῶσα προσδεχομένη τὸν ὑετόν, οὕτως οὗτοι τὴν ἐμὴν λαλιάν.*

5 *εἰς διετῆ χρόνον*: The two-year period extended from fall/winter 996 to the fall of 998, when this letter was written.

5 *τὴν πρώτην γεῦσιν*: As Schramm points out,[2] "the first taste" refers to the Philagathus affair rather than to previous negotiations on the marriage.

12 *Λογγιβαρδίαν*: Byzantine southern Italy.[3]
13 *τὸν βασιλέα*: Basil II.

14 ff. The legate for whom Leo waited during September 998 (at Otranto; see Ep. 2.22–23) was Arnulf, who was elevated to the see of Milan in this year.[4] Three years later, in the summer of 1001, Arnulf renewed Otto's suit for a porphyrogenita in Constantinople. He succeeded and returned with the bride early in 1002, only to be met at Bari with the news of Otto's death.[5]

19 Because of damage to P, Darrouzès has here adopted the reading of Sakkelion's manuscript, *Atheniensis 1896*, *δυστυχοῦντος*, a variant that is incompatible with the traces in P.

[1] Scylitzes, p. 322 (= Cedrenus, II, 427, Bonn ed.).
[2] Schramm, "Briefe," 104 note 3.
[3] *Ibid.*, 96 note 1.
[4] *Ibid.*, 95.
[5] P. E. Schramm, "Kaiser, Basileus und Papst in der Zeit der Ottonen," *Historische Zeitschrift*, 129 (1924), 472–73.

4

This letter presents a dating problem. As it stands, it seems to have been written sometime early in 998, after Leo's trip to Germany, since this is the last event mentioned. Schramm, however, places it last in his collection of nine and assigns it to the fall of 998.[1] He notes verbal similarities between this letter and the two preceding it: *ἐν Φραγγίᾳ* and *τὰ τῆς συμπενθερίας*.[2] In addition, he believes that the text of the letter is broken off at the end, but the brevity of the factual information may be due to the fact that this is primarily a letter of condolence. Another factor in favor of the later date is that although the letters do not appear in chronological order, they do appear to be arranged in groups. This letter could be considered a member of the group written in the fall of 998, i.e., Epp. 2–4.

This letter also appears in O (NE, 19 [1925], 187–88), but the variations it offers are of no independent value. Nothing more is known of this Methodius, who seems to have been a close personal friend of Leo's. See Epp. 40–41.

3 *τοῦ κοινοῦ πατρὸς*: Cf. Ep. 41.3 where Leo speaks of Methodius' natural father as being his by adoption. Darrouzès suggests that Leo's use of the term "spiritual brother" could indicate that the father had entered the religious life and consequently was known as his spiritual father.[3] However, this does not seem necessary to explain Leo's use of the phrase, especially in a letter of condolence. Cf. Ep. 5.2.

[1]Schramm, "Briefe," 105.
[2]*Ibid.*, 90.
[3]Darrouzès, *Epistoliers*, 168 note 2.

5.

Schramm puts this letter, written from Rome (cf. line 5), first in the collection and dates it in the spring of 997.[1]

2–3 *τὸ τούτῳ ἢ ἐκείνῳ προσρυῆναι*: Schramm comments, "Also den beiden Parteien: Papst und Kaiser, Crescentius und Philagathos."[2] The context of the letter as a whole, however, seems to indicate that Leo's "refuge" is in Constantinople rather than in Rome. He acknowledges Myron's help and asks for his continued support despite his (Leo's) personal shortcomings; perhaps Leo is referring to his hesitation in seeking Myron's assistance in the first place.

[1]Schramm, "Briefe," 97.
[2]*Ibid.*, 97 note 3.

6.

This letter was written shortly after the appointment of Philagathus, i.e., in the early months of 997. Leo assumes the possibility of his correspondent's not knowing the news. On the identity of John, see note to Ep. 1.

6 I disagree with Schramm, who comments, "Die unmassigen Ansprüche des Philagathos? Oder die unmassige politische Tätigkeit des Absend-

ers"?[1] I take *θἀτέρου* as neuter, referring to the addressee's excessive ignorance or knowledge of the affair. In other words, John is laughing because he already knows about Philagathus or else because the news comes as a complete shock.

12–13 *ὁ . . . βασιλεύς*: Basil II.

15 *τοῖς βασιλεῦσι*: Basil II and his brother Constantine VIII.

[1]Schramm, "Briefe," 98 note 1.

7.

The heading, *τῷ γενικῷ*, is an abbreviated form of the title *ὁ λογοθέτης τοῦ γενικοῦ*, a minister of finance who ranked just below the *σακελλάριος*.[1] He was responsible for the assessment and collection of taxes.[2] The addressee of this letter may be assumed to be the same as that of Ep. 44 (q.v.), but no further identification is possible.[3] Schramm dates this letter to the spring of 997.[4]

10 It would be interesting to identify this Lord Calocyrus. Schramm suggests that he may be the *λογοθέτης τοῦ δρόμου*.[5] It is not clear in what way he is related to the patrician Calocyrus Delphinas[6] who was catepan of southern Italy for the years 982–85 and who, as a partisan of Bardas Phocas, was executed in 998.[7] Darrouzès mentions a Calocyrus who was an ambassador to the Russians in 967 and adds that this family, or one related to it, had connections with Euchaïta.[8]

[1]Oikonomides, *Listes*, 303; F. Dölger, *Beiträge zur Geschichte der byzantinischen Finanzverwaltung besonders des 10. und 11. Jahrhunderts* (Leipzig-Berlin, 1927; reprint, Hildesheim, 1960), 19.

[2]Oikonomides, *Listes*, 313–14; Dölger, *Finanzverwaltung*, 19–20.

[3]Cf. R. Guilland, "Les logothètes: études d'histoire administrative de l'empire byzantin," *REB*, 29, (1971), 23.

[4]Schramm, "Briefe," 98.

[5]*Ibid.*, 91.

[6]*Ibid.*

[7]Scylitzes, 336 (= Cedrenus, II, 444, Bonn ed.).

[8]Darrouzès, *Epistoliers*, 169 note 3.

8.

Schramm dates this letter around February 997, shortly after the elevation of Philagathus to the papal see.[1]

2–3 The present-day (or very recent) formula is: "Ecce annuntio vobis gaudium magnum: habemus pontificem." One wonders how old it is.

8–9 *ἀποσφριγάσαντα καὶ ἐξανδήσαντα*: Darrouzès[2] dismisses the interpretation of Schramm, who, on the basis of an incorrect manuscript reading, *ἀποσφραγίσαντα* (an error retained by Darrouzès), sees an allusion to Apoc. 8.13.[3] Darrouzès continues: "Léon veut dire précisément que l'ambassadeur byzantin a *brisé les sceaux et fait* la proclamation, c'est-à-dire qu'il a agi comme ayant pouvoir de confirmer l'élection du nouveau pape au nom de la nouvelle Rome." Leo is here drawing a contrast (*μὲν . . . δέ*) between the bold vigor of Philagathus, pope of the Old Rome, and the feeble condition of the aged Sisinnius, patriarch of the New, who died after less than three years in office. This is a state of affairs which by all rights (λῆξιν) should be reversed.

17 On Lord Calocyrus, see Ep. 7.10 and notes.

[1] Schramm, "Briefe," 93 and note 1.
[2] Darrouzès, *Epistoliers*, 170 note 4.
[3] Schramm, "Briefe," 99.

9.

Schramm dates this letter around February 997.[1]

2 *πάτερ καὶ δέσποτα*: This phrase leads Schramm to suggest that the patriarch (Sisinnius) may be the intended recipient of this letter,[2] but it could refer to a simple bishop.

4–5 *τὸν ἀρχιεπίσκοπον Φραγγίας*: It was through the favor of the empress Theophano, mother of Otto III, that Philagathus became archbishop of Piacenza in 988. Further, Piacenza was removed from the jurisdiction of the bishop of Ravenna and its bishop given the status of metropolitan.[3]

5 *ἰουλίῳ*: In 995, Philagathus and Bernward of Würzburg were sent to Constantinople by Otto III or his ministers "ob Graeci imperatoris filiam sibi matrimonio adquirendam."[4] Philagathus alone returned in 996:

"inde cum Graecorum revertentem legatis."[5] This places Philagathus in Constantinople in July 996 where he could have received the prayers of Sisinnius who was installed in April of that year.

8 τὸν ἴδιον . . . πάπαν: Gregory V. See Ep. 11.26 ff. and note.

11 τοῦ κυροῦ Καλοκυροῦ: See Ep. 7.10, note.

11 ff. This is an indication that Leo's involvement in the Philagathus affair was unknown to Basil II and subject (or so Leo feared) to the emperor's disapproval.

[1] Schramm, "Briefe," 94.
[2] *Ibid.*, 92.
[3] Schramm, "Kaiser," 446.
[4] *Annales Quedlinburgenses*, MGH *SS*, III, 74.
[5] *Ibid.*

10.

The combination of the office of sacellarius and the honorific title magister in the heading indicates that Leo's correspondent is the imperial rather than the patriarchal sacellarius.[1] The sacellarius was "a sort of comptroller, with authority over all the financial ministries."[2] This letter was written in the early months of 997. See *infra*.

6 τοῦ Σοφίας λιμένος: The Port of Sophia (also known as the Port of Julian, Λιμὴν τοῦ Ἰουλιανοῦ) was located in the southern part of Constantinople, on the Sea of Marmora. See R. Janin, *Constantinople byzantine: Développement urbain et répertoire topographique*, 2nd ed. (Paris, 1964), 231–34.

9ff. The Mediterranean is notoriously unpredictable and dangerous in the fall and winter months.

12 Perhaps it was during this rough crossing that Leo's secretary (Epp. 7.11–12 and 11.23) and Bernward, bishop of Würzburg, died.[3]

13 ff. Darrouzès believes that the hardships Leo describes are those encountered on his return from Germany ("Frangia") and that the letter was, consequently, written early in 998.[4] He does not think "l'insistance sur les pluies, les neiges, les fleuves" can be otherwise explained. It seems peculiar at the very least that Leo would begin his letter with an account of the voyage from Constantinople to Rome, then, after passing over a

whole year in silence, proceed to give the details of his return to Italy. In Ep. 3, Leo states that as of the end of September (998) he has been gone two years. This puts his departure from Constantinople sometime in the fall of 996. The winter in question would then be that of 996–97 and the letter written in the early months of 997.

[1]Guilland, *Recherches*, I, 51 and 56.

[2]J. B. Bury, *The Imperial Administrative System in the Ninth Century* (London, 1911; reprint, New York, 1958), 85; Oikonomides, *Listes*, 312.

[3]*Annales Quedlinburgenses*, MGH *SS*, III, 73.

[4]Darrouzès, *Epistoliers*, 172 note 6.

11.

Leo's correspondent is Patriarch Sisinnius II. The letter appears to have been written in the spring of 997.

2 ff. Leo refers to the short period of time between Sisinnius' elevation to the patriarchal throne (April 12, 996) and his (i.e., Leo's) departure in the fall of 996.

11–12 Cf. Ep. 10 for an enumeration of the difficulties of the voyage.

18–19 *τοῦ . . . βασιλέως*: Basil II.

20 *του κρατοῦντος* Κρισκένζου: The patrician John Crescentius II. Papal harassment seems to have been a family tradition with the Crescentii in the continuing struggle between the old Roman aristocracy and their Saxon rulers.[1]

23 See Ep. 10.12 and note.

26 ff. Pope John XV died in March 996. Otto III appointed as his successor his kinsman Bruno, known as Gregory V. He was enthroned on May 3, 996, and crowned Otto on May 21. Shortly thereafter, Otto returned to Germany and Crescentius expelled Gregory, "nudum omnium rerum,"[2] from Rome in the fall of the same year.

29 ff. The exact date of Philagathus' usurpation is not agreed upon. Schramm argues for February 997,[3] Duchesne for March,[4] and Mercati for April.[5]

[1]*Liber Pontificalis*, ed. L. Duchesne, II (Paris, 1892), 261 note 3, and 255 note 1.

[2]*Annales Hildesheimenses*, MGH *SS*, III, 91.

[3]Schramm, "Briefe," 93.

[4]Duchesne, II, 262.

[5]A. Mercati, "The New List of Popes," *Mediaeval Studies*, 9 (1947), 76.

12.

The Metropolitan of Sardes to whom the present letter is written can be securely identified as Leo, since he signed a synodal decree in Constantinople in February 997.[1] The letter should be dated about this same time, in the spring of 997, since Philagathus has not yet been deposed.

2–3 See Ep. 10.

13 ff. These lines imply that the Philagathus affair was not a preconceived plan or, at the very least, that Basil II was not involved in it. It is likely that Leo found the situation in Rome an irresistible opportunity.

19 Philagathus was a native of Rossano in Calabria, as was his contemporary, St. Nilus.

23–24 In 982, Philagathus became abbot of the monastery of St. Sylvester at Nonantola near Modena. A year later, after the death of Otto II, he played a role of increasing importance at the court of the regent Theophano.[2]

33 *τὸν αἱρετικόν*: In the absence of any qualifying statement, one assumes that Philagathus' heresy consists in his acceptance of *filioque* in the Creed, but one need not make too much of this.

35 ff. In all fairness to Philagathus, it must be pointed out that he was alleged to have been sexually involved with Theophano, Otto III's mother.[3]

40 At this point Darrouzès wonders about the morality of elevating such a creature to the throne of St. Peter.[4] One may also question the wisdom of allowing him to stand as sponsor for Otto III (and Bruno/Gregory V) at their baptism.[5]

50 ff. After his expulsion from Rome, Gregory "per Italiae urbes merens imperatoris expectando adventum versabatur."[6] Otto began his march on Rome in late 997, and he and Gregory entered the city toward the end of February 998.

[1] PG, 119, col. 740D.
[2] Schlumberger, *Epopée*, II, 262.
[3] Peter Damian, PL, 144, col. 253; cf. *Annales Quedlinburgenses*, MGH *SS*, III, 74.
[4] Darrouzès, *Epistoliers*, 175 note 10.
[5] *Ex Vita Sancti Nili*, MGH *SS*, IV, 616.
[6] *Chronicon Venetum*, MGH *SS*, VII, 31.

13.

The heading, *τῷ κανικλείου*, is an abbreviated form of the title, *ὁ ἐπὶ τοῦ κανικλείου*. This official was responsible for the imperial inkpot (and red ink) and the contents of imperial documents.[1] This position was often held in conjunction with another office.[2]

The recipient of this letter has been identified as Nicephorus Uranus[3] on the basis of a golden bull of Constantine IX Monomachus from the year 1052 found in the archives of Mt. Athos.[4] The purpose of this document is to entrust the Lavra of St. Athanasius to the protection of John, *πραιπόσιτος*, *ἐπὶ κοιτῶνος*, and *ἐπὶ τοῦ κανικλείου*. As a justification for this action, Constantine notes the intimacy (*οἰκειότης*) that exists between the emperor and *ὁ ἐπὶ τοῦ κανικλείου* by virtue of the nature of that office and cites the success of the Lavra's previous patron, Nicephorus, also an *ἐπὶ τοῦ κανικλείου* who is described in the following terms: *Ἀλλ' ἐπεὶ καὶ πάλαι ὁ τὴν μόνην ἐξ ἀρχῆς ἱδρυσάμενος, ὁ ὅσιος Ἀθανάσιος . . . εὖ ποιῶν ἀνέθετο ταύτην τῶ πότε προέχοντι (καὶ) παρὰ τῶ τηνικαῦτα βασιλεῖ τὰ μέγιστα δυναμένω τῶ μαγίστρω Νικηφόρω καὶ ἐπὶ τοῦ κανικ(λείου).*[5]

In addition to serving as *ὁ ἐπὶ τοῦ κανικλείου* (a title which also appears in Arabic sources but not in Cedrenus),[6] Nicephorus Uranus also enjoyed a distinguished military career, hence the address *θαυμάσιε στρατηγέ* in the opening lines of the letter. Since the internal evidence of the letter indicates that Leo is in the West (*κατὰ τὴν Ἰταλίαν πᾶσαν . . . κατ' αὐτὰς τὰς Γαλλίας, Ἱσπανίας*, lines 2–4), the letter ought to antedate Nicephorus Uranus' appointment as governor of Antioch late in 999.[7] Prior to this, in 997, *πάσης δύσεως ἄρχων ὁ μάγιστρος Νικηφόρος ὁ Οὐρανός*[8] inflicted a crushing defeat on the Bulgarian tsar Samuel at the Sperchius River.[9] It is this victory that must have prompted the present letter, which will then have been written in 997.[10]

The correspondence of Nicephorus Uranus has been edited by J. Darrouzès[11] and, not surprisingly, one finds that Leo and Nicephorus have several mutual correspondents: John the Ostiarius, Malacinus the Judge, Nicholas of Neocaesarea, Stephen of Nicomedia, and (possibly) John the Chartophylax.

5 *ἑξηκοντούτης*: This casual remark has made this letter the linchpin in determining the chronology of Leo's life. Since the letter may confidently be said to have been written in 997, Leo will therefore have been born in 937.

7–9 The text here is problematic. The corruption appears to lie within *ἴσον τι* (if nowhere else) and I have chosen *οἰήσονται* as the emendation most compatible with the reading of P and the sense of the passage. The meaning of *μὴ ἐμβλέψαι . . . γενέσθαι*, apart from any textual considerations, remains obscure.

10 A similar expression of this sentiment may be found in von Arnim, *SVF*, III, 164.23–26 = Plut., *De tranq. animi*, 472A): *ἀλλ’ ἔνιοι τοὺς μὲν Στωϊκοὺς οἴονται παίζειν, ὅταν ἀκούσωσι τὸν σοφὸν παρ’ αὐτοῖς μὴ μόνον φρόνιμον καὶ δίκαιον καὶ ἀνδρεῖον, ἀλλὰ καὶ ῥήτορα καὶ ποιητὴν καὶ στρατηγὸν καὶ πλούσιον καὶ βασιλέα προσαγορευόμενον.*

[1] Oikonomides, *Listes*, 311.
[2] Bury, *System*, 117.
[3] P. Lemerle et al., *Actes de Lavra*, I (Paris, 1970), 191.
[4] *Ibid.*, no. 31, 189–92.
[5] *Ibid.*, 191, lines 11–17.
[6] M. Canard, "Deux documents arabes sur Bardas Skléros," *SBN*, 5 (1939), 56 note 4.
[7] *Histoire de Yahya-Ibn-Sa'id d'Antioche*, ed. and trans. I. Kratchkovsky and A. Vasiliev, Patrologia Orientalis, 23 (1932), 459–60; Scylitzes, 341 (= Cedrenus, II, 454, Bonn ed.).
[8] Scylitzes, 341 (= Cedrenus, II, 449, Bonn ed.).
[9] *Ibid.*, 342 (= Cedrenus, II, 450, Bonn ed.).
[10] Without knowing the identity of the addressee, Darrouzès suggested 997 as the date of this letter in "Inventaire," 122.
[11] Darrouzès, *Epistoliers*, 217–48.

14.

The identity of Leo's correspondent here and in Epp. 15, 16, and 32 is somewhat problematic since there are two patriarchs of Antioch whose reigns are compatible with Leo's period of activity: Agapius I (January 20, 978–September 996) and John III (October 4, 996–July 1021). Further, the internal evidence of the letters, which otherwise might be expected to resolve the difficulty, can be applied equally to the known biographical data of each patriarch. Darrouzès favors John III[1] and is almost surely right, although his reason for doing so ("son prédécesseur était plutôt brouillé avec la cour") does not in itself seem conclusive. He is right in a sense, because the choice between the two amounts to deciding whether Leo was more likely to have rubbed shoulders with Agapius or with John, who had been the chartophylax of Hagia Sophia before his election. Agapius' internment in a monastery in the capital (a direct result of his falling into imperial disfavor) certainly decreased his social mobility and thus his opportunities for contact with Leo.

Theodore II, patriarch of Antioch, was summoned to Constantinople by Basil II shortly after the outbreak of Bardas Sclerus' revolt, but died en route (May 28, 976).[2] The Antiochans then drew up a list of candidates from which the emperor was to choose a successor, and Agapius, at that time bishop of Aleppo, set out to deliver it to Basil–but not before he finagled the addition of his own name to the list.[3] Once in Constantinople, he apprised the emperor of the situation in Antioch

(which was held by Sclerus) and the obvious advantages of having a loyalist on the patriarchal throne. Thus a deal was struck whereby Agapius would be named patriarch in return for winning over the magister Oubeïdallah (Sclerus' man in Antioch) and for inserting Basil's name in the diptychs to the exclusion of Sclerus'.[4] Using cloak-and-dagger techniques, Agapius kept his part of the bargain[5] and was installed as patriarch of Antioch on January 20, 978.[6] As patriarch, Agapius encountered initial opposition from Elias (963–1000), his colleague in Alexandria, who refused to enter his name in the diptychs on the grounds that his translation from the bishopric of Aleppo to the patriarchate was illicit[7] (which, technically, it was, though not without precedent). Agapius successfully argued his case and was thenceforth commemorated in the diptychs.[8]

Agapius' downfall came about in a typical fashion: in the aftermath of Bardas Phocas' defeat, Basil II found a compromising letter from the patriarch of Antioch among Phocas' belongings. Agapius was consequently summoned to Constantinople and interned in one of the monasteries there after holding the see for twelve years (i.e., early 990).[9] During his exile Agapius continued to exercise the prerogatives of office (i.e., performing ordinations for the diocese, etc.).[10] In September 996, Basil induced Agapius to write his letter of resignation by offering a financial settlement in addition to promising that his (Agapius') name would be retained in the diptychs.[11] Agapius died a year later, on September 8, 997.[12]

In the meantime, Basil had named John, the chartophylax of Hagia Sophia, patriarch of Antioch on October 4, 996.[13] The nomination had no sooner been made than Agapius regretted his resignation, with the consequence that John not only declined to go to Antioch for his installation but also ceded the right of the patriarch of Antioch to be installed by his own metropolitans in favor of the patriarch of Constantinople.[14]

There are reasons to suppose that John did not take up residence in Antioch immediately after his accession: first, his predecessor was still alive (until September 8, 997); second, the political situation in the Middle East was grave,[15] became worse when the duke of Antioch, Damian Dalassenus, fell in July 998,[16] and by the fall of 999 had deteriorated to the point of requiring the emperor's personal intervention.[17] According to Nikon of the Black Mountain,[18] John was in Antioch when he met with Orestes, the patriarch of Jerusalem, and ceded to him the income from property in Iberia held by the patriarchate of Antioch. Since Orestes died in Constantinople in 1006 after a stay of four years,[19] this meeting ought to have taken place between the early months of 1000 (after the conclusion of a treaty between Basil II and the calif al-Hakim which Orestes had helped negotiate)[20] and 1002. Unfortunately for the dating of this letter and Ep. 32, the date of John's arrival in Antioch cannot be determined more precisely. He died in July 1021.[21]

The contents of the letters do not offer a clear choice between Agapius and John. The expressions of concern for safety and health which recur throughout them are not in themselves chronologically significant since then, as now, the Middle East was anything but a picture of tranquility. The evaluation of Ep. 32 is especially diffi-

cult. At first glance, it seems to coincide exactly with the circumstances in which Agapius found himself—living out his last years in exile at a monastery in Constantinople during the interregnum between Nicholas II Chrysoberges and Sisinnius II (December 991–April 12, 996). On the other hand, if, as I have tried to suggest, John III postponed his departure for Antioch for a year or so after Agapius' death, the situation described in the letter would equally suit a John who was languishing in the capital and far from his see during the vacancy between Sisinnius II and Sergius II (August 998–June/July 1001). In the face of these ambiguities, the tone of the letters assumes a critical importance. It is one that indicates a relationship of great warmth and familiarity. Leo would surely have had more opportunities to develop a friendship with the former chartophylax of Hagia Sophia than with Agapius. An additional factor is the series of letters to the Chartophylax (Epp. 47–49), which would confirm an ongoing relationship if, as seems likely, they were written to John. John III should therefore be identified as the patriarch in question.

If the "cadaverous or pasty-faced" individuals of lines 7–8 refer to (the corpses of) the patriarch's predecessors, the letter should have been written after Agapius' death.

7 ff. John's immediate predecessors were Eustratius (December 969—), an appointee of Nicephorus Phocas who died before he could be installed; Theodore I (January 23, 970–May 29, 976); and Agapius I (January 20, 978–September 996).[22]

22–23 This quotation (from II Cor. 1.13) becomes less cryptic when taken in the context of the preceding and succeeding verses. The general import is that in view of their intimacy and high mutual regard the patriarch could not possibly take what Leo says in the wrong way.

25 *τῷ δώροις ἁπλῷ*: The allusion is to James 1.5, where the "liberal giver" is God (cf. line 28, *ἰσόθεος*): *Εἰ δέ τις ὑμῶν λείπεται σοφίας, αἰτείτω παρὰ τοῦ διδόντος Θεοῦ πᾶσιν ἁπλῶς καὶ μὴ ὀνειδίζοντος, καὶ δοθήσεται αὐτῷ.*

26 *οὗ μὴ ἄξιος ὁ κόσμος*: By this phrase, which is slightly adapted from Hebrews 11.38, Leo compares his friend to the prophets and other Old Testament figures who, through their faith, prevailed in disastrous circumstances but also suffered the gravest afflictions: *ὧν οὐκ ἦν ἄξιος ὁ κόσμος, ἐπὶ ἐρημίαις πλανώμενοι καὶ ὄρεσιν καὶ σπηλαίοις καὶ ταῖς ὀπαῖς τῆς γῆς.*

34 *τοὺς ... λόγους*: See Ep. 47 and commentary.

[1] Darrouzès, *Epistoliers*, 177 note 12.
[2] *Histoire de Yahya*, 375.
[3] *Ibid.*
[4] *Ibid.*, 376.

[5] *Ibid.*, 377.

[6] V. Grumel, "Le patriarcat et les patriarches d'Antioche sous la seconde domination byzantine," *EO*, 33 (1934), 135 and note 1.

[7] *Histoire de Yahya*, 379.

[8] *Ibid.*, 380–89.

[9] *Ibid.*, 428.

[10] *Ibid.*

[11] *Ibid.*, 445.

[12] *Ibid.*, 446.

[13] *Ibid.*, 445.

[14] V. Grumel, "Les patriarches grecs d'Antioche du nom Jean," *EO*, 32 (1933), 283–84 and note 6. Grumel's source is Nikon of the Black Mountain.

[15] *Histoire de Yahya*, 447 ff.

[16] *Ibid.*, 456.

[17] *Ibid.*, 457–61.

[18] Cited by Grumel, "Patriarches grecs," 284.

[19] *Histoire de Yahya*, 415 and 461.

[20] *Ibid.*, 461.

[21] *Ibid.*, 445.

[22] Grumel, "Patriarcat," 130–36.

15.

On the identity of the patriarch of Antioch, see the introductory note to Ep. 14. There is no indication of the date on which this letter was written, but the following letter (especially lines 9 ff.) indicates that there has been a flurry of correspondence from Leo of which this and the preceding letter may be part. If this is so (and it is only conjecture), the letter may be dated ca. 1000.

8 *Δημήτριον*: I have been unable to find any further information about this paragon of a nephew.

16.

On the identity of the patriarch of Antioch and a tentative date for this letter, see the introductory notes to Epp. 14 and 15 respectively.

2–3 *τὸν Θεουπόλεως*: Theopolis was a common epithet for Antioch, since it was here that the followers of Christ were first called Christians. See Acts 11.26.

14 *χόλος ἐν στήθεσι μετόπισθε*: Leo has adapted this phrase (which refers to Agamemnon) from the response of Calchas to Achilles' query about the cause of Apollo's anger. The source of this adaptation is the *Iliad*, 1.81–83: *εἴ περ γάρ τε χόλον γε καὶ αὐτῆμαρ καταπέψῃ, / ἀλλά τε καὶ μετόπισθεν ἔχει κότον, ὄφρα τελέσσῃ, / ἐν στήθεσσιν ἑοῖσι· σὺ δὲ φράσαι εἴ με σαώσεις.*

17.

Darrouzès remarks that the series of letters to Arsenius is written in "le plus pur style de la plaisanterie 'ecclésiastique'" and that "l'exagération évidente de l'épistolier dévoile cependant quelques pittoresques scènes de moeurs."[1] I believe Darrouzès' judgment of Arsenius errs on the side of charity: Leo's anger is very real. Although the dating of the Arsenius letters is problematic—the only certainty is that he was not (any longer?) in possession of his see in February 997[2]—still I think we may see reflected in Arsenius' behavior a grave situation among the episcopacy in the late tenth century which Basil II attempted to remedy by imperial novel and the patriarch Sisinnius by synodal decree. See *infra*, Epp. 18.14 ff. and 19.5 ff., notes.

15–17 Leo refers again (cf. Ep. 20.10) to this passage from Plutarch's *De Pythiae oraculis*, 396E: *ἐκλαβὼν γὰρ ὡς ἔοικεν ἵππον ἀλινδούμενον γράψαι τρέχοντ' ἔγραψεν. ἀγανακτοῦντος δὲ τἀνθρώπου γελάσας ὁ Παύσων κατέστρεψε τὸν πίνακα, καὶ γενομένων ἄνω τῶν κάτω πάλιν ὁ ἵππος οὐ τρέχων ἀλλ' ἀλινδούμενος ἐφαίνετο. τοῦτό φησιν ὁ Βίων ἐνίους τῶν λόγων πάσχειν, ὅταν ἀναστραφῶσι.*

17–18 Leo's allusion to Hebrews 7.26 is especially appropriate for an errant bishop. His adaptation gains point by comparison with the full text of the verse: *τοιοῦτος γὰρ ἡμῖν καὶ ἔπρεπεν ἀρχιερεύς, ὅσιος, ἄκακος, ἀμίαντος, κεχωρισμένος ἀπὸ τῶν ἁμαρτωλῶν, καὶ ὑψηλότερος τῶν οὐρανῶν γενόμενος.*

21 This is an indication that the letter was written shortly after Arsenius' appointment, as may also be the *ἐπιβατήρια* of line 12.

[1]Darrouzès, *Epistoliers*, 179 note 13.
[2]PG, 119, col. 740C–D.

18.

10–11 Cf. Ep. 17.10.

14 ff. *πρόεδρον*: Although the title proedrus can be applied to church officials, the present context seems to rule this out. The secular title was created for Basil the paracoemomenus by Nicephorus Phocas between 963 and 969.[1] Apparently the title was purely honorific[2] and was held by Basil alone, while he lived,[3] and after his fall from grace in 985 was "retired" from use by the emperor Basil II because of "une rancune trop tenace" toward his former advisor.[4] After Basil II's death in 1025, his brother Constantine VIII conferred it on several eunuchs.[5] It is very likely, then, that the proedrus mentioned here is Basil the paracoemomenus. Unfortunately, the terminus ante quem of 985 suggested by this identification is made much less secure by the fact that the manipulations in question antedate Arsenius' appointment (*τότε*, line 16). There is not enough information to gauge how long ago these events took place.

σεβαστοφόρον: This office was also of recent origin (between 963 and 975) and generally held by eunuchs.[6] At an earlier point, Oikonomides suggested that the sebastophorus in question is Romanus, son of Stephen Lecapenus, grandson of the emperor Romanus I Lecapenus, and the first to hold the office, and that this letter was written before 985.[7] This is possible, but, as with the proedrus, there is simply not enough information in either the letter or in other sources to make a positive identification.[8] Further, even if this identification is correct, it does not necessarily determine the date of the letter. Another possibility is presented by an unpublished tenth/eleventh-century seal cited by Guilland. It belongs to the sebastophorus Theophilus, but he is a mere name.[9]

δέσποιναν: "Official" use of the title despoina was confined to the regent or empress until the end of the eleventh century,[10] but it was "unofficially" applied to other women as well.[11] The title itself did not confer any rank or prerogatives but merely "qualifie un état de fait."[12] In nonimperial usage, the title "est réservé aux relations du type maître-serviteur; même si cela est purement formel."[13] The present context is too vague to determine whether this despoina is simply a lady of some importance or the empress herself.

τοὺς ἀπεμπολουμένους ... τοὺς καλοὺς ἀγρούς: Although there is some ambiguity about the actual agent(s) of the sale (Arsenius? the carpenters and cooks?), it is clear in any case that a transference of prime real estate is involved, and this to persons who could be classed among "the powerful." The transaction calls to mind Basil II's novel of January

1, 996,[14] which severely restricts the ability of "the powerful" to acquire land from "the poor" and forbids their acquiring it from metropolitans and bishops. The incident also agrees with what we know of Basil the paracoemomenus, whose voracious appetite for power and possessions was notorious.

[1]Oikonomides, *Listes*, 299.

[2]C. Diehl, "De la signification du titre de 'proèdre' à Byzance," in *Mélanges offerts à M. Gustave Schlumberger à l'occasion du quatre-vingtième anniversaire de sa naissance, 17 Octobre 1924* (Paris, 1924), 110.

[3]*Ibid.*, 107.

[4]*Ibid.*, 110.

[5]*Ibid.*, 112.

[6]Oikonomides, *Listes*, 308.

[7]In an unpublished study, *Un Taktikon inédit du Xe siècle, cod. Scorial. gr. R-II-11*, 81, cited by R. Guilland in "Le sébastophore," *REB*, 21 (1963), 201 note 19.

[8]Guilland expresses the same reservation; see *ibid.*

[9]*Ibid.*, 205.

[10]E. Bensammar, "La titulature de l'impératrice et sa signification," *BYZ*, 46 (1976), 286.

[11]*Ibid.*, 284.

[12]*Ibid.*, 285.

[13]*Ibid.*

[14]J. and P. Zepos, *Ius graecoromanum*, I (Athens, 1931), 262 ff.; Dölger, *Regesten*, I, 783.

19.

5 ff. Episcopal abuse was a continuing problem for the Church, and repeated efforts were made to keep the situation under control. However, it may be significant that there is a synodal decree from the patriarchate of Sisinnius II "interdisant certains abus qui transforment en trafic la charge épiscopale."[1] It continues: "les évêques sont vivement exhortés de n'appliquer les clercs qu'à la louange divine et de ne point leur imposer d'autres charges, et s'ils sont pauvres, de les aider plutôt que de les accabler comme des serfs." Failure to comply will result in "la déposition perpetuelle." Unfortunately, this document is not dated. Yet, the similarity between the type of behavior condemned by the decree and the particular misbehavior of Arsenius leads one to suspect temporal proximity. Since Leo was out of the country from ca. August 996 to ca. September 998, a date before or after this period is required. The earlier dating, i.e., before August 996, seems more likely. It would not be surprising if, during the vacancy in the patriarchate (991–96), certain bishops had indulged in rather dubious practices. Nor would it be surprising if the new patriarch dealt with this problem soon after his accession (April 996), especially in

view of the fact that the emperor himself had already taken strong measures against the abuses of rank and wealth early in 996. Cf. Dölger, *Regesten*, I, 783, and Ep. 18.14 ff. and note.

13 Rhaedestus (Bisanthe, Rhodosto), suffragan see of Heraclea, is located on the northern shore of Propontis. The bishop in question is unknown.

[1]V. Grumel, *Les Regestes des Actes du Patriarcat du Constantinople. I: Les Actes des Patriarches, fasc. II, 715–1043* (Kadiköy, 1936), no. 808.

20.

10 Cf. Ep. 17.15–17.

11 and 16–17 Darrouzès sees here an allusion to the proverb *οὐ δύνῃ Φωκίωνι φίλῳ χρῆσθαι καὶ κόλακι*. Given the circumstances in which Arsenius found himself, it seems more likely that his reference to Phocion is intended to conjure up the image of a man of the utmost probity who is unfairly condemned (and executed) by his compatriots. It is perhaps not irrelevant to note that the Phocion affair reminded the Greeks of Socrates' fate. Cf. Plutarch, *Phoc.*, XXVIII.2 and Ep. 21.

12 *τοῖς δὲ ἔσω*: Christian authors.

17 *κατακριθήσῃ*: If this letter was written during the patriarchate of Sisinnius, this threat of condemnation may be taken literally. Cf. Ep. 19.5 ff., note.

21.

2 A lacuna is indicated in the Greek text. I have attempted to supply the sense of the missing portion in the translation, where it appears in brackets.

3–5 The following passage from Galen's *In Hippocratis aphorismos* (I.12) sheds some light on Leo's remark to Arsenius: *ἄλλο δὲ γένος ἔστι σημείων, τῶν κρισίμων ὑπ' αὐτοῦ προσαγορευομένων*... (here follows a list of the various symptoms) . . . *εἰ μὲν ἐπὶ πεπεμμένῳ τῷ νοσήματι γίγνοιτο, σωτηρίαν ὑπόγυον, εἰ δὲ ἐπὶ ἀπέπτῳ, κρίσιν οὐκ ἀγαθήν, ἤτοι γε εἰς ὄλεθρον ἄξουσαν ἢ εἰς χρόνου μῆκος.*

9 ff. If by his mention of Phocion Arsenius intended to represent his position as that of a martyr in the fashion of Socrates, Leo's extensive quotation from a "Socratic" dialogue has special point.

25 *τῶν συγκέλλων*: Leo and his colleague Stephen, metropolitan of Nicomedia, and syncellus from before 976 until 1003 (or later).[1] Cf. Epp. 34 and 35.

[1] Oikonomides, *Listes*, 309 note 116.

22.

The contents of this letter do not permit accurate dating. Since Leo is in Constantinople (line 6), the letter must have been written before fall 996 or after fall 998. The terminus ante quem, 1039, when Nicholas' successor Theodulus is known to have held the see,[1] is of minimal value here. His seal is extant.[2] Nicholas seems also to have enjoyed a cordial relationship with Nicephorus Uranus. Three of his letters to Nicholas, which are mainly concerned with the pain of separation, survive.[3]

[1] V. Laurent, *Le corpus des sceaux de l'empire byzantin*, V, 1 (Paris, 1963), 361.
[2] *Ibid.*, no. 492.
[3] Darrouzès, *Epistoliers*, V, 15, 21, and 26.

23.

In 997 Malacinus the protospatharius, a man *ἐπὶ συνέσει καὶ λόγῳ ἐμπρέπων*, was accused of Bulgarian sympathies and transferred from Thessalonica to Byzantium.[1] He also appears to have held the office of *κριτής*: cf. line 3, *ὁ κριτὴς ἡμῶν*, and the two letters to Malacinus the Judge from Nicephorus Uranus.[2]

The protospatharius was originally the head of the imperial bodyguard (Spatharii), and although at this period it was an honorific title its holders retained a ceremonial function.[3]

2 ff. Two years of this separation may be assigned to Leo's embassy to Italy. If the remaining two years belong to the preceding period (when Malacinus was presumably in Thessalonica), the letter will have been written in the fall of 998, shortly after Leo's return.

5 ff. If this letter was written in late 998, Leo's misfortunes are no doubt those encountered en route to and in Italy. Cf. Epp. 10.5 ff. and 3.4–5.

[1]Scylitzes, 343 (= Cedrenus, II, 451, Bonn ed.).
[2]Darrouzès, *Epistoliers*, V, 31 and 34.
[3]Oikonomides, *Listes*, 291.

24.

Evidently there has been some problem in the delivery of letters. It is not clear from the letter exactly who is where, but the mention of the Anatolikon theme leads one to suspect that Leo is in Synada. Perhaps Leo received a letter from Malacinus and was slow to reply because his own courier had no urgent reason to leave the theme.

25.

It is tempting to identify Leo's correspondent with the poet Christopher of Mitylene,[1] whose lifetime roughly spanned the first half of the eleventh century. He held the rank of patrician and, later on, became the *κριτής* of Paphlagonia.[2] It is not impossible that Leo wrote to Christophorus Mitylenaeus, but that he wrote to him as *κριτής* seems much less likely.

[1]Darrouzès, *Epistoliers*, 84 note 16.
[2]K. Krumbacher, *Geschichte der byzantinischen Litteratur (527–1453)*, 2nd ed. (Munich, 1897), 737; cf. H. Hunger, *Die hochsprachliche profane Literatur der Byzantiner*, II (Munich, 1978), 171.

26.

For this letter it is the abundance of information rather than a lack of it that has created problems. Nicephorus Uranus, who was roughly contemporary with Leo, wrote to a metropolitan of Euchaïta named Symeon.[1] It seems agreed, at least provisionally, that Michael succeeded Symeon as metropolitan of Euchaïta[2] and that consequently this letter, written soon after Michael's accession, belongs to the end of the tenth[3] or the beginning of the eleventh century.[4] The question now arises whether this Michael is to be identified with the kinsman of Romanus Argyrus who was appointed syncellus by that emperor soon after his accession in 1028.[5] Janin

thinks not and postulates a second Michael of Euchaïta as syncellus.[6] Darrouzès believes they are one and the same and that Michael (as also the Judge Mitylenaeus?) represents the younger generation in Leo's correspondence.[7] V. Laurent shares the latter judgment and attributes two extant seals to Leo's Michael: the first[8] has as its legend +Μιχαὴλ *μητροπολίτῃ* Εὐχαῖτων; the second,[9] +Μιχαὴλ *ἐλέῳ* Θεοῦ *μητροπολίτῃ* Εὐχαῖτων *καὶ συγκέλλῳ*.

12–13 Darrouzès wishes to see in these lines an allusion to theological concern with the afterlife and more particularly the place in which it was spent.[10] Although Leo is ordinarily not very interested in theology, and even confesses his lack of interest (cf. Ep. 31.19), such a concern is not narrowly theological, especially if it involves oneself. Still, Leo may simply mean: "whether 'earth' refers to this life or the hereafter."

[1] Darrouzès, *Epistoliers*, V, 39.
[2] R. Janin ("Euchaïtes," *DHGE*, 15, col. 1313) inclines to the opposite view.
[3] *Ibid.*
[4] Darrouzès, *Epistoliers*, 185 note 17, and Laurent, *Corpus*, V, 1, 588.
[5] Scylitzes, 375 (= Cedrenus, II, 486, Bonn ed.).
[6] Janin, "Euchaïtes."
[7] Darrouzès, *Epistoliers*, 185 note 17.
[8] Laurent, *Corpus*, V, 1, no. 767.
[9] *Ibid.*, no. 768.
[10] Darrouzès, *Epistoliers*, 185 note 17, where he cites A. Wenger, "Ciel ou Paradis," *BZ*, 41 (1951), 560–69, and Nicetas Stethatus, *Opuscules et Lettres*, Sources chrétiennes, 1961.

27.

There are indications (e.g., line 7, *γέροντα* 'Αβραάμ, and line 13, *τῇ νεοπαγεῖ φιλίᾳ*) that Leo's correspondent may be one of the younger members of the ecclesiastical hierarchy. On the other hand, the lively tone of this letter seems to signify a relationship of longer standing. In any case, the letter ought to have been written before 1022, when the metropolitan of Nicaea was Constantine.[1] A Gregory of Nicaea is known as the author of a treatise on the baptism of Jews,[2] but Darrouzès elsewhere seems to identify him with Gregory of Caesarea,[3] a correspondent of Nicephorus Uranus.

15 The word *κορδάκιον* is unattested but seems to be a diminutive of *κόρδαξ*, and the adjective *κακέμφατα* supports this notion. It would then mean something small which exhibits frenzied or suggestive movements. Lake Ascania was known as a veritable treasure trove of therapeutic aids. There were tiny green fish that cured fever; crayfish, whose broth was "un remède souverain" for paralysis; and light, yellow stones

that insured a speedy delivery if hung about the hips of the expectant mother.[4] Κορδάκιον may be a popular local expression for one of these. Another possibility is offered by L. Robert who argues that the *κορδάκιον* is the bleak (*alburnus lucidus*), a small fish whose scales are used in the making of artificial pearls, and that it received the name *κορδάκιον* from its habit of leaping out of the water to catch flies.[5] However, Robert does not seem to have been aware of the passage in Edrisi's *Geography*.

[1] M. LeQuien, *Oriens Christianus*, I (Paris, 1740), col. 648.

[2] J. Darrouzès, "Les catalogues récents de manuscrits grecs," *REB*, 7 (1949), 64.

[3] Darrouzès, *Epistoliers*, 220 note 6.

[4] P. A. Jaubert, *La Géographie d'Edrisi*, II (Paris, 1836–40; reprint, Amsterdam, 1975), 304.

[5] L. Robert, "Les kordakia de Nicée, le combustible de Synnada et les poissons-scies. Sur des lettres d'un métropolite de Phrygie du Xe siècle. Philologie et réalités," *Journal des Savants* (1961), 111.

28.

This letter is as puzzling as it is interesting. It is evidently a reply to a summons (quoted by Leo in the letter) to attend a synod which, in this period, ought to have been held in Constantinople (cf. lines 4–5, *εἰσήλθομεν* and *εἰσελθέτω*). This curt invitation seems to have been issued in the name of the bishops (to whom Leo apparently addresses lines 17–22), probably by order of the patriarch, although Leo pretends to be in the dark on this last point (cf. line 26, *ὅστις ἂν ᾖς*). Unfortunately, the scarcity of documentation for this period in Eastern church history, as well as the lack of any concrete information in the letter itself, hinders attempts to ascertain the date of the synod and the letter, the identity of the addressee, and the subject of the vote. One does wonder, though, whether the vote referred to could be the same as in Epp. 53 and 54, i.e., the election of a new patriarch, which Leo was prevented from attending. In this case, the frame of reference for lines 22–24 would extend beyond the note cited in lines 4–7, and line 26 would take on a different meaning since Leo might really not have known the identity of the patriarch to whom he was writing. While a connection between this letter and Epp. 53 and 54 seems to make tolerable sense, it would be well to remember that there must have been more than one occasion during his career as syncellus when Leo was called upon to vote. We simply do not know about the others.

19 It is hard to tell if this is mere bluster on Leo's part or if it has any application to the dispute over precedence between metropolitans and their colleagues who were also syncelli. At issue was whether a metropolitan, by virtue of being a syncellus, could be elevated in the ecclesiastical hierarchy above the rank determined by the see he held and thus above his brother metropolitans. This question became quite heated in the eleventh

century, but because of a lack of information we do not know if it arose earlier and affected Leo (and his colleague Stephen of Nicomedia).[1]

It is also interesting to note the use of the term *πρωτόψηφος* in the treatise *Περὶ τῆς ἐν τῷ πατριαρχείῳ γινομένης φιλονεικίας διὰ τὰς ψήφους* by Nicetas of Amasia (see Ep. 53 and notes): *Καλοῦμαι ἐν ταῖς ψήφοις ὡς σύμψηφος καὶ τίνι συμψηφίσομαί τε καὶ συναινέσομαι; Ἆρα τῷ πατριάρχῃ, ὡς πρωτοψήφῳ καὶ ἀρχηγῷ;*[2] The word means "prime-elector," not in the sense that his vote is first, but that it is the final or decisive one.[3] We know that the office of syncellus was frequently a stepping-stone to the patriarchate,[4] but I have been unable to find a case of a syncellus replacing the patriarch during a vacancy. If Leo were patriarch pro tempore, one would like to know where he was when this letter was written, since he does not seem to be in Constantinople, and why he himself did not oversee the arrangements for the synod.

20 ff. Leo also addresses, more earnestly, the issue of residence in one's see in the conclusion of Ep. 54.

24 *τὸν μειζότερον*: There were patriarchs for whom these would be fighting words, but here the emperor Basil II is probably meant.

[1] V. Grumel, "Titulature de métropolites byzantins. I. Les métropolites syncelles," *REB*, 3 (1945), 94 ff.

[2] J. Darrouzès, *Documents inédits d'ecclésiologie byzantine* (Paris, 1966), p. 160, 1–2. Cf. p. 162, 3.

[3] *Ibid.*, 162 note 1.

[4] Metropolitan Athenagoras, Ὁ *θεσμὸς τῶν συγκέλλων ἐν τῷ* Οἰκουμενικῷ Πατριαρχείῳ, EEBS, 4 (1927), 9–12.

29.

The addressee and exact circumstances surrounding this letter are unknown. Apparently, as in Ep. 42, Leo has taken up the cause of his aged uncle, the bishop, who may be one of Leo's own suffragans. In any case, the mention of the protonotarius (line 18) indicates that the situation involves the provincial administration. The *πρωτονοτάριος τοῦ θέματος* was responsible for the civil administration of the theme[1] and was its chief fiscal officer.[2] He was subordinate to the *στρατηγός* in the theme and to the *χαρτουλάριος τοῦ σακελλίου* in Constantinople.[3] Since church property was subject to taxation[4] (and confiscation in times of distress), it would appear that in the course of his duties the protonotarius removed some items from the bishopric of Leo's uncle. At this point, Leo sought the aid of a third party, possibly either one of the protonotarius' superiors. This man acquired for Leo's uncle a golden bull, which probably granted exemption from the levy, and in addi-

tion wrote to the protonotarius and ordered the restitution of the objects that had been taken.

Darrouzès calls attention to a series of letters written by Nicephorus Uranus.[5] These letters accompany copies of a letter written by the emperor to *ὁ ἐπὶ τῆς σακέλλης* which *τὸ ἀσφαλὲς τοῦ λοιποῦ τοῖς χρυσοβούλλοις προσνέμουσαι*.[6] These golden bulls, of indeterminate content, affect the metropolitans of Laodicea, Nicomedia, and Caesarea and the bishops of Corone and Lophus. Darrouzès suggests that Leo's letter may date from the same period.[7] If this is true, they must antedate 985 since in one of the letters[8] the paracoemomenus (Basil) is spoken of in glowing terms, *τῇ τε θείᾳ καὶ ἱερᾷ ψυχῇ τοῦ θείου ὡς ἀληθῶς ἀνδρὸς τοῦ παρακοιμωμένου*, and has the power to grant an *excusatio*, *τοῦ παρακοιμωμένου ἐξκουσσείας ἐδεήθη τινός*. The crucial difference seems to hinge on the fact that in the letters of Nicephorus Uranus golden bulls already in existence are reconfirmed by an imperial directive to the official in charge of the saccellium, whereas in the present letter Leo's anonymous benefactor, in addition to some other unnamed favor, seems to have brought about the issuance of a golden bull for Leo's uncle. See Ep. 37.

8–9 The allusion is to Heb. 4.12: *ζῶν γὰρ ὁ λόγος τοῦ Θεοῦ καὶ ἐνεργὴς καὶ τομώτερος ὑπὲρ πᾶσαν μάχαιραν δίστομον καὶ διϊκνούμενος ἄχρι μερισμοῦ ψυχῆς καὶ πνεύματος, ἁρμῶν τε καὶ μυελῶν, καὶ κριτικὸς ἐνθυμήσεων καὶ ἐννοιῶν καρδίας.*

16–17 Other references to Leo's uncle may be found in Ep. 42.5–6 and possibly Ep. 50.

18 On the protonotarius, cf. Ep. 37.

[1] Oikonomides, *Listes*, 315.
[2] Dölger, *Finanzverwaltung*, 69.
[3] H. Glykatzi-Ahrweiler, *Recherches sur l'administration de l'empire byzantin aux IXe–XIe siècles* (Athens–Paris, 1960), 43.
[4] Dölger, *Finanzverwaltung*, 63–64.
[5] Darrouzès, *Epistoliers*, 218–20.
[6] *Ibid.*, V, 4.5 and 5.20.
[7] *Ibid.*, 218 note 3.
[8] *Ibid.*, V, 5, to Stephen of Nicomedia.

30.

This letter is a verbatim copy of one (no. 333) written by St. Basil of Caesarea. Although there were secular and ecclesiastical *νοτάριοι* attached to various administrative offices, in both Constantinople and the themes, it seems most likely

that Leo's correspondents are ecclesiastical *νοτάριοι* in the service of the patriarchate. One should note that while Leo has adapted the address of Basil's letter, he has left unchanged the text with its singular reference (lines 3–4, *Σὺ οὖν, ὦ παῖ*).

31.

Leo's will is certainly one of the most fascinating documents in the corpus. His self-examination tells us much that we have known or suspected all along, e.g., that he was not always as charitable as he might have been, that his affection for classical literature sometimes got the better of him, that he yielded to emotion. Leo adds to his candor a generous dash of humor–humor that is all the more appealing because it is turned upon himself.

Substantial variations in P and C, the two manuscripts containing the will, indicate that we are dealing with two versions, one earlier, one later and revised. Although there are some points of ambiguity (e.g., in lines 4–5 *οἴδαμεν μὲν*, and in line 16, *ἐθήλυνέ με*, which could be, according to one's perspective, instances of haplography or diplography), the readings of P in general seem the more expressive and correct. Therefore, as a rule, they appear in the text at the expense of the variants offered by C.

Since 937 has been established as Leo's date of birth (see Ep. 13 and notes) and since Leo states in line 7 that he is 66 years old, the date of composition for this document is 1003.

8 These lines contain a reminiscence of Job 31.26: *Ἦ οὐχ ὁρῶμεν ἥλιον τὸν ἐπιφαύσκοντα ἐκλείποντα, σελήνην δὲ φθίνουσαν; οὐ γὰρ ἐπ' αὐτοῖς ἐστί.*

49 The phrase "hewers of wood and drawers of water" is biblical. Leo may have in mind Deut. 29.11–12: *ἀπὸ ξυλοκόπου ὑμῶν καὶ ἕως ὑδροφόρου ὑμῶν*, the climax of an enumeration of the assembled Israelites; or Josh. 9.27, where hewing wood and drawing water is the fate of the people of Gabaon.

52–54 Leo is alluding to Matt. 7.13 (cf. also Luke 13.24): *Εἰσέλθατε διὰ τῆς στενῆς πύλης· ὅτι πλατεῖα ἡ πύλη καὶ εὐρύχωρος ἡ ὁδὸς ἡ ἀπάγουσα εἰς τὴν ἀπώλειαν, καὶ πολλοί εἰσιν οἱ εἰσερχόμενοι δι' αὐτῆς.*

57 This phrase is an adaptation of the *Odyssey*, 4.511: *ὣς ὁ μὲν ἔνθ' ἀπόλωλεν, ἐπεὶ πίεν ἁλμυρὸν ὕδωρ.* The victim is Aias, son of Oileus, who perished as the result of an ill-advised boast quoted in line 504 by Proteus for the benefit of Menelaus: *φῆ ῥ' ἀέκητι θεῶν φυγέειν μέγα λαῖτμα θαλάσσης.*

32.

For a discussion of the identity of the patriarch of Antioch (John III), see the introductory note to Ep. 14. The letter must have been written sometime after August 24, 998, while John was still in Constantinople. However, the circumstances described here are so similar to those in which Agapius I found himself while interned and the tone of this letter so different from the others addressed to the Patriarch of Antioch (Epp. 14–16) that one is led to suspect that the recipient of the present letter was someone other than John III, namely, Agapius I. If this is true, the failure to distinguish between the two men in the addresses might be accounted for by the fact that this letter appears in V, while the others are found in P.

7–9 This anecdote is recorded by Diogenes Laertius, II.35: *τῆς γυναικὸς εἰπούσης, "ἀδίκως ἀποθνῄσκεις," "σὺ δέ," ἔφη, "δικαίως ἐβούλου;"*

11 *ἡ γείτων*: This should refer to the see of Constantinople and the vacancy between the death of Sisinnius II (August 24, 998) and the election of Sergius II (June/July 1001), although there was a vacancy in the patriarchate of Jerusalem between 1006 and 1012.

14 ff. Basil's preoccupation with military affairs caused two interregna in the see of Constantinople in one decade, a situation that seems to have been accompanied by a considerable backlog in lesser appointments as well.

33.

Although the unqualified title canstrisius may refer to either a patriarchal or an imperial official,[1] the relationship between Leo's canstrisius and the cubuclisius (Ep. 46.4 ff. and note) indicates that the addressee of this letter is attached to the patriarchate. The canstrisius was responsible for the patriarch's insignia, assisted him in dressing on ceremonial occasions, and offered the censer for his blessing.[2] Cf. Ep. 46.

2–3 Leo expresses himself similarly in Ep 17.3–4. This could be an indication that the two letters are contemporaneous.

6–7 Here Leo has adapted Job 39.35. The unquoted remainder of the verse reiterates the sense of the preceding clause: *χεῖρα θήσω ἐπὶ στόματί μου. Ἅπαξ λελάληκα, ἐπὶ δὲ τῷ δευτέρῳ οὐ προσθήσω.*

8–10 The allusion is to Aelian, *De natura animalium*, I.37: ὄφεως δὲ εἰ καθίκοιο καλάμῳ, μετὰ τὴν πρώτην πληγὴν ἀτρεμεῖ καὶ νάρκη πεδηθεὶς ἡσυχάζει· εἰ δὲ ἐπαγάγοις δευτέραν ἢ τρίτην, ἀνέρρωσας αὐτόν. The present context, based as it is on Aelian, demands that the sense of ἀποναρκᾶν be "become unnumb." However, this meaning for the verb (and for ἀποναρκοῦν as well) is unattested in both Liddell-Scott and in Lampe's *Patristic Greek Lexicon*. Apparently Leo was being creative, or was just mistaken.

[1] J. Darrouzès, *Recherches sur les 'Οφφίκια de l'église byzantine* (Paris, 1970), 46.
[2] Laurent, *Corpus*, V, 1, 103; cf. Darrouzès, *Recherches*, 47–49.

34.

Although Darrouzès expresses some reservations about the identity of the metropolitan of Nicomedia and the dating of this letter, he does concede the likelihood that Leo's correspondent is his colleague, the (in)famous syncellus Stephen.[1] This conjecture is surely right. Stephen appears to have played a very energetic and controversial role in affairs at Constantinople and elsewhere and to have enjoyed a position of influence with the emperor and the patriarch.[2] In 975 ὁ σύγκελλος καὶ τῆς Νικομηδείας πρόεδρος was sent to Bardas Sclerus to persuade him to lay down his arms.[3] Around 1003[4] he became embroiled in a dispute with Symeon the New Theologian over the cult of Symeon's spiritual father, Symeon Studites. According to Symeon's biographer, Nicetas Stethatus, Stephen had resigned from his see by the time his problems with Symeon began;[5] but, according to Demetrius of Cyzicus, "son collègue de Nicomédie ne déposa sa charge pour revêtir l'habit monacal qu'avant sa mort."[6] He was still alive in 1010 or 1011[7] and died sometime before May 1030, when the metropolitan of Nicomedia named John attended a synod on the Jacobite heresy.[8] If the chronology of I. Hausherr and Nicetas Stethatus is correct, this letter and Ep. 35 will antedate 1003, since Stephen is still in possession of his see (Ep. 35.8). But if, on the other hand, the information provided by Demetrius (who was in a position to know) is accurate, the issue of Stephen's resignation loses its value as a chronological determinant and the dating of these letters remains as much as ever an open question. Stephen's seal is extant.[9]

5 ff. An accurate date for the letter would help determine whether this is simply hyperbole on Stephen's part or whether something more than sloth kept Leo and Stephen from communicating.

23–24 Leo elsewhere gives evidence of a special relationship with Constantine VIII; see Epp. 53.13–14 and especially 54.43–45. Apparently Stephen

is now in Constantinople, while Leo was there recently but left without their crossing paths.

[1]Darrouzès, *Epistoliers*, 192 note 21.
[2]I. Hausherr, ed. and G. Horn, trans., *Un grand mystique byzantin: Vie de Syméon le Nouveau Théologien (949–1022) par Nicétas Stéthatos* (Rome, 1928), 100, no. 74.
[3]Scylitzes, p. 317 (= Cedrenus, II, 420, Bonn ed.).
[4]Hausherr, *Vie de Syméon*, XC.
[5]*Ibid.*, 100, no. 74.
[6]*Cod. Ambros. Gr. 682*, fol. 369^v, cited by Laurent, *Corpus*, V, 1, 272.
[7]Hausherr, *Vie de Syméon*, XC.
[8]Laurent, *Corpus*, V, 1, 272.
[9]*Ibid.*, no. 378.

35.

6 ff. Even Stephen's adversaries acknowledged his intelligence, erudition, and eloquence.[1] His character, however, was open to vigorous debate. Nicetas Stethatus portrays him as conceited, jealous, and unable to endure any threat to his reputation for knowledge—but, then, Stephen is alleged to have called his holy Symeon an ignorant, inarticulate boor.[2] Stephen, too, found his defenders: in Cedrenus, he is *καὶ ἐπὶ σοφίᾳ καὶ ἀρετῇ διαβόητος*,[3] and in the manuscript *Paris 1162*, fol. 89^r, he appears as *τοῦ ὁσίου πατρὸς ἡμῶν Στεφάνου.*[4]

8 *θρόνος*: Stephen still holds his see. For the chronological significance, see the introductory note to Ep. 34.

20 *τὸ Μηδικὸν*: Median oil, i.e., naphtha. The allusion is to Plutarch, *Quaestiones conviviales*, 681C: *τοιαύτη γὰρ γίγνεται διάδοσις καὶ ἀνάφλεξις ἀπὸ τῆς ὄψεως, ὥστε παντελῶς ἀπειράτους ἔρωτος ἡγεῖσθαι τοὺς τὸν Μηδικὸν νάφθαν θαυμάζοντας ἐκ διαστήματος ὑπὸ τοῦ πυρὸς ἀναφλέγομεν· αἱ γὰρ τῶν καλῶν ὄψεις, κἂν πάνυ πόρρωθεν ἀντιβλέπωσι, πῦρ ἐν ταῖς τῶν ἐρωτικῶν ψυχαῖς ἀνάπτουσιν.* The point, then, is that Leo's love, like "Median oil," has blazed up even though the flame, his beloved, is distant. An author himself,[5] Stephen seems to have brought out the best (or the worst) in his correspondents as far as literary allusions are concerned. Four letters to him from Nicephorus Uranus survive,[6] one of which in particular[7] contains an amusing reference to the story of Cronus' eating a rock wrapped in swaddling clothes instead of the infant Zeus—this is apropos of the jaw-breaking bread Nicephorus found on his journey! I have been unable

to find the second allusion, but it seems to concern a pagan magician who poured oil into a bath and set it on fire by incantations.

23 ff. One wonders whether Leo's protestations of friendship and loyalty are to be taken simply at face value as "the rhetoric of affection" or whether the metropolitan of Nicomedia for some reason really did need assurance of Leo's support. It has been suggested that toward the end of his life Stephen had "moins de crédit auprès de l'empereur."[8]

[1]Hausherr, *Vie de Syméon*, 100, no. 74.
[2]*Ibid.*, 102, no. 74.
[3]Scylitzes, 317 (= Cedrenus, II, 420, Bonn ed.).
[4]Hausherr, *Vie de Syméon*, LII.
[5]A treatise on the tripartition of the soul survives, and Hausherr believes he had a hand in the Menologion of Basil (*Vie de Syméon*, LIV–LVI).
[6]Darrouzès, *Epistoliers*, V, 5, 7, 9, and 47.
[7]*Ibid.*, V, 47.33: *τὴν κρονικὴν κατάποσιν*.
[8]Hausherr, *Vie de Syméon*, LVI.

36.

The metropolitan of Ephesus in this letter can be identified with a fair degree of confidence as Theodore. Although the exact period during which Theodore held the see cannot be determined, V. Grumel, by piecing together various scraps of evidence, including two inscriptions,[1] has established the approximate end-points of his reign from between 984–89 until 1018–19.[2] Theodore is associated with another of Leo's correspondents, John III, the patriarch of Antioch and former chartophylax, who addressed to him a treatise on baptism.[3] He may also have been a member of the embassy that escorted the emperors' sister Anna to Kiev for her marriage to Vladimir.[4]

The phrase *διὰ χρυσοβουλλίου* is something of a puzzle. In the strictest sense, golden bulls were simply seals of gold, as opposed to lead or wax, which were attached to official imperial documents. They served more to ornament and verify the authenticity of the documents than to secure their contents.[5] The use of these golden seals was the exclusive prerogative of the emperor.[6] The term "golden bull" also came to signify the document which it accompanied, and it is in this sense that Leo uses the word *χρυσοβούλλιον* elsewhere (Epp. 29.16, 18 and 43.6–7, 17). While Darrouzès acknowledges the difficulty with *διὰ χρυσοβουλλίου*, he stops short of offering an explanation of it. What he does say, however, namely, that the tone of the letter is too serious to warrant interpreting the word in an ironic sense,[7] is no doubt right since Leo usually does take steps to prevent such a misunderstanding on the part of the reader. Be that as it may, Leo's actual intention here

remains baffling. Perhaps this letter was dispatched with a golden bull from Constantinople; or, as L. G. Westerink has pointed out, since the abridged form that appears in the address of V might also stand for χρυσοβούλλιον, an imperial missive might have been the occasion that prompted this letter. Finally, Leo's use of the term may be figurative to underscore the urgency and importance of his plea. Admittedly, none of these suggestions are very satisfactory. Equally unclear are the circumstances that prompted Leo to seek Theodore's guidance. Darrouzès hazards a guess that there may be some connection between the situation in this letter and that of Epp. 53 and 54,[8] but it seems that this would make the "golden bull" even more difficult to explain.

4–5 κεφαλὴ ... ἐκκλησίας: This is probably a diplomatic exaggeration, but it could be literally true if both the patriarchate of Constantinople and the see of Caesarea in Cappodocia were vacant at the time this letter was written, since Ephesus was ranked second among metropolitan sees after Caesarea.

[1] H. Grégoire, *Recueil des inscriptions grecques chrétiennes d'Asie Mineure* (Paris, 1922; reprint, Amsterdam, 1968), no. 115 bis and ter.

[2] Grumel, "Patriarches grecs," 283.

[3] *Ibid.*, 281–82.

[4] Dölger, *Regesten*, no. 778.

[5] F. Dölger and J. Karayannopulos, *Byzantinische Urkundenlehre, I. Die Kaiserurkunden* (Munich, 1968), 140.

[6] *Ibid.*, note 5.

[7] Darrouzès, *Epistoliers*, 194 note 22.

[8] *Ibid.*

37.

Neither the address nor the contents of this letter make it clear to which protonotarius Leo is writing. Among the more likely possibilities are: (1) the protonotarius of the theme (in this case, the Anatolikon), who was its chief civil administrator;[1] (2) the protonotarius who was the head of the patriarchal secretariat;[2] (3) the protonotarius of the drome who was attached to the logothete of the drome and who took over for him in absentia.[3] John, ὁ περίβλεπτος ἐκεῖνος ἀνὴρ ἐν βασιλείοις,[4] was protonotarius of the drome during the reign of Basil II, but later, in fulfillment of St. Symeon's prophecy, was the victim of the emperor's condemnation and punishment.[5] The emperor Romanus Argyrus appointed him syncellus.[6] Since Leo's correspondent appears to be different from the protonotarius in Ep. 29, for whom the intercession of a third party was necessary, the protonotarius of the Anatolikon theme may be eliminated. Of the remaining two, one is inclined to give

preference to John the protonotarius of the drome. However, the patriarchal protonotarius (and other anonymous protonotarii) was no doubt a learned man, at least to his friends, and equally capable of inspiring affection. See Ep. 29.

10 The allusion is to the *Iliad*, 23.536, and refers to Eumelus who came in last in the chariot race at the funeral games for Patroclus: λοῖσθος ἀνὴρ ὥριστος ἐλαύνει μώνυχας ἵππους.

[1]Oikonomides, *Listes*, 315.
[2]Laurent, *Corpus*, V, 1, p. 98.
[3]Oikonomides, *Listes*, 311.
[4]Hausherr, *Vie de Syméon*, 158, no. 113.
[5]*Ibid.*
[6]Scylitzes, 375 (= Cedrenus, II, 486, Bonn ed.).

38.

The address of this letter adds further complications to an already controversial problem, i.e., the connection or lack thereof between ἰδικός and εἰδικός. In (my photograph of) the manuscript, the τῆς is fully and clearly written out. However, the proximity of the final ς to the ε of the following word indicates that V originally had ἰδικ; further, the abbreviation for ῆς is unusually ambiguous. Lambros' reading of εἰδικόν is not, at least prima facie, implausible.

Bury maintains that there is no relationship whatsoever between ὁ ἐπὶ τοῦ εἰδικοῦ (ὁ εἰδικός) and ἡ ἰδικὴ περιουσία (= res privata) or ἡ ἰδικὴ κτῆσις (= sacrum patrimonium),[1] while Dölger believes that the λόγος εἰδικός had its origin in the (eastern) pretorian prefect's ἰδικὴ τράπεζα,[2] which was in turn connected with the res privata.[3] He further observes that before the tenth century, εἰδικός is consistently spelled ἰδικός, and that in works "welche mit der literarischen Tätigkeit des Kaisers Konstantinos Porphyrogennetos zusammenhängen, ebenso konsequent die Schreibung εἰδικός durchgeführt ist."[4]

Leo's use of the feminine substantive ἡ εἰδική (i.e., κτῆσις, περιουσία, τράπεζα?) appears to be unusual, if not unique: the normal expression for the bureau is τὸ εἰδικὸν (σήκρητον) and its chief officer, ὁ εἰδικός or ὁ (ἐπὶ) τοῦ εἰδικοῦ. In any case, it is beyond doubt that this official formed part of the Byzantine financial administration. He served as a sort of quartermaster general for military expeditions; and the imperial workshops (ἐργοδόσια) and their products (e.g., of gold and silk) also fell under the supervision of his department.[5]

Around the year 1000, a piece of silk bearing the names of Michael, primicerius, coetonites, and eidicus, and Peter, archon of Zeuxippus, was placed in the tomb of Charlemagne by Otto III.[6] Charles Diehl attributes the fabric to the tenth

century, probably the middle, on stylistic grounds.[7] He also observes that Otto III had access to such material through his mother, Theophano, and cites, without accepting it, the conjecture of Martin who thought to identify this Michael with Michael *κατάρχων τοῦ κοιτῶνος*, mentioned by Leo the Deacon in 969.[8] But surely Otto III himself had equal opportunity for acquiring Byzantine silk in view of the continuing negotiations (initiated by Philagathus in 995) with Byzantium for a porphyrogenita. The question then becomes whether Otto III chose to place a family heirloom in Charlemagne's tomb or whether the silk was of more recent manufacture. If the latter is true—and at this point it is purely conjecture—then it is most likely that Leo's correspondent preceded Michael as *εἰδικός*, and we have at least a terminus ante quem for the letter.

[1]Bury, *System*, 98.
[2]Dölger, *Finanzverwaltung*, 35.
[3]*Ibid.*, 36.
[4]*Ibid.*, 36 note 4.
[5]Oikonomides, *Listes*, 316–17; Bury, *System*, 99.
[6]C. Diehl, "L'étoffe byzantine du reliquaire de Charlemagne," in *Bulićev Zbornik* (Zagreb, 1924), 446.
[7]*Ibid.*, 447.
[8]*Ibid.*; Leo the Deacon, *History*, ed. C. Hase (Bonn, 1828), V, 6, p. 86.

39.

On the addressee, see the preceding letter and note. This letter is preserved by both P and V. As with Ep. 45 (also found in P and V) and Ep. 31 (P and C), the variants here seem to be deliberate and not the results of copying errors. Since the two versions do not differ substantially in terms of meaning, the choice between them is to be made chiefly on stylistic and aesthetic grounds. Taken collectively, the readings of V seem to be superior to and present fewer problems than those of P and for these reasons appear, with one exception, in the text.

13–14 Leo's excuse, which alleges generals, emperors, et al. as his reason for not writing, could very well be applied to almost any point in Basil II's reign. The information that can be gleaned from the letter is slight and far from certain. Lord Leo, as *εἰδικός*, was normally based in Constantinople and presumably was there when the letter was written, although this official could and did accompany imperial expeditions as a chief supply officer.[1] Leo, likewise, presumably wrote from the Anatolikon theme. If Leo's use of the plural *βασιλεῖς* is significant and not rhetorical exaggeration, the implication is that both Basil II and Constantine VIII are involved in some sort of military situation. This dovetails nicely with one of our scraps of information about Constantine VIII for the years

976–1025: he was present at the battle of Abydos on April 13, 989.[2] It seems just possible to suggest as a tentative date for this letter the period during or shortly after the revolt of Bardas Sclerus and Bardas Phocas (987–89) which involved the whole of Asia Minor. Leo was certainly in a position to be affected by this civil turmoil, but again it should be emphasized that our information is too vague to allow any chronological certainty.

[1] Dölger, *Finanzverwaltung*, 38.
[2] Scylitzes, 337 (= Cedrenus, II, 444, Bonn ed.).

40.

The circumstances that prompted this letter are obscure, as are the identities of Leo's secretary and his "most esteemed lord." Methodius appears to have been a close personal friend of Leo's. Cf. Epp. 4 and 41.

41.

This letter was written before 998, for in that year Leo wrote (from the West) to console Methodius on the loss of his father. Cf. Epp. 4 and 40.

42.

The identity of the judge is unknown. Darrouzès suggests that it could be Mitylenaeus,[1] the addressee of Ep. 25. The unqualified title, though, indicates that the judge of Leo's theme, Anatolikon, is meant, and the difference in tone between the two letters also militates against identifying the judge of this letter with Mitylenaeus; however, the address may be abridged.

2 *οἱ τῆς μετάξης* seem to be people in the silk industry, which was subject to stringent regulation in all its phases.[2] They appear to be different from *οἱ πονηροί* of line 4, but the brevity of the context allows some leeway in interpretation.

5–6 If Leo's correspondent is the judge of the Anatolikon theme, then the uncle should be one of Synada's twenty suffragan bishops. Leo intervened on behalf of his uncle on at least one other occasion. Cf. Ep. 29.

[1]Darrouzès, *Epistoliers*, 197 note 24.
[2]Cf. R. S. Lopez, "Silk Industry in the Byzantine Empire," *Speculum*, 20 (1945), 1–42.

43.

This letter, apart from the information it yields on the economy of Anatolia, is of value for giving an insight into the personality of Basil II. Michael Psellus[1] paints a portrait of a man who had little or no patience for either learning or the learned and who, so far from adopting the stylistic pretensions of his day, employed a prose that was plain and utilitarian. Leo has very sensibly taken into account his sovereign's literary predilections and written a letter that, unlike some of his other efforts, is a paradigm of simplicity and lucidity.

Leo employs the term *χρυσοβούλλιον* twice in this letter (lines 6–7, 17), but it is not clear whether it is a question of two different documents or of a single one which originated in the reign of Romanus II (959–63) and which evidently provided the metropolitan see of Synada with an (annual?) allotment of oil and wine, among other things. The golden bull of lines 6–7, if it is to be distinguished from that of Romanus II, ought to be connected in some way with the latter as well as with the nondelivery of goods that had been granted by it and that seem to have become expected. Although it was customary for a new emperor to confirm the privileges granted by his predecessor(s) soon after his accession,[2] Leo makes no mention of any subsequent renewals of Romanus II's golden bull. However, Leo's silence would be understandable if his difficulties originated in the period following Basil's assertion of independence from Basil the paracoemomenus in 985. After Basil's deposition, the emperor ordered that all golden bulls from the years 976–85 be submitted for ratification.[3] In his novel of 996,[4] Basil II declares that all such golden bulls that do not bear the word *ἐτηρήθη* in the emperor's own hand are null and void. It may be that Basil II, acting on the advice of "some people" (lines 22 ff.), has declined to affix the mark of validation and has returned to Leo the golden bull that was issued earlier by the paracoemomenus and that confirmed the provisions contained in the golden bull of Romanus II; or, as a result of the same advice, the emperor may have issued a second golden bull that eliminated many, if not all, of the former benefits. Unfortunately, there is simply not enough information to determine the number of golden bulls involved or the date when this letter was written.

9 τῷ ζαρζάκῳ: As Darrouzès notes,[5] this word is otherwise unattested and seems to be a local expression. L. Robert, in what must be the definitive work on the processing of dung in Anatolia, identifies this substance with the Turkish *tezek*.[6] Herewith the recipe: Collect dung, add water and straw. Knead well, form into desired shape, and dry.[7]

16 τοῦ μακαριωτάτου σου πατρὸς καὶ βασιλέως: i.e., Romanus II. Leo apparently hopes that filial devotion may prompt the emperor to resume the delivery of goods to Synada if he won't respond to a plea based on actual need.

[1]Psellus, *Chronographie*, ed. and trans. E. Renauld, I (Paris, 1926), 30–31.

[2]Dölger, *Regesten*, no. 758, from the year 976, which confirms privileges granted by Romanus II, Nicephorus Phocas, and John Tzimisces to the monastery of the Lavra on Mt. Athos.

[3]Zepos, I, 270.

[4]*Ibid.*

[5]Darrouzès, *Epistoliers*, 198 note 25.

[6]Robert, "Kordakia," 116.

[7]*Ibid.*, 130.

44.

One assumes that the addressees of the present letter and of Ep. 7, written in the spring of 997, are identical. Neither the date nor the circumstances of this letter can be determined from its contents, although one wonders whether there is any connection between it and the preceding one to Basil II. However, Leo's request for aid may be a purely personal one and involve the see of Synada indirectly, if at all. For the title and duties of ὁ γενικός, see Ep. 7.

2 The allusion is to Job 30.20: κέκραγα δὲ πρὸς σὲ καὶ οὐκ ἀκούεις μου, ἔστησαν δὲ καὶ κατενόησάν με.

3 μοι: The manuscript reading has been retained as a "hyper-correct dative."

5 ff. Leo has rephrased an anecdote about Diogenes of Sinope found in Diogenes Laertius, VI.49: ᾔτει ποτὲ ἀνδριάντα· ἐρωτηθεὶς δὲ διὰ τί τοῦτο ποιεῖ, "μελετῶ," εἶπεν, "ἀποτυγχάνειν."

9 γενικῶς: a pun on the title of Leo's correspondent.

45.

The recipient of this letter is unknown, but, as Darrouzès suggests,[1] he is doubtless one of Leo's ecclesiastical colleagues, a metropolitan or patriarch.

2 This letter is found in both P and V. As is evidenced by the very first line, the two copies show variations that are the result of deliberate changes by an editor (probably Leo himself) rather than carelessness on the part of a copyist. Since these textual variations (as opposed to omissions) are slight and do not substantially affect the meaning, the choice between them is not a clear-cut one. Therefore, in the interests of consistency, I have preferred the text of P because it is more complete.

7–8 *ὡς νιφάδας ἐπιστολῶν πέμψας*: I take this to be the "humor" mentioned in line 6 and translate accordingly.

9–10 See note on line 2.

15–17 Although the endings of letters are vulnerable to loss, the omission of these lines in V is most likely the work of an editor or copyist: the deletion of obscure references or those lacking immediate interest to the general public is not an uncommon phenomenon in collections of letters.[2] The present difficulty centers on the definition of *οἱ πρίσται*. Darrouzès notes without discussion that they are sawfish,[3] an interpretation that prompts Robert to a rather entertaining rebuttal.[4] He proposes instead that they are marble cutters from the famed quarries near Synada.[5] (Synnadic marble, also known locally as *Δοκιμίτης* or *Δοκιμαῖον*, from the nearby village *Δοκιμία*, is white with veins in shades of purple, and enjoyed great popularity from the imperial Roman period onward.)[6] Such a request on the part of Leo's correspondent is not prima facie implausible, especially since work on architectural elements (e.g., revêtements, for which Synnadic marble was frequently used) was completed at the construction site itself;[7] and it is one that should evoke the sympathy of anyone who has ever tried to engage the services of a reliable, skilled workman. However, two objections may be made to this ingenious suggestion. First of all, the evidence for taking *πρίστης* in the sense of "stonecutter" instead of the usual "woodcutter" is rather slight: of the attestations Robert offers, the only bona fide one is a papyrus (albeit from the Byzantine period) which mentions a certain Leontius *πρίστης σκληρῶν πλακείων*;[8] and a more contemporary witness, Nicholas Mesarites (12th–13th c.) in his ekphrasis of the Church of the Holy Apostles at Constantinople, uses the word *τεχνίτης* for the person who covers the church's walls with marble revêtement (*πριστὸς λίθος*).[9] Second, although the quarry retained the potential for excavation as recently as the late nineteenth cen-

tury,[10] Robert does not demonstrate that the quarry was actually in production during the late tenth century: the latest attested use of Synnadic marble is in the Sacred Palace built by the emperor Theophilus in the second quarter of the ninth century.[11] The absence of any mention of the quarries, or the income therefrom, in Ep. 43 (to the emperor) may be excused on the grounds that it was in Leo's best interests to suppress this information. Still, given the limited corroborative evidence, Robert seems to go too far when he says: "La lettre de Léon de Synnada atteste l'activité des scieurs à Synnada au Xe siècle et leur renommée . . . Les carrières n'étaient pas abandonnées."[12] In addition to "sawyer," Liddell-Scott (s.v.) also defines *πρίστης* as "saw" or "file." While this interpretation may be less dramatic than Robert's, it is also less complicated. In addition, a present of files or saws is more in line with the gifts exchanged in Ep. 48, a cowl and some pomegranates.

[1]Darrouzès, *Epistoliers*, 199.
[2]L. Robert, "Les kordakia de Nicée," *Journal des Savants* (1962), 6.
[3]Darrouzès, *Epistoliers*, 200 note 27.
[4]Robert, "Kordakia" (1962), 5–10.
[5]*Ibid.*, 13.
[6]*Ibid.*, 13 ff.
[7]*Ibid.*, 36–37.
[8]*Ibid.*, 12.
[9]*Ibid.*, 38.
[10]*Ibid.*, 40 and note 3.
[11]*Ibid.*, 32–33.
[12]*Ibid.*, 39.

46.

On the role of the canstrisius, see Ep. 33, note.

4 *κουβουκλείσιος*: The title of cubuclisius first appears in the hierarchical lists at the beginning of the tenth century.[1] Although the original function of the cubuclisius remains unclear, the proliferation of this title among persons representing all grades in the church hierarchy, as evidenced by seals, indicates that it became honorific in nature.[2]

6 *ὁ ἀδελφὸς*: Leo most likely means his own brother. Elsewhere (e.g., Epp. 1.10, 4.2, and 5.2), Leo uses the noun to refer to his correspondent, and it is clear, sometimes explicitly, that the fraternal relationship is a spiritual one. Cf. Ep. 47.9.

[1]Darrouzès, *Recherches*, 39.
[2]*Ibid.*, 42.

47.

As Darrouzès notes,[1] Leo's correspondent here and in the two following letters is doubtless the (grand) chartophylax of Hagia Sophia in Constantinople, a position, in the late tenth century, of some importance and responsibility. In addition to maintaining the patriarchal archives and supervising the publication and distribution of the acts of the patriarchate,[2] the chartophylax also responded to those questions of a canonical nature that could be handled without the benefit of a synod.[3] It is in connection with this last function that we meet the man who is the most likely recipient of this letter, the chartophylax John (later John III, patriarch of Antioch). Grumel attributes to him during his tenure as chartophylax a treatise entitled *Responsa de baptismo ad Theodorum metropolitanum Ephesinum*, which has been transmitted under the name of John of Antioch.[4]

John's tenure extended from sometime after 987, when the chartophylax Stephen is known to have been active,[5] until October 4, 996, when he was named patriarch of Antioch.[6] This period of activity, combined with the fact that we are relatively well informed about John and that, as patriarch of Antioch, he is the probable recipient of four more of Leo's letters, makes him an attractive candidate for the addressee in this series as well. Cf. Epp. 14–16 and 32 to the patriarch of Antioch and Ep. 36 to the metropolitan of Ephesus. The chartophylax John was also the recipient of a letter which Nicephorus Uranus wrote jointly to him and to Symeon of Euchaïta; see Darrouzès, *Epistoliers*, V, 39 (pp. 238–39).

6 *τὸ γειτονεῖν*: The exact location of the "neighborhood" is unclear. Presumably it is in Constantinople where the chartophylax naturally spent the majority of his time and of which John was perhaps a native—as patriarch of Antioch he is surnamed *ὁ πολίτης*.[7] As a metropolitan, Leo, too, would have occasion to visit the capital, and the reference would then be to his quarters in Constantinople (shared with his brother? cf. line 9). On the other hand, the two following letters, which place the chartophylax in Synada (or the vicinity) and Dorylaeum, suggest the possibility that the chartophylax or his family had property in Asia Minor.

9 *τοῦ ἀδελφοῦ*: In the absence of any statement qualifying this relationship as a purely spiritual one, it is simplest to take *τοῦ ἀδελφοῦ* to mean Leo's own brother, as in Ep. 46.6.

[1] Darrouzès, *Epistoliers*, 201 note 29.
[2] Laurent, *Corpus*, V, 1, 67. See also Darrouzès, *Recherches*, 334–53.
[3] Grumel, "Patriarches grecs," 282.
[4] *Ibid.*
[5] Laurent, *Corpus*, V, 1, 70.
[6] *Histoire de Yahya*, 445.
[7] Grumel, "Patriarcat," 136 and note 5.

48.

On the identity of the chartophylax, see Ep. 47.

7 *τὰ συνήθη δῶρα*: The exchange of small gifts between correspondents was not an unusual practice and apparently a regular (*συνήθη*) one for Leo and the chartophylax. Cf. Ep. 45.15–17 and note.

8–9 *τὴν οὖν δίοδον*: If this letter is connected with the following one, as seems likely, Leo ought to be referring to his passing through Dorylaeum and promising to announce his arrival to the chartophylax. On the other hand, this line could also be translated "we shall give you directions for passing through." In this case, since Leo seems to be in Synada, the chartophylax ought to be traveling through it or its environs.

49.

On the identity of the chartophylax, see Ep. 47.

2 *τὸ Δορύλαιον*: Dorylaeum, located in the Opsikion theme and approximately equidistant from Constantinople and Synada, was an excellent site for a rendezvous since it was accessible by highway from the four cardinal points. It lay on an important military route (to Arab territory), and the Thracesion and Opsikion themes mustered their troops there.[1]

3 *ἀδελφὲ*: This form of address might be intended to recall Leo's gratitude in Ep. 48 for the kindness shown to Leo's brother by the chartophylax, acting *in loco fratris*. But this might also be reading too much into an expression that was in common use between clergymen and others.

[1] S. Vryonis, Jr., *The Decline of Medieval Hellenism in Asia Minor and the Process of Islamization from the Eleventh through the Fifteenth Century* (Berkeley, 1971), 32.

50.

Darrouzès suggests that the recipient of this letter is the chartophylax or Leo's uncle[1] (cf. line 4). Ἄλλος at the beginning of a new entry in a manuscript can signify that the author (or, in this case, the addressee) is the same as the preceding

one. Yet, even allowing for the difference in subject matter, the contrast in tone between this letter and those to the chartophylax makes it difficult to believe that they were written to the same person. The more likely candidate is Leo's uncle the bishop, to whom he has referred on other occasions (e.g., Epp. 29.16–17 and 42.5–6) and in language which at least does not make the identification impossible, e.g., *τὸν γέροντα καὶ θεῖόν μου*, Ep. 42.7.

6–7 The adaptation is from Ps. 142.2: *Καὶ μὴ εἰσέλθῃς εἰς κρίσιν μετὰ τοῦ δούλου σου, ὅτι οὐ δικαιωθήσεται ἐνώπιόν σου πᾶς ζῶν.*

[1] Darrouzès, *Epistoliers*, 202.

51.

Nicetas' brother is very likely Theodegius, who served as metropolitan of Athens from ca. 981 to 1006.[1] As Darrouzès observes,[2] the following letter (Ep. 52) seems to be written to a metropolitan, and it may be that the part of the address giving Nicetas' own title and see has been omitted here, since it is unlikely that a metropolitan would be identified by his brother's see. Darrouzès also expresses doubt that the recipients of these two letters are identical,[3] but it does not seem necessary to assume the existence of a second correspondent in order to account for the contrast between the levity of this letter and the gravity of the following one. The radical difference in subject matter goes far in explaining the letters' difference in tone: this letter is nothing more than a follow-up note after a (chance?) meeting between Leo and Nicetas at Pylae; the other, a status report on what appears to be a power struggle involving Nicetas and an unnamed villain in the capital. However, this does not resolve the problem of the address (i.e., the identification of Nicetas as the brother of the metropolitan of Athens), and Darrouzès may be right after all in suspecting that V, which is not overly reliable in the matter of headings, has erred in assigning the Nicetas of the present letter as the recipient of Ep. 52.

The mention of Pylae leads to the speculation that this letter was composed around the same time as Ep. 54. This may be the case, although if, as seems likely, Leo's usual route to Constantinople involved taking the ferry from Pylae, the proximity of the letters in the Vienna manuscript and their mention of Pylae may also be mere coincidence.

3 *ἐν Πύλαις*: Pylae was located on the Asiatic side of Propontis. According to Leo (Ep. 54.28 ff.), Pylae was not much of a town—for people, at any rate. Its chief asset apparently lay in its being a terminal from which livestock were ferried to the capital. However, since Leo went there with

the expectation of gaining passage to Constantinople (and it was here that a successful attempt was made to intercept him), it is reasonable to assume that a "regular" ferry service operated between Pylae and Constantinople and that, at least occasionally, it formed the final leg of Leo's journey from Synada to the capital. Pylae also figures in Constantine VII Porphyrogenitus' *De cerimoniis*,[4] in which he relates the procedures preliminary to the emperor's crossing from Constantinople and the ceremonies attending his arrival there.

14 Ἀναξιμένης: Anaximenes of Lampsacus, active in the second half of the fourth century B.C., was a historian and rhetorician whose *Rhetorica ad Alexandrum* is our only extant pre-Aristotelian handbook on rhetoric. Since, however, the *Rhetorica ad Alexandrum* was transmitted under the name of Aristotle and was not attributed to Anaximenes until the sixteenth century, Leo's knowledge of him will have been acquired at second hand through such sources as Plutarch, *Praecepta gerendae reipublicae*, 803B (*ἐπὶ δὲ τῶν Ἐφόρου καὶ Θεοπόμπου καὶ Ἀναξιμένους ῥητορειῶν καὶ περιόδων, ἃς περαίνουσιν ἐξοπλίσαντες τὰ στρατεύματα καὶ παρατάξαντες, ἔστιν εἰπεῖν οὐδεὶς σιδήρου ταῦτα μωραίνει πέλας*) and Dionysius of Halicarnassus, *De Isaeo*, 19 (*Ἀναξιμένην δὲ τὸν Λαμψακηνὸν ἐν ἁπάσαις μὲν ταῖς ἰδέαις τῶν λόγων τετράγωνόν τινα εἶναι βουλόμενον ... οὐ μέντοι τέλειόν γε ἐν οὐδεμιᾷ τούτων τῶν ἰδεῶν ἀλλ' ἀσθενῆ καὶ ἀπίθανον ὄντα ἐν ἁπάσαις θεωρῶν*). It will be observed that neither of these remarks is particularly flattering to Anaximenes.

[1]Laurent, *Corpus*, V, 1, 444 (no. 395).
[2]Darrouzès, *Epistoliers*, 203 note 31.
[3]*Ibid.*
[4]Constantine Porphyrogenitus, *De cerimoniis aulae byzantinae*, I, ed. J. J. Reiske (Bonn, 1829), 474 and 493.

52.

For a discussion of the identity of Leo's correspondent, see the introductory note to Ep. 51. The circumstances that prompted this letter, apparently written from the capital, remain obscure, as does the interval of time between it and the preceding one.

53.

This letter and the one following should be taken together as a two-pronged effort on Leo's part to gain admittance to the synod being held for the purpose of electing a patriarch—and even to the capital itself, which he has been kept from entering, apparently on orders from the emperor himself. Although V does not transmit the addressees of either of the two letters, Leo's repeated use of apostrophe allows us to identify his correspondents with certainty: in the present letter they are the bishops participating in the synod; in Ep. 54, the emperor Basil II. The approximate date at which the letters were written is also established with a relative degree of ease and confidence. The concurrence of events mentioned by Leo, i.e., the synod for the election of a patriarch (53.33 ff. and passim), the emperor's return from the Bulgarian front (54.8 ff.), and the restoration of Hagia Sophia (54.12 ff. and 54.26), point to the early months of 996, before the consecration of Sisinnius II on Easter Sunday, April 12, 996.

More difficult to ascertain is the nature of the controversy which resulted in the exclusion of Leo (and others) from the synod. In the context of the tenth century, the affair of the tetragamy immediately comes to mind as the most likely source of Leo's predicament, and it may be that Leo was involved in a final convulsion of the internal schism that had resulted from Leo VI's fourth marriage to Zoe Carbonopsine in 906. In support of this, it may be observed that Leo implies the existence of a state of schism among the bishops of the Church (53.26–28) and that of the eleven acts extant from the patriarchate of Sisinnius II, whose election is the topic of these two letters, three (four?) are concerned with marital legislation,[1] and moreover that the Tome of Union was repromulgated during his reign.[2] Taking into consideration the notorious longevity and acrimony of dissension in the Eastern Church, one might consider the matter settled were it not for the relatively recent publication of two tracts which present opposing arguments on another point of contention in the tenth century.[3] These tracts consider the relationship between the patriarch of Constantinople and the other bishops, particularly as it applies to episcopal elections. The first treatise, whose author remains anonymous and which is dated ca. 963–69 by its editor, Darrouzès,[4] maintains that these bishops (specifically the metropolitans) are independent of the patriarch and that he is not entitled to participate in the actual electoral process but is restricted to performing the ordination of the candidate chosen by them. The second one, by Nicetas of Amasia, is believed by the same editor to have been written some thirty years later, or, in other words, to be approximately contemporary with Leo's Epp. 53 and 54.[5] Nicetas argues that not only does the patriarch have the right to vote but also that the other bishops stand in the relation of suffragans to him.

The controversy had its antecedents in the patriarchate of Theophylact (933–56), whose lack of interest in church affairs allowed (or required) the bishops to assume a more powerful role in their management. The situation came to a head

during the reign of Polyeuctus: *καὶ τῶν μὲν* (i.e., *ἀρχιερέων*) *εἰς ἑαυτοὺς ἑλκόντων τὴν ἄδειαν τοῦ ψηφίζεσθαι οὓς ἂν ἐγκρίνοιεν, τοῦ δὲ* (i.e., *Πολυεύκτου*) *τὰς ψήφους αἰτιωμένου, ὡς οὐκ ἀπαθῶς γινομένας οὐδὲ κατὰ γνώμης εὐθύτητα, καὶ σπεύδοντος κοινοῦσθαι αὐτῷ τοὺς ἀρχιερεῖς περὶ τῶν μελλόντων ψηφίζεσθαι.*[6]

Unfortunately for both parties, their wrangling succeeded only in provoking the emperor Nicephorus II Phocas to dispense with their services altogether by appropriating for himself the selection (*προχείρισις*) of bishops.[7] Although some bishops (*τῶν εὐριπίστων καὶ κολάκων*)[8] did actually subscribe to the document conferring this power on the emperor,[9] it did not remain in effect for long (from 964 until the accession of John Tzimisces)[10] and certainly cannot be said to have resolved the conflict which appears to have festered for another thirty years and to have been kept alive by the checkered history of the patriarchate during this period.[11]

Darrouzès is thoroughly convinced that the dispute in which Leo was embroiled is the very one that forms the subject of the two treatises—so convinced, in fact, that he uses Leo's letters 53 and 54 to date the one written by Nicetas of Amasia; and, citing a "parenté de tempérament" between Leo and Nicetas, puts forward the opinion that it was Leo's support of the primacy of the patriarch of Constantinople that caused his exclusion from the synod.[12] Yet even if the treatise by Nicetas is correctly dated and if it is more than a purely rhetorical exercise, Leo's own words would seem to place him in the opposite camp, i.e., with the group favoring the autonomy of the metropolitans. Still, regardless of the side Leo took in it, this controversy seems to require the presence of a patriarch, and one wonders if the mere anticipation of his election were enough to bring matters to a head. Knowing the nature of the legislation (*νόμος*) that was placed before the synod (53.32–33) would surely help to resolve the difficulty of interpreting these two letters, but unfortunately neither Leo himself nor the documents extant from the patriarchate of Sisinnius are of use here. One would like to know more about Basil II's interest in the affair, since Leo gives the impression that he is somehow at the back of it. Unclear, too, is the connection, if any, between these two letters and Epp. 28 and 36, to the patriarch and to the metropolitan of Ephesus respectively.

6–8 In his *De fraterno amore* (478D), Plutarch mentions the "fraternal" and cooperative relationship between the various pairs of bodily parts: *ἀλλ' ἐν αὐτῷ σώματι τὰ πλεῖστα τῶν ἀναγκαίων διττὰ καὶ ἀδελφὰ καὶ μηχανησαμένη* (i.e., *ἡ φύσις*), *χεῖρας πόδας ὄμματ' ὦτα ῥῖνας, ἐδίδαξεν ὅτι ταῦτα σωτηρίας ἕνεκα καὶ συμπράξεως κοινῆς, οὐ διαφορᾶς καὶ μάχης οὕτως διέστησεν.*

10–13 Plutarch cites the examples of Lucullus and Polydeuces in *De fraterno amore*, 484D–E: *ὁ γοῦν Λεύκολλος οὐκ ἠξίωσε τἀδελφοῦ πρότερος τὴν ἀρχὴν λαβεῖν πρεσβύτερος ὤν, ἀλλὰ τὸν αὑτοῦ παρεὶς καιρὸν τὸν ἐκείνου περιέμεινεν. Ὁ δὲ Πολυδεύκης οὐδὲ θεὸς ἠθέλησε*

μόνος ἀλλὰ μᾶλλον ἡμίθεος σὺν τἀδελφῷ γενέσθαι καὶ τῆς θνητῆς μερίδος μετασχεῖν ἐπὶ τῷ μεταδοῦναι τῆς ἀθανασίας ἐκείνῳ.

19–20 Leo has adapted this from a passage in Aristotle's *Physica*, I.2, 185A11–12 (= I.3, 186A9–10), which is critical of the eristic arguments of Parmenides and his pupil Melissus and refers to the latter in particular: *καὶ γὰρ ψευδῆ λαμβάνουσι καὶ ἀσυλλόγιστοί εἰσιν.* Μᾶλλον δ' ὁ (i.e., λόγος) Μελίσσου *φορτικὸς καὶ οὐκ ἔχων ἀπορίαν, ἀλλ' ἑνὸς ἀτόπου δοθέντος τὰ ἄλλα συμβαίνει. τοῦτο δὲ οὐδὲν χαλεπόν.* A similar phrase occurs in the anonymous treatise defending the rights of metropolitans against the encroachment of the patriarch: *ἀρχῆς δοθείσης ἀτόπου.*[13]

21 ff. Darrouzès has suggested that the victim of the slight may have been Theodore of Cyzicus and his defender, the anonymous author of the treatise on behalf of the metropolitans. The *βασιλικὸς τόμος καὶ δόγμα* would then refer to that law of Nicephorus II Phocas which in 964 conferred upon him the prerogative of appointing bishops.[14] This hypothesis, which places the incident of Leo's youth in the milieu of the power struggle between the patriarch and his bishops is an attractive one, apart from the speculative identification of the principals. However, as Darrouzès himself recognizes, its bases are somewhat less than secure. First, there is the question of whether a twenty-seven-year-old man can properly be called a *παιδάριον*. The second point is that the quarrel that prompted Nicephorus II's high-handed measure seems to have been one between the patriarch and the bishops as a group rather than between two factions of bishops. While neither of these obstacles is insurmountable, they do seem to leave the door open for another interpretation of these lines.

22–23 This line contains an allusion to Oration 29.2 of Gregory of Nazianzus (PG, 36, col. 76B): *Διὰ τοῦτο μονὰς ἀπ' ἀρχῆς εἰς δυάδα κινηθεῖσα, μέχρι τριάδος ἔστη.*

38–40 The source of this allusion has eluded both Darrouzès and myself, as well as Westerink. Our ignorance on this point is particularly unfortunate since knowledge of the context in which it is found ought to be helpful in determining whether Leo here intends a reference to some patricular person (e.g., the emperor or the patriarch) as well as the cause of the schism—there is, naturally enough, talk of "freedom" in the anonymous treatise.[15]

65 ff. In his *Ecclesiastical History*, IV.6.3, Eusebius, citing Ariston of Pella as his source, makes mention of a decree which was promulgated by the emperor Hadrian after quelling the revolt of Bar Chochebas. This

notice, however, does not specify the three-mile or six-mile limitation: τὸ πᾶν ἔθνος ἐξ ἐκείνου καὶ τῆς περὶ τὰ Ἱεροσόλυμα γῆς πάμπαν ἐπιβαίνειν εἴργεται νόμου δόγματι καὶ διατάξεσιν Ἀδριανοῦ, ὡς ἂν μηδ' ἐξ ἀπόπτου θεωροῖεν τὸ πατρῷον ἔδαφος, ἐγκελευσαμένου·

[1]Grumel, *Regestes*, vol. I, fasc. II, nos. 804, 805, 807, and perhaps 812.

[2]*Ibid.*, no. 813. Although the accuracy of Scylitzes-Cedrenus, who provides the only historical evidence for the reissue of the Tome of Union under Sisinnius II, has been questioned (Grumel, *l.c.*), L. G. Westerink has shown this information to be correct in *Nicholas I, Patriarch of Constantinople: Miscellaneous Writings*, Dumbarton Oaks Texts, 6 (Washington, D.C., 1981), 149. The source of confusion on this point is the conflation in the editions of the appendix commemorating the reunion under Basil II and Constantine VIII with acclamations originating in the patriarchate of Nicholas II Chrysoberges —a combination not found in the manuscripts.

[3]Darrouzès, *Documents*, 116–59; 160–75.

[4]*Ibid.*, 30.

[5]*Ibid.*, 32.

[6]Zonaras, *Annales*, ed. Pinder, III (Bonn, 1897), 505.

[7]*Ibid.*

[8]Scylitzes, 274 (= Cedrenus, II, 368, Bonn ed.).

[9]*Ibid.*

[10]Scylitzes, 285 (= Cedrenus, II, 379–80. Bonn ed.).

[11]Darrouzès, *Documents*, 32.

[12]*Ibid.*

[13]*Ibid.*, 138.6 and 154.26.

[14]*Ibid.*, 31 and note 2; 32 and note 1.

[15]Darrouzès, *Documents*, 136–38.

54.

This letter was written to the emperor Basil II in the early months of 996. Se Ep. 53 and notes.

8–12 This piece of information dovetails perfectly with the evidence of Yahy of Antioch who explains that Basil II's campaign against the Bulgarian during the years 991–95 was responsible for the vacancy in the patr archate of Constantinople between Nicholas II and Sisinnius II.[1] It shoul also establish once and for all that the Greek sources, Cedrenus an Zonaras, who place this vacancy after the abdication of Anthony Stu dites, are simply wrong.[2]

12 Ἀνταρκτικὸς: Leo's sense of world geography seems a trifle shaky, bu he may intend here a reference to Basil's rescue mission to Syria in th spring of 995.

13–15 Leo the Deacon[3] informs us that it took six years to repair the extensive damage suffered by Hagia Sophia in the earthquake on the night of October 25, 989.[4]

28 Πυλῶν: See Ep. 51.3 and note.

43–45 Leo elsewhere gives evidence of a special relationship between himself and Constantine VIII, who seems to have been pretty much of a silent partner in his brother's reign. Cf. Ep. 34.23–24.

48–49 The quotation is from the *Iliad*, 6.58 ff.: *μηδ' ὅν τινα γαστέρι μήτηρ / κοῦρον ἐόντα φέροι, μηδ' ὃς φύγοι, ἀλλ' ἅμα πάντες / Ἰλίου ἐξαπολοίατ' ἀκήδεστοι καὶ ἄφαντοι.* In this passage, Agamemnon reminds Menelaus of the grievous personal injury done to him by the Trojans and urges him not to spare Adrestus whose offer of ransom Menelaus is on the verge of accepting.

59–60 Leo may have had in mind these lines from the *Iliad* 6.495–496, which describe Andromache's return to the palace after her meeting with Hector on the walls of Troy: *ἄλοχος δὲ φίλη οἶκόνδε βεβήκει / ἐντροπαλιζομένη, θαλερὸν κατὰ δάκρυ χέουσα.* It may be well at this point to comment again on the adjustment Leo makes in his literary style when writing to Basil II. This can be seen quite clearly by comparing the number and variety of literary references in the preceding letter, addressed to his brother clergymen, with those in the present letter: there are only two, and both are from the sixth book of the *Iliad*, with which even the Bulgaroctonus ought to have been familiar. Cf. Ep. 43 and commentary.

74–76 I have been unable to locate this canon. However, curiously enough, an apparently obsolete law specifying a six-month time limit on episcopal elections is cited by the anonymous author of a treatise on the rights of bishops:[5] *Εἰ δὲ οἱ ὀφείλοντες τὰ ψηφίσματα ποιεῖν, ἐντὸς μηνῶν ἕξ μὴ ποιήσουσι, τηνικαῦτα τῷ κινδύνῳ τῆς ἰδίας ψυχῆς ἐκεῖνος ᾧ ἁρμόζει τὸν ἐπίσκοπον χειροτονείτω.*

83–84 This seems to be a standard phrase, probably adapted from a classical author, although the exact source remains elusive. It was also used by Theophylact of Achrida in the conclusion of his speech to the emperor Alexius Comnenus (PG, 126, col. 305B).

[1] *Histoire de Yahya*, 444.

[2] Scylitzes, 328 (= Cedrenus, II, 434, Bonn ed.); Zonaras, III, 547 (Bonn ed.). Cf. also Grégoire and Orgels, "Chronologie," 159–78, and V. Grumel, "Chronologie patriarcale au Xᵉ siècle," *REB*, 22 (1964), 45–71.

[3] Leo the Deacon, *History*, X, 10, p. 176 (Bonn ed.).

[4]The error of Cedrenus (Scylitzes), who says the earthquake occurred in 986 (Scylitzes, 331–32; Cedrenus, II, 438, Bonn ed.), has been discussed by several scholars, most recently by A. Poppe, "The Political Background to the Baptism of Rus'," *DOP*, 30 (1976), 211–12.

[5]Darrouzès, *Documents*, 154, 1–3. Darrouzès has identified the source as Justinian's Novella 123.1.2. (Zachariae [1881], II, 296.15–18). In a note (*l.c.*, note 1), he adds, "Le choix de ce passage de la Nov. 123 est un signe évident de mauvaise foi, puisqu'il paraît aboli et par Nov. 137 et par les Basiliques 3, 1, 8–9 qui ne reproduisent pas le passage."

INDICES

I. NAMES and TERMS

II: INCIPITS

CORPUS FONTIUM HISTORIAE BYZANTINAE

SERIES WASHINGTONIENSIS, EDITOR JOHN M. DUFFY

DUMBARTON OAKS TEXTS

De Administrando Imperio
Constantine VII Porphyrogenitus
Gyula Moravcsik | R. J. H. Jenkins
CFHB 1 • DOT 1

Nicholas I, Patriarch of Constantinople: Letters
R. J. H. Jenkins | L. G. Westerink
CFHB 6 • DOT 2

Nicholas I, Patriarch of Constantinople: Miscellaneous Writings
L. G. Westerink
CFHB 20 • DOT 6

The Correspondence of Athanasius I, Patriarch of Constantinople
Alice-Mary Talbot
CFHB 7 • DOT 3

The Letters of Manuel II Palaeologus
George T. Dennis
CFHB 8 • DOT 4

The Synodicon Vetus
John Duffy | Thomas S. Parker
CFHB 15 • DOT 5

Letters of Gregory Akindynos
Angela Constantinides Hero
CFHB 21 • DOT 7

The Correspondence of Leo, Metropolitan of Synada and Syncellus
M. P. Vinson
CFHB 23 • DOT 8

Three Byzantine Military Treatises
George T. Dennis
CFHB 25 • DOT 9

Nikephoros, Patriarch of Constantinople:
Short History
Cyril Mango
CFHB 13 • DOT 10

The Correspondence of Ignatios the Deacon
Cyril Mango |
Stephanos Efthymiadis
CFHB 39 • DOT 11

The Taktika *of Leo VI*
George T. Dennis
CFHB 49 • DOT 12

The Life of Patriarch Ignatius
Nicetas David
Andrew Smithies | John M. Duffy
CFHB 51 • DOT 13

COMMENTARIES

De Administrando Imperio*: A Commentary*
R. J. H. Jenkins

A Critical Commentary on the Taktika *of Leo VI*
John F. Haldon

Please visit www.doaks.org/publications

for other books in this series and many other books about Byzantium.